THE LAND OF THE CROOKED TREE

THE

Land of the Crooked Tree

U. P. HEDRICK

NEW YORK

OXFORD UNIVERSITY PRESS

1948

*Map used on binding by courtesy of the New-York
Historical Society, New York City*

PRINTED IN THE UNITED STATES OF AMERICA

TO THE MEMORY OF MY PARENTS
PIONEERS IN THE LAND OF THE CROOKED TREE

Preface

THE Land of the Crooked Tree, found on old maps as L'Arbre Croche, is on the northern tip of the lower peninsula of Michigan and was one of the last forest regions in eastern America to be settled by whites. It is with the activities of the early settlers there, in the 1870's and 80's, after it was opened to homesteaders, that this book is concerned.

The Land of the Crooked Tree is not an autobiography, although it is brazenly personal from beginning to end. The people all lived, though a few in real life bore different names. The incidents recorded all took place, though the order in which they are related is not strictly chronological. Some invention has been used to reconstruct conversations that took place so many years ago.

There is no development of plot through the text; there is no climax at the end; in fact, there has been no effort to use the devices dear to the hearts of professional writers. Spontaneity, it is hoped, will enable the reader to share more fully the physical and mental pleasures, the adventures, dangers, and inconveniences of pioneer life in a forest.

U. P. HEDRICK

23 June 1948

Contents

THE LAND OF THE CROOKED TREE

The Migration

IT was the year 1874. We were on the steamboat *Menominee* in the northern part of Lake Michigan, having left Detroit four days before. Three small children were squabbling at a tiny cabin window for the right to see what was outside. I claimed the right, since my brother, two years older, belonged in another cabin with Father, and our sister, two years younger, was not tall enough to see out of the porthole.

From the tiny window through which I looked, across a mile of billowing whitecaps, a forest floated before my eyes. It was without length or breadth, light and dark green, dropping down a long, high, rolling slope from lazy clouds to snowlike drifts of sand where land and water met. I had never before seen trees or hills.

We had been living in Iowa, where my sister and I were born. Our birthplace was a log cabin that stood on the steep bank of a creek running through the rich black earth of our farm. The land for miles about was as flat as a millpond, except for the steep banks of the creek, up and down which wagons loaded with corn spilled off bushels on autumn days when they crossed the bridge, my big sisters picking up the ears for the cabin cookstove.

I do not know whence came the logs for our solid little log house. In the country round about there was only one tree; all the others, one of my sisters told me, had been cut to build houses. The lone tree belonged to my Uncle John Simpson.

Now, as I stood in the cabin on the *Menominee,* peering with drowsy eyes at a real forest, fear seized me. The wilderness, distant though it was, stirred my imagination as did childhood's nightmares. The dark shadows in the forest took on the semblance of monstrous animals, an endless procession of them. I expected a sudden leap of some wild beast or the war whoop of Indians, who I knew lived in the land to which we were going. In vain I looked for a house, a road, a cultivated field. There were none; the forest began and ended in caves of pitchy blackness.

I asked my mother: 'Are there Indians in those woods? . . . Do white people live in the forest? . . . Can children climb the hills? . . . Can I find my way among so many trees? . . . Are there wild animals there?'

To stop the flow of questions, my mother, who, I suspect, shared in some degree my fears, drew me from the porthole and hurried me into my clothes. My brother was called to take me on deck to my father.

We found Father far up in the bow of the boat talking to a man we had seen the day before, and by whom we had been charmed. Father told us that the man's name was St. Leger; that he was a Frenchman; that he had often been in Little Traverse, the town to which we were going; that he could talk to Indians in their own language; that he had been a trapper; and that he had had many fights with Indians.

The Frenchman was remarkable in appearance. He was tall and straight, wore his jet-black hair long, and had coal-black chin whiskers. His cheeks were purplish-red, his teeth white and even, his eyes black and sharp under heavy eyebrows. He wore a suit with stripes like a zebra and was crowned with a broadbrimmed black hat that made his red face look even redder. St. Leger took us in hand to give us a lesson in the geography of the region bordering the eastern shore of upper Lake Michigan, the country he called in broken English 'my lan'.'

Far off to our right was a long, broken, blue line of islands. On the end of one of them, to our rear, was a flashing light. St. Leger said it was Big Beaver Light, and that the one directly behind us was Ile aux Galets, which, he said, 'de Yankee call "Skillagalee." ' Behind Skillagalee was Waugashance, and directly ahead was Charlevoix Light. The mainland the French had long ago named L'Arbre Croche.

The musical names, Big Beaver, Skillagalee, Waugashance, Charlevoix, L'Arbre Croche, sang in my ears. With such names the country to which we were going must be a land of enchantment. Besides, there must be white men to take care of the lighthouses. With the knowledge that there were men of our color about, and with the brightness of the mounting sun, I forgot the terrors of the forest.

As the lesson in geography came to an end, the *Menominee's* captain came up, and, after speaking to Father, turned to St. Leger and asked him whether he had been up to any of his tricks.

St. Leger began feeling in his pockets and looking at his hands.

'Som'body 'ave rob' me!'

Suddenly his hand flashed to the little pocket in my jacket, and out came a gold watch and a huge chain.

'Ha! ma gol' wa'ch!'

Again his hand flashed, this time to my brother's pocket, and out came a fat pocketbook.

'Ha! ma mon'y! . . . Now ma ring, ma gol' ring!'

Seizing me by nose and chin, he opened my mouth and pulled out an enormous gold ring set with a big stone.

Had I not seen smiles on the faces of the captain and Father, and so sensed some sort of joke, I should have jumped overboard in embarrassment.

The breakfast bell was ringing, there was a smell of cooking in the air, and our family were glad enough to make for the dining room for breakfast. As we ate, Father tried to enlighten his sons on the mysteries of sleight-of-hand tricks.

Breakfast over and the family again on deck, we heard a jangling church bell seemingly out of the black wilderness. Then there came in view on the near shore a sparse clearing and a cluster of shabby cabins. In the center of the wretched hamlet was a church with a steeple belfry surmounted by a shining cross. Mother must have been sore at heart as she looked at the little village, since she knew our future home was to be but a few miles away. Much as she had disliked Iowa, no doubt she would gladly have turned and gone back to the prairie with its grasshoppers and cyclones.

St. Leger again joined us and told us the whites called the hamlet we were looking at 'Middle Village,' but to the Indians it was 'L'Arbre Croche, or w'at you say, Crooked Tree.' Then he told us, in his soft broken English that I shall not attempt to reproduce, how the region came to have so curious a name:

'There is where the big crooked tree stood, high up on that hill. When the French priests, the first white people to come this way, paddled their canoes along this shore, they saw there a very big pine tree. Its body was perfect, but its branches were bent and crooked. The tree stood all alone against the sky and could be seen far out in the lake, so that the priests, who had hard work finding names for all the parts of this new land, called the place "L'Arbre Croche." The tree was once perfect, the trunk thicker and the top higher than those of any other pine round about. Then an unhappy accident befell the great tree. An Indian chief, a famous warrior and hunter, stronger than any other man that ever lived, was climbing the bluff with his canoe on his shoulder. When he came under the big pine tree, one of its branches caught the canoe and gave him a nasty fall. Rising in his wrath, the chief struck the trunk and twisted the branches of the pine. The branches were ever after awry.'

Our boat was now turning from the open waters into a spacicus harbor formed by a long arrowhead of land jutting a mile into the lake. On the tip of the point was a huge cross of hewn timber. St. Leger told us this cross was a guide to sailors, and then whimsically added:

'Ze *croix* is ev'ryw'ere an' for all leeving t'ings abo't here, as you can see; even ze feesh swim in its shadow.'

Sure enough, a school of herring was jogging slowly by in the shadow of the cross.

The *Menominee* headed straight for the single wharf in the town. Her voice, that of a bull magnified a thousand times, bellowed three long blasts to send notice of her coming miles away into the forest. As we came slowly to dock the eyes of our family scanned the place that was to be our home and the people on the wharf who were to be our neighbors.

The autumn before, Father had visited this northern wilderness to spy out the land. On the dock stood several men he had met on his visit: Blackbird, an Indian chief, postmaster and government agent; Father Zorn, the village priest; Queen Margaret Boyd, sister to Blackbird; Bell, the real-estate agent who had sold my father his land; and Joutel, a half-breed, who had been Father's guide. There were many others of lesser note—sailors, timber buyers, homesteaders, half-breeds, and Indians.

Before the gangplank could be shoved from the *Menominee* to the wharf, several men had leaped aboard; and Joutel, who had recognized Father, came at once to our family group.

'*B'jou! B'jou!*' he said in a hearty voice.

Strange words, but not unexpected, since Father had told us that *bon jour* was the greeting of northern Indians. Joutel grabbed the bags and led the way through the crowd to the shore, talking with strange oaths.

To Father, he said: 'Joseph! Jesus! Mary! God A'mity! I'm glad to see you.'

Then to Mother: 'Ma gosh! I lak seein' you.'

As I write, I sniff the ghosts of the scents that came to our nostrils on that June morning as Joutel took us ashore. There were the smells of a dozen essences strange to those familiar only with the odors of a farm: the fishy smell of the lake; the ancient smell of the decaying wharf; the pungent tang of tanbark and newly cut lumber; the tarry exhalations of fishnets drying on the shore; the smell of a fire of driftwood; the effluvium of putrid fish offal; the exquisite perfume of some minty weed crushed by our feet.

The waters that touch the shores of the Land of the Crooked Tree have as their seaward boundary a line drawn from the point of one to that of the other of two well-marked capes, Waugashance and Charlevoix. From point to point it was some forty miles. The boundary line on the water can be seen as a bright thread of blue, the *ba-esk-ko-be* of the Indians, the horizon of the whites. The shore itself measures more than twice forty miles, because it is broken by bays and coves. The southern boundary is marked by a nearly circular bay some five or six miles in diameter, called La Petite Traverse to distinguish it from La Grande Traverse, a larger bay a half-day's sail southward.

Sometimes this shore is bordered and bottomed with glistening boulders, rocks, and pebbles of many colors. The forest, always of several species of evergreens and white birches, comes down to the water. Sometimes the shore and bottom are of glistening yellow sand, of which there is a windblown waste of drifting dunes supporting a curious dune-land flora. Always the lake is kept in its basin by a high bluff, which in places is lapped by the water; but mostly bluff and water are separated by dunes or swamps. Every mile or two, brooks or little rivers ripple and gurgle through the sands or roar down the bluffs and over the rocks from the tangles of the forest.

Until long after the beginning of the nineteenth century, these waters and the great lake of which they are a part had been a solitary sea on which were seen only the canoes of traders, trappers, and Indians. Jesuit missionaries first saw the country three centuries ago and gave it the name L'Arbre Croche, as St. Leger had told us, from a large crooked tree standing prominently on a high bluff overlooking Lake Michigan. Priests, explorers, trappers, fishermen, and Indians long knew this land as the home of the Ottawa and Chippewa before whites were allowed to own any piece of it.

When, in 1874, Washington permitted whites to 'take up' land from the government as homesteads and to buy it from Indian owners, there was a rush of farmers, lumbermen, fishermen, pigeon trappers, and summer resorters to settle the new country. Now the horizon marked one of the world's great travel routes. Men from the Atlantic seaboard had discovered the Middle West and now were building western states and cities. Steamships crowded with passengers were hourly passing to and fro. Fleets of sailing ships, rich with wealth from western farms or eastern factories, sailed across the sea between our capes. Steam, as yet, could not compete with wind.

Travel by land had but recently reached the forests of the Land of the Crooked Tree. A trail led north and south from the old town to which we had come, but it was almost impassable in summer, and in winter only travelers on snowshoes could make use of it. To the people of the town, the world beyond was 'outside'; its people, 'outsiders.'

This was the land to which my father was bringing his family.

Our New Home

THE mainspring in my father's life was a desire to subdue wild lands. Before middle age, his tireless feet had thrice traveled to new frontiers. To him the fight gave more pleasure than the victory. His triumphs were those of Man over Nature. He loved to transform prairies and forests into smiling fields of golden grain and grazing herds.

In early manhood, he left his boyhood home in Virginia to carve out a farm in a walnut and butternut forest in northern Indiana. After a few years of forest life, the rolling prairies of Illinois seemed more to his liking. Soon he again traveled toward the setting sun to the flat prairies of Iowa. Now he was migrating once more, this time to a beech and maple forest in northern Michigan, as yet scarcely touched by white men.

At the time of this migration, Father was in his middle forties, well-built, straight, showing his age but little. His hair and beard were slightly grizzled; toil and care had lined his forehead and brought crow's-feet about his eyes; his hands were rough, calloused, and a little distorted, so that I used to wonder if they pained him; prairie suns and winds had given his face the tan of a sailor. Somewhere I had heard the saying, 'A blue eye is a true eye,' which made me proud of my father's blue eyes. I have seen few countenances in my time better than my father's: serene, kindly, courteous, distinguished, shining with hope and pleasant daydreams.

You would have known from his appearance and manner of speaking that Father was a Virginian. He had come to the North before the Civil War, but remained always a Southerner at heart. He had, I am afraid, been a rank Copperhead. We three children were our father's second brood. His first, three daughters and a son, were now of an age to care for themselves, and in this move had been left behind as a rear guard.

Father's life was one of paradoxes. A Southerner, he lived in the North; ever a strait-laced Democrat, from boyhood he had incarcerated himself in Republican strongholds. A member, and always an officer, of the Presbyterian Church, he would declare time and again that anyone who read the Bible ought to be either a Jew or a Roman Catholic. Almost a teetotaler, he would now and then go in a crowded saloon and down a glass of whiskey to show disagreement with the prohibitionists among whom he lived. He had a fair education, yet he lived always by the labor of his hands. He left to each of his seven children two great blessings: industry and a love of books.

Mother was a slight, frail woman, but very active in mind and body, and she had remarkable powers of resistance to fatigue in the hard life of pioneering. I do not remember ever having heard her say, 'I am tired.' All her life crudeness and toil had prevailed over refinement and ease; and her associates were for the most part people of little culture. She had compensations in the blessings of perfect health, a companionable spirit, and peace of mind; pity for her would be out of place.

Mother had a keen mind, but her early education was negligible, so that she was not Father's intellectual equal. She, too, was of Virginia stock, 'a Garnet,' she would proudly say. (Whoever met a Virginian who did not belong to a 'first family'?)

Mother understood Father as wives seldom understand husbands. She looked after his every want and used common sense and cheerfulness in treating his slightest ailments and in tolerating his foibles. With sublime patience, she swept her floors, washed and mended, kept food in her cupboard, and gave hospitality to all. She numbered as her friends all who had white faces and Christian names; Indians, in Iowa and Michigan, regardless of age or sex, were to her of Satan's brood.

Always her inquiring mind was at work, curious about everything on earth. This trait was inconvenient to her children, about whom she must know the most minute details of life, everything that they had done, seen, or heard. All that appeared on a printed page, or that she heard from a pulpit, she believed, and out of a remarkably good memory she would often quote bits of strange information, prefaced by: 'The preacher said . . .' 'They say . . .' or 'I read . . .'

Quite without religious cant, she tried to bring her children up in the straight and narrow path, to accomplish which her hand was well practiced in the use of a switch. I doubt if any children ever had a mother with more talent for switching just enough and not too much, or who punished with a better grace or a more virtuous feeling of having done her duty. Much more bothersome than the mild switchings was her energy in keeping us well scrubbed, in seeing that we were early in bed and properly fed.

Named after the bay, Little Traverse, the harbor town to which we had come, was the capital and metropolis of the Land of the Crooked Tree. The name and the description given by Father to his open-eared children had carried our interest to a high pitch. Now, at sight of the primitive little trading-post, we were all eyes.

From the deck of the *Menominee* we had seen that the habitations were small and shabby, but the three or four trading houses and a golden-steepled church looked large and fine. Close at hand, however, we saw that these great buildings, and the lesser ones as well, were about to tumble down. There was not a patch of paint, a new board, or a bright shingle on any one of them.

The hotel to which Joutel took us was the weather-beaten remains of an old government warehouse. Swinging and creaking over the front entrance was a signboard with a huge golden star painted on a brilliant blue background. At the bottom of the board we read 'The Star Hotel.' Sun, wind, and rain had warped the walls and roof, warped the shingles, and painted the building an ashy gray, which in the morning sun seemed luminous. The glare of the shining walls was relieved by splashes of green moss in joints between shingles and cornices.

Yet to me, the Star Hotel was a palace, and, despite its disreputable exterior, had a homelike atmosphere when compared with the *Menominee*, which had no semblance of a home, whatsoever. The words 'landlord' and 'landlady' had a strange fascination for me. They seemed to suggest very superior human beings. Now, at last, I was to see what these lords of creation were like.

How disappointed I was! The mistress of the Star was a tall, lean, withered, stoop-shouldered woman in a plain gray, worn, soiled garment. She welcomed my mother in a high-pitched, tremulous voice, so nearly a sob that I wondered what she was crying about and wished Mother would say something to comfort her.

At night the landlady's face and figure troubled me in a strange way. I would waken with the fear that the old woman was approaching her end. This was the period of my life when I had a dread of facing the fact of death. The landlady dead, however, would have been little different from the landlady living, so worn, thin, and pale she was.

As the hostess of the Star and my mother went about the business of getting acquainted inside the house, we children were attracted by a commotion outside. We heard derisive hoots and calls: '*B'jou, Cochon!* '*allo, Cochon!*' from the throats of a pack of red-skinned urchins.

The cause of the excitement was an enormous, unwieldy man. Never before had I seen a man so rolling in fat. Folds of flesh filled out his bagging clothes and padded the bones of his legs and arms. The knuckles of his hands were completely lost. His feet were hidden from his own sight, so that he could not see where to place them and must shuffle and stumble along, feeling his way. You would expect a man of his bulk to have a booming bass voice; but as he stopped to chide his tormentors, it turned out that he spoke in a shrill falsetto, with a tremor in his voice that gave it a strangely pathetic note like the mournful cry of some bird.

Father had told us about this fat man, and we knew him at once as the landlord of the Star, *Le Cochon* to the Indians, 'Hog Smith' to the whites. Later, I learned that the introduction of the pig by the French in this part of the world had furnished the aborigines with several words to describe human beings.

After what seemed ages, the landlady took us to our rooms in the second story. This part of the building, once a storeroom, had been divided by unpapered partitions into a dozen bedrooms, with rough boards and uncarpeted floors creaking at every step. The ramshackle stairs possessed the one note of beauty in the building. The railing was curly bird's-eye maple, beautifully polished by hands that had slid down it. Father said we had many maples on our farm, and that some day we should live in a home finished in curly maple.

Without his airy hopes, how could my father have lived?

The two rooms in the hotel for our family looked out on a rough, weedy yard, pastured by the domestic animals of the village; beyond was a road deep in sand, from which a cloud of dust arose. Up and down the street were Indian habitations, mostly log cabins. Through our open windows came the noise of drowsy insect voices, and now in the heat of the day there was a rank odor from fish litter, mingled with the more pleasant smell of tarred nets. My mother looked out of the window to see the blue waters of the harbor, drew a long breath, and began unpacking.

Our night in this hostelry was anything but pleasant. Fleas swarmed in the beds. They at once scented fresh, young blood, and soon there were dozens on my body. Long afterwards I read of a monk who for some sin was punished by being made to sleep in a bed where fleas abounded. If he suffered as did I in the Star, the penance should have secured him pardon for his most damning sins. Even Father, who enjoyed a good bed, was upset by this scourge of fleas, but to Mother's denunciations of a human habitation overrun with this pest of dogs he could only say: 'It might be worse!'

There were other troubles in the night. A thunderstorm with a gale of wind came up, and the Star creaked and swayed like a boat at sea. The howling of dogs made the night unearthly. Little Traverse, we soon came to know, was a dog's paradise.

The daylight hours for the next few weeks in the land of our adoption were spent in exploration. The old town is now so changed that ghosts of those old days, returning, would recognize only two landmarks, both of which will endure to the end of time. One of these is the harbor into which we came. A hundred ocean ships could safely anchor here. In the summer, few craft made use of this anchorage, but in the storms of autumn, sailing vessels of all descriptions, from little schooners to great six-masters, and side- and stern-wheel steamers anchored in the harbor. Always the sight of a storm-driven boat heading our way brought a thrill of excitement to old and young. This shipping brought business to the traders, but left work for Father Zorn, the village priest, in mending the morals of his people.

Most of the life of the town was along the water front, and here, where there was much to see and do, was our playground.

Besides the sailing craft of commerce, there were fishing smacks pulled up alongside fish houses, about which were all the gear of the industry: nets, barrels, anchors, sails, and kettles of tar. On the shore and the long wharf were tiers of pungent hemlock bark and lumber awaiting ships. Through the town ran a brook in which minnows were netted for bait to catch larger fish off the wharf.

The point of land that separated the waters of the harbor from those of the lake was sand, tortured into monstrous shapes by wind and water. The sand, the wind, and a climate slightly different because of the temperature of water on its three sides made a home for plants unlike those of the mainland. These peculiarities set 'the Point,' as all called it, apart as a special place. To the Indians it was a home of ghosts and spirits, hallowed by legend and story. This long-pointed, tree-covered, arrowhead of land was to white children, in the days before summer colonists took it over to the last square inch, a fairyland, all the more delightful for being a sanctuary from the superstitious young Indians.

The other of the two landmarks was a high perpendicular bluff back of the town. The face of the bluff was cut with paths on which adventures with the roving domestic animals of the town could be undertaken by boys with a slingshot or a bow and arrow. From the top, we could see the harbor and far out over the lake.

The largest trees on the face of the bluff were aspens, junipers, scrub oaks, and thorns. In June, violets, hepaticas, and yellow dogtooth violets filled the open spaces between the clumps of small trees; in July, the slope was covered with a cloak of wild-rose blooms; in August, the bluff was a piece of porcelain, enameled with daisies, milfoils, and red grasses; September found the high bank hung with a shaggy Persian rug splashed with the yellow and purple of goldenrods and asters on a background of red sumac, scarlet scrub oak, the yellows of aspens, and the greens of junipers.

My father had a rare eye for natural beauty. On Sunday afternoons he often took the family up the bluff for 'a view.' On the transparent crystalline days of the northern summer, the outlines of distant objects were sharpened as from alpine heights. We saw from the top of the bluff every detail of the shabby Indian village beneath, the harbor and its shipping, the curiosities in land formation of the long point, the deep-curving bay surrounded by undulating wooded hills, and far to the west in the lake the blue *ba-esk-ko-be* of the Indians. Bending over all was the clear blue sky—no purer blue this side of Paradise.

Much of the region east of the village was a treacherous swamp carpeted with deep sphagnum moss, tempting to walk on, but through which our feet might sink into bottomless ooze. It was a place of strange odors from fetid fungi and spicy foliage. On summer nights the swamp blazed with fireflies and phosphorescent woods. It was a sanctuary for birds, and the northern songsters gave concerts morning and evening, whether or not human beings were there to hear—or, if there, wanted to hear. In winter this swamp was a trapping ground for the great northern hare caught by boys who dreamed of becoming mighty hunters.

One night at the Star was quite long enough, and on our second day we set up housekeeping in a small, square, clap-boarded house, shingled with home-split shakes, through which rain drove and later snow sifted. It was a wretched little shack into which our belongings had to be crowded, with a living-room below, a sleeping-room above, and a lean-to kitchen, which could be used only in summer; in winter it became a woodshed.

Yet ours was a better house than most. Some of the neighboring houses were shingled with sheets of cedar bark. Several were enclosed in high palisaded fences in the style of the earlier fortified dwelling places of the region; now the warlike palings served only to keep out cows and ponies, which roamed at will in the town. The houses built to stand siege appealed greatly to us children, as did the circular wigwams of the Indians, which dotted the shore of the harbor. We wished that our parents had chosen a palisaded house or a wigwam as a dwelling.

Our little house had board walls and ceilings, none too clean, fouled with smoke. Wallpaper was not to be had, and my tidy mother was hard pressed for wall coverings; finally she papered the walls with newspapers. Father had brought with our household goods a number of unbound volumes of *Harper's Weekly* he had treasured. These my mother used to decorate her walls, with the illustrated front pages laid on as a dado, and the text and advertisements above. The walls became to the children in the family a university. During times of childhood diseases, and in winter days and evenings, the secular gospel of *Harper's Weekly* was before our eyes. We had to kneel, bow, prostrate ourselves, climb, twist, stretch, and squint to get all of the text, and thus got physical as well as mental exercise.

Here on the walls of our cottage were the battles on land and sea of the Civil War; all the parts of our country and many foreign places, with the human endeavors pertaining thereto; Indian and white hunters shooting buffalo; stories and poems; the great men of the nation, Presidents, statesmen, and generals; cartoons depicting the good and bad men of the country. Had the children in our family had no other education than what we got from our wallpaper, we should have been fairly well informed about what had been going on in the world for the years just before we came into it. A wallpaper education continued in all the houses in which we lived for several years to follow.

Exploring the village was difficult during the first weeks in our new home, for as soon as my brother and I stuck our noses out of doors we were pounced upon by youthful red devils who made us fight for our lives. My brother stuck by Father, but I was too small to keep pace with a man, and had to stay with

Mother. I soon began taking walks, hand in hand, with *Le Cochon,* as ample a human bulwark as the Lord ever created.

As a child I was fascinated by *Le Cochon* when he became excited in either anger or mirth, for he would flop his great bulk in a chair, open wide his mouth, draw in his breath with a prolonged hiss, and then discharge it in a cyclonic rush accompanied by an owl-like screech. I expected at such times to see him stiffen and froth at the mouth, but he never gratified me by going quite so far. My brother and I often mocked him in this breathing performance, to amuse ourselves or frighten our little sister.

It may seem strange that the proprietor of the Star would choose a small boy for a companion, but my short legs just kept pace with his shuffling feet. Besides, the old man was starving for company. Grown-ups would not put up with his stuttering, wheezy, wind-blown conversation; so he chose a child. I did not, however, see much of the town with *Le Cochon* as a guide, since he could waddle only over ground that was level; no steps, ascents, or descents for him. Having been upset once in a rowboat, weighted to the edge by his bulk, he could not be tempted on the water, great as was my desire to travel that way.

After a week or two, my walks with the landlord of the Star ceased. It happened that I, too, in Indian eyes had some resemblance to a pig, not a huge, overgrown swine, such as Hog Smith, but a plump, well-rounded porker, just right for the roasting pan. After a few outings with my friend, the little redskins began to greet me:

'*Allo, 'Tite Cochon!*' '*B'jou, 'Tite Cochon!*'

When the significance of the name became known to me, the humiliation was more than I could bear. In our home circle the new name was strictly forbidden, for at its sound I would strike, bite, kick, and scratch. Outside I fought young savages with clubs or stones, and murder in my heart. They soon dropped the name.

My brother and I had a hard time of it at first with the young

Indians, who in malice and cruelty were fiends. Out of sight of white men, they would have tortured us without mercy. By instinct they thirsted to kill, and woe to the stray dog, cat, or unfortunate wild creature that came into their clutches. Given an opportunity, they would murder, despoil, or steal as slyly as the predatory fox—or as any other small boy, for that matter. Our time came the next spring when the Indian youngsters were half starved and weak from cold and winter ailments. Then the white skins, numbering one to a dozen redskins, would charge the multitude of Midianites.

I am afraid my brother and I quickly became savages among savages. Even our games were battles, whites against Indians. In summer we battled with stones and sticks; in winter, with hard-packed snowballs. 'Lickety-cut' was a favorite game. Two boys with blue-beech gads, five or six feet long, stood foot to foot, each thrashing the other in alternate strokes. The one who first cried or turned tail was defeated. In this game my brother and I excelled, since we could put on two or three pairs of pants and an extra shirt or two, while an Indian boy wore but one each of these garments, and often I saw blood trickling down a young Indian's legs. Even thickly dressed as we were, the pain sometimes drew tears.

Before spring, however, our relations with the Indian rapscallions had begun to mend. We quickly learned that an Indian could not 'take it' on the nose or chin, and my brother and I were soon handy with our fists. Fisticuffs won a fair degree of respect, but food brought more friends. When Mother had her household running, we could give our Indian companions cookies, prunes, dried apples, and other delicacies from the family larder. Such gifts brought us from the starving Indian horde more retainers than we could support.

Our Neighbors

AFTER a few busy days in settling our belongings, we began to cast about to see who our neighbors were. There were not more than a dozen white families in Little Traverse, although at the hour of our arrival there had been perhaps forty white men on the wharf—traders, timber buyers, sailors, and fishermen. Of Indians and half-breeds there were perhaps two or three hundred, few of whom counted as neighbors.

The first summer, there was but one house in the village from which we could borrow and return, and where Mother could hear the talk of the town. This was the home of Madame Pettier, a widow who owned the house in which we lived and who was a near neighbor in a much better house.

It is easy to describe Madame Pettier's features to anyone who has studied Roman history. She had the shape of face and forehead, the same aquiline nose and thin lips, of a Roman matron. It was a rather masculine face, its masculinity emphasized by a faint mustachio, as is often found with the dark complexion of French-Canadian women. Her dress was simple and black, almost straight up and down, with a white embroidered collar. On special occasions she wore a high tortoise-shell comb and gold earrings with heavy black pendants. In chilly weather, indoors and out, her shoulders were draped with a dark shawl. Madame Pettier's counterpart is often to be seen in French-Canadian villages today.

There was much visiting back and forth between Madame Pettier and my mother, so that our family came to know her well. She was good to small boys, giving them titbits from her pantry, in return for which she asked an occasional errand. Indeed she was kind to all living things, plants and animals as well as humankind. Everyone in the village esteemed her as a good and wise woman, in spite of a very masterful voice and manner, which enabled her to have her way with the villagers as though they were children. She had acquaintances in every part of the region and all the way from our village to Quebec. True, she was feared by some, but so many had found unexpected kindnesses in her heart that she was loved by most of those who knew her.

Madame Pettier gossiped about all that went on in the village. She spoke English, French, and Ottawan, and people of all of these languages came to her with nuggets of news. She specialized in the genealogies of the illegitimate offspring of white men and red-skinned damsels. Gossiping was Madame Pettier's one fault, yet no one could say that she was a scandalmonger, or that she was mean or spiteful about the irregularities of her neighbors.

Madame Pettier was happy in having a hobby that yielded her great pleasure. She was a collector of Indian art, not only from the Ottawa and Chippewa about her, but from many other tribes far away. On her floors were beautifully tanned deer skins with the color and pile of a peach; fine Indian blankets covered her beds; luxurious furs from bear, fox, and otter cushioned her chairs. There were mats, screens, gummed woven jars and bottles; wampum belts with symbolic figures of ancient Indian worship; baskets of barks and of sweet grasses, worked with beads and porcupine quills in geometrical figures.

When Madame Pettier let me take my time with them, her treasures held me spellbound. Whether I was most pleased with the designs or with the colors, it would be hard to say. Most of the pieces had designs worked in beads or porcupine quills, in patterns of checks, coils, scrolls, herringbones, and latticework. The gamut of colors ran through the yellow-greens of grasses to browns, soft reds, and sooty blacks. The old lady would not allow in her home the hard colors of foreign dyes; her works of art must be colored in the soft tones of dyes made from roots, barks, fruits, fungi, and lichens, colors that became soft and mellow as they ripened with age.

Besides her Indian work, Madame Pettier had some pieces of silver on her table—solid silver, it was said—each piece kept so brilliantly polished that, standing on her sideboard, it reflected sunlight like a mirror. I had never seen silverware before. It gave Madame Pettier's ugly little house a charm no other home in which I had ever been could approach.

Madame Pettier's father, of whom she spoke with great pride, was a partner in the great Hudson's Bay Fur Company—presumably a junior partner. He spent much of his time in the active life of the fur trader in the wilderness about Hudson Bay, up the Mackenzie, or in other remote parts of the far North. Several times she and her mother went with him, and she often told us of these adventures in the best story-book style.

Who Madame Pettier's husband was, I never knew, though she and St. Leger spoke of him time and again, calling him by his first name, Antoine. I gathered that Antoine Pettier and St. Leger had both served in some capacity under Madame Pettier's father. The father, by the way, was a Scotsman and a Protestant, while the mother, half French and half Indian, was a Roman Catholic.

For more than two centuries the harbor on Little Traverse Bay had been a rendezvous for the *coureurs de bois*. Of these trappers and traders, many of whom were unscrupulous adventurers and vagabonds, there remained in our parts but three that I knew: St. Leger, Joutel, and Joseph Pyant, the patriarch of the village.

There is little to be said about St. Leger. Truth is, none in the harbor village talked about his past; his present greatness in the eyes of his neighbors furnished material for endless conversations. Madame Pettier and Joutel could have given the history of his life had there been any reason to do so. To our family he often spoke of his youth in Saint Malo, France, and of his reasons for coming to the New World. Now he was long past sixty and getting old—younger than Madame Pettier by several years. He had come to Quebec some forty years before we knew him and, after years of service in the Hudson's Bay Company, had settled down as a merchant trader from post to post in this northern region.

Joutel's given name was Alphonse, but all, whites and Indians, called him by his surname. The story of his own life was a favorite theme with this babbler, but it varied so much with the tellings that no one could make out where he was born, what his parentage was, or where and how he had spent his early years.

Asked where he was born, he would say: 'De plase I'm born' is ma fader's affaire.'

He had so much to say about Sault Ste. Marie we decided he had been born there on the Canadian side of the river, since on every possible occasion he shouted: 'Me, I'm Canadien.'

He could not read or write a word, yet whenever he heard the children in our family talking about school, he announced: 'I'm spen' t'ree year on school in Soo San Marie.'

His family, of whom he often spoke, and for whom he bore much affection, was a large one: 'I'm got ten brudder and t'irteen seester.' He reeled off their names from the oldest to the youngest in a sort of song and always in the same order. None of them ever came our way.

Joutel was in his element in the woods, where no matter how hard the labor or how severe the punishment from Arctic weather or from mosquitoes and black flies, his cheerfulness and gaiety were never impaired. He would end the day by the fireside, a pipe between his teeth, contentedly telling stories. Though a twice-told tale is proverbially tedious, Joutel could dress a story so well that I am sure I listened to some of his stories a hundred times without tiring. He had only to begin, 'W'en de canoe came down from de nord . . .' to draw me from whatever I was doing.

Joutel had a hobby. Though he could not read a word, he collected almanacs—no bibliophile ever treasured books more carefully. On the cover of almanacs a generation ago, as every oldsters knows, there was a picture of a man with his internal organs exposed to the light of day, from which lines radiated to the signs of the Zodiac. This man, with abdomen opened wide and the face of a martyr, encircled by strange symbols, was the most wonderful picture in the world to Joutel. The cuts illustrating seasons and rural tasks, the jokes, the bits of advice, gave him almost all the spice he had for his impoverished intellectual life.

I blush with shame to think how my brother and I imposed on Joutel's credulity. Almost never did we read correctly what the almanac said. He lied to us—why should we not lie to him? We exaggerated, mystified, perverted, wrongly interpreted. He was so little accustomed to telling the truth himself, however, that he did not expect it from anyone else.

Joutel was a good Roman Catholic and had as much religion as men of his class usually have. You always knew when he was in a religious mood, for then his tongue was stilled from vehement oaths and he would say again and again in a scarcely audible voice: '*O ma conscience!*' Always he feared that hell yawned for him, and he went often to confess his sins to Father Zorn; but never did he make a concrete atonement. He frequently called Father a heretic, though never to his face. But Father's heresy did not keep Joutel from listening to grace when he could squeeze in a place at our table.

We all had great respect for Joutel's opinions about the weather. Usually his forecasts began: 'W'en I'm in ze Nor'-Wes'

I'm l'arn ze wedder.' In early morning and again at bedtime he made daily forecasts by taking note of wind, temperature, and the heavens. As we basked in Indian summer, he had a hundred signs of the coming winter weather. Fat squirrels and chipmunks meant much snow and cold; plump, fuzzy sumacs and cattails indicated an Arctic winter; brittle autumn leaves presaged bitter cold in January and February. A long run of starry nights and a moon surrounded night after night with blue were signs of mild winter weather. When pines and hemlocks whispered loudly day and night in winter, they were 'talking' of months of pleasant weather when summer came again.

Joseph Pyant, 'Zozeep' to the Indians, was very different from the scapegrace Joutel. As I have said, he was the patriarch of our little parish, a grave, dignified old man with refined features that gave evidence of good blood. Of the men who had lived long on Little Traverse Bay, Joseph Pyant was by far the most worthy of remark. Years before we knew him he had been an independent fur trader, a man of substance; but when our family landed from the *Menominee*, he was a poorly paid clerk in one of the village stores. Early in life he had married an Indian wife and now had children and grandchildren as plentiful as blackberries, mostly ne'er-do-wells, whom he supported as best he could.

His father had come from Montreal to Mackinac as an employee of the old Northwest Fur Company and had married a half-breed Chippewa, of which union Joseph was one of several offspring. Though a quarter-breed, now in his gray and wrinkled old age he showed no trace of Chippewa blood. His good breeding came from his father, who was a cultivated Englishman. Most of the *habitants* spoke English with an accent and interlarded what they had to say with more or less *patois*. Joseph's English was as good as that of anyone in the region. He had a habit of beginning an answer to every question with: 'Oh, God, yes!' or 'Oh, God, no!' with not the least irreverence but as a means of emphasis.

What a life he had lived! Joseph remembered much about the two battles between the Americans and the British that were fought on Mackinac Island in the War of 1812. His father was a British subject, and when Mackinac Island was taken over by the Americans, the Pyant family fell on evil days. Joseph was apprenticed to a baker on the island, but ran away to become a fur trader. Madame Pettier remembered him well as a trader, for he had kept an eye open for treasures in furs and Indian work for her collection. In these early days he dealt in finery for women and in knives and ammunition for men. He wore, Madame Pettier said, bracelets on his arms, pendants in his ears, ovals, disks, and crescents on his coat, all glittering and jingling, and made a dashing figure among the dusky belles. In due time, gentle, kindly Joseph Pyant vanished out of our lives, but not until he had made an enduring impression as a good man.

There were two left-overs of Indian royalty in our little village, Chief Blackbird and his sister, Queen Margaret. They were children of a family that once had reigned in the kingdom of the Ottawa, a family now reduced in royal functions to helping the descendants of former subjects bear as best they could the miseries of the new regime. At the time of our arrival in the village, Chief Blackbird was walking in full splendor as the great man of L'Arbre Croche. He was interpreter for the Government, and was at that moment postmaster. He had married a white woman, and though their mansion was a plain little frame building, it was the nearest approach to a palace in the region.

Chief Blackbird's white wife seemed never in her proper element and had the look in eye and color of a woman suffering from a strange disease. She was so blond as to be almost an albino; because of her color, the Indians regarded her as more foreign than the general run of whites. White women were not friendly because she was the wife of an Indian. In spite of lack of friends, however, she seemed happy in her home and in her strange surroundings, for strange indeed they must have been to her, since she had been born and reared in England. There were four offspring of this marriage, three boys and a girl. Never have I known children so badly spoiled by their parents, nor human beings with less care beyond the day, as if, poor things, they knew they had no future.

Blackbird was born a pagan, bred a Roman Catholic, and lived his mature life as an Episcopalian. A long and pleasant acquaintanceship between the old chief and me was brought about through his churchly zeal. One day when I had gone to the post office for mail I was asked to go to a storekeeper in another part of the town for a prayer book. For this small errand, Chief Blackbird gave me a two-cent piece. Thus I suddenly became rich. Never before had I been given more than a penny at one time. For two cents, Blackbird purchased by lifelong friendship.

Blackbird was a small man with hands and feet no larger than those of a woman, body straight and trim. He wore a high, stovepipe hat and a voluminous Prince Albert coat. Always on weekdays he was shod in soft deerskin moccasins, but on Sundays he wore stringless shoes with elastic sides. Footwear of any kind must have pinched the old man's feet, for often he went puttering around the post office at ease, his feet devoid of both shoes and stockings. When we came to the village, Chief Blackbird was well past middle life; his hair, once coal black, was turning gray, an indication of age that he tried to hide by wearing his 'stovepipe' indoors and out.

Late in life, Chief Blackbird wrote a book, the *Complete History of Ottawa and Chippewa Indians of Michigan and Grammar of their Languages*. The best pages in the book are those in which he gives a description of the Eden in which he was born and bred. The air, in this earthly paradise of his childhood, in the summer was perfumed with wild strawberries, raspberries, blackberries, and blueberries. The woods were filled with wild pigeons and feathered songsters. Every draw of the fish net brought up so many whitefish and trout that the net and its sinkers floated. His people did not want for anything to eat or wear, there being plenty of fish, corn, vegetables, wild fruits, and wild animals for food and furs.

Despite his boyhood delights, Blackbird early adopted the life of the whites. He earned money to pay for an education and progressed from life in a wigwam to that in a school dormitory. He made long journeys to and from school and college and endured many hardships. In one part of his story he dwells on how hard it was to stay indoors at his books when the sun shone, and tells how he ran away time and again for a day in the woods. Sometimes, he writes, he would run away in a rainstorm and take off his clothes and let the rain beat on his body. I do not remember having read another tale of school life more pathetic.

Blackbird came home from college to find his relatives and friends little better than the beasts of the forest. The passing of the fur traders and the encroachment of whites on the Ottawa hunting and fishing grounds had left the Indians in a terrible plight. He quickly took leadership among them and for fifty years was a wise counselor.

The story of Blackbird does not end happily. As old age came on, he was ousted from government positions by whites and there was little left upon which he could subsist. His high hat and frock coat degenerated into castoff garments given him in charity. Who could wonder that he fell into a state of profound melancholy? Probably his book, on which he had spent years of work, brought him a few dollars. For the rest, during the summer he gave lectures at tourist hotels and received charity from whoever would give.

I saw the old man last when I was in vigorous, youthful manhood; he, old and palsied. The years had stolen all the fire from his eyes, the strength from his body. I went to ask him about the Ottawa. As he tried to answer my questions, the old Indian steadied his palsied head with his hands, saying to himself before he would try to answer me: 'Be calm, Blackbird! Be calm!'

If I hurried my questions, he would say: 'Wait! Wait! One thing at a time!'

Even his English, fluent in earlier years, had almost gone, and he mumbled in the language of his childhood. Again and again he tapped his forehead, muttering: 'So many things gone from here! Gone! Gone!'

Before I left him, the old man asked me to loan him a dollar. I gave him ten. Had I given him a hundred times as much, it could not have made him happier than his two-cent piece had made me.

Blackbird's sister, Margaret, a few years older, was more of a personage among the Indians than the chief even in the height of his authority. She was a woman of remarkable energy and enterprise, as well educated as her brother, and constant in her loyalty to the Roman Church. Queen Margaret had married a half-breed, more Indian than white, named Boyd.

To me, her image was vague for several years, even though I must have seen her often. Then tourists were beginning to visit our shores, and we heard them say as Queen Margaret passed: 'What a fine-looking squaw!' Of course I took note. She was of medium height, with an intelligent, rather distinguished face, which no one could mistake for Caucasian, as one might that of her brother. Indian blood showed not so much in her coppery-red skin, tinged with a purple especially high in her lips, as in her straight, black hair and the way she carried her body; she had the gliding motion of the Indian. She spoke in a loud voice, with the authority of one used to command. The old lady was very proud of her royal descent and the title 'Queen Margaret.' We whites ought to have been proud to have as our next-door neighbor a highborn forest queen, but I am afraid none of us were.

Until a year before we came to the north woods, Queen Margaret had had charge of the government school in the village. Many of our Indians had been her pupils and out of habit took orders from her. Like school teachers the world over, she knew all that was going on in her school district, which included the country for miles about. She and Madame Pettier could have written the genealogy of every person, red or white, in all L'Arbre Croche. Yet the two old ladies were not friends, each jealous, no doubt, of the other's authority in our little empire.

A little before we came to the harbor village, Queen Margaret had been sent to Washington in the interest of the Ottawa. When she returned, she made much ado about her interview with President Grant. She said: 'The President was very courteous and made many good promises. After a long talk,' she was proud of telling, 'he took me by the arm and led me to another room, where he introduced me to his wife and some other ladies.'

She had much to tell about the wonders she saw—railroads, steamboats, the Capitol, the White House, a theater, the Patent Office, a balloon ascension. Had she been any other than Queen Margaret, her neighbors would have said she was a great liar.

Queen Margaret once cornered me in one of the village stores and cross-examined me about the origin, history, religion, and politics of my father. She asked if he had ever been in Washington, and seemed much impressed when I told her that he had lived there. I spoiled the good impression, however, when I told her that my father thought Lee a greater man than Grant.

Queen Margaret had a son, Sammy, with whom I fought at every chance. For the first few years I took some terrible beatings from Sammy Boyd, but, finally, being better fed, I could pummel him at will, and he thereafter kept out of my way. Long years afterward, I found that I had not only been fighting with a prince of the Ottawa, but possibly a nephew of a President of the United States. A man conversant with the affairs of Mackinac Island told me that Queen Margaret's husband, George Boyd, was, without question, the illegitimate son of George Boyd, Indian agent on Mackinac Island from 1824 to 1833. The elder Boyd's legitimate wife was the sister of the wife of President John Quincy Adams.

Queen Margaret's last days were as sad as those of her brother. In old age, she was thin and gray, with a thousand wrinkles on her face; she was bent nearly double with rheumatism and had to hobble about with two sticks, her eyes on the ground, for she was nearly blind. Disease and old age had brought low another queen.

Most of my boyhood friends were white, sons of families from the outside world. There were always some dickerings and bickerings with Chief Blackbird's three sons, and fights with Sammy Boyd. My Indian friend, Leander, had a host of Indian playmates when we came to the village, with whom I had dealings of one kind or another, mostly unfriendly; but, as more and more whites came, Indian families moved to Canada or to other villages in the Land of the Crooked Tree.

It was astonishing how many of our Indian neighbors had French, English, Irish, and Scotch names. The explanation is that the human fruits born out of wedlock were nearly as common in our land as those of marriage; 'children of the wind' the Indians called them. The custom was to give them the names of their fathers. If one traced the non-Indian names, strange relations came to light. There were names of traders, merchants, men from ships, government officials—and, of course, a ne'er-do-well might have his surname handed down to several offspring. Any amorous male in our parts, in the early days, might, at the low cost of a word or a glance, procure the affection of an Indian mistress.

Probably few of these children of the wind suffered agony of mind because of having one parent 'from the sky.' Yet some of them groaned in spirit at thought of the birth fortune had given them. Leander was such a one. He was, he knew, a mixture of very diverse human elements. His father, once a man of note in the harbor village, was separated by a great mortal abyss from his mother, a full-blooded Indian, descended from an Indian chief. Leander lived with his mother, bearing the name of a father he had never seen but of whom he often heard from the gossip-loving villagers.

Throughout my boyhood Leander and I were playmates and schoolmates; we were in the same graduating class in high school; and, finally, we were in college together for four years. I very well remember when his face and figure appeared upon my horizon. In our first years in the harbor village, all Presbyterians met for worship in a hall over a store. One Sunday, looking out of the window as the preacher droned his hour-long sermon, I saw a dozen happy little heathens running, jumping, wrestling. One boy was champion in all. It was Leander.

Leander's mother was known only as 'Leander's mother.' Madame Pettier told my mother that Leander's mother was by far the most attractive Indian girl in the village when Leander's father was paying attention to her. In those days her face had been bright and joyous and she had dressed in gay frocks with ribbons and beads and wore a hat at a time when most Indian women covered their heads with shawls. After Leander came, she wore only black dresses with a shawl in place of a hat. One seldom saw her except as she came and went to Father Zorn's church. Leander, when I first knew him, was an acolyte in the Roman Catholic Church, but, after much association with heretics, became a Presbyterian. Happily, Father Zorn died before Leander, the apple of his eye, became a Protestant.

When I knew Leander's mother she was tall and straight, alluring in her sinewy body, which looked firm of flesh and was beautifully molded. Her face, when I occasionally saw it, was calm and serene but sad, with eyes like bottomless pits. It was

her eyes that especially interested me because to my child's
mind they seemed supernatural, as though they could look into
the future. Everybody admired her well-formed figure and free,
graceful movements; sailors and woodsmen would stop to look
at her as she passed. She never returned the looks and would
have nothing to do with the whites, although she was occasionally kind to me. She smiled only when I tried to speak in
the Indian tongue.

As a rule, the half-breeds in our community passed as Indians.
Leander was an exception. By the time he was ready for college,
he was all white in appearance except for a tinge of copper in
his skin, his straight black hair, and a face devoid of beard. Still,
he was not a white, but fundamentally as different from either
race as if he had slipped in from some unknown land. He was
not large, even though most people at first sight would think,
'What a man!' He was straighter than an Indian, if that is
possible; his shoulders were broad and well-filled; his muscles
moved beneath his skin like rippling waters. He was a beautiful
figure in motion, yet those of us who knew him most admired
his body motionless, especially if he were nude. Vitality and
alertness glowed from bright black eyes that quailed before no
man, either in a mental or in a physical contest.

Everybody in our part of the world was proud of Leander.
He did very well as a student in school and college and eventually became a mechanical engineer of some note. His athletic
prowess brought our little town state-wide renown. In inter-
collegiate meets, he took prizes in whatever athletic events he
entered and was famous as a pitcher in baseball. Poor Leander
lived but a few years after leaving college; tuberculosis, the
great enemy of those with Indian blood, carried him off before
he had reached full manhood.

One girl with Indian blood was a familiar of our household
in the first years of our living in the harbor village. She came

to us on occasions, through Madame Pettier, to look after my little sister. She had a French father and an Indian mother. The father we never knew, but her mother later married an Indian and lived in the village.

There was nothing remarkable about Juliette as a child. I remember her as a mean little grub, poorly dressed, never clean, and not careful in language or actions, even for a half-breed. I lost track of her in the nymph stage. Then, behold, a rare butterfly! No girl in all the country round about could boast so large a share of beauty. She was old ivory in color and had blue-black hair, her braids hanging below her waist. Her lips were as red as wild rose hips; her teeth the color of pearls. Face, neck, and hands—I have seen few more beautiful. Her body was straight, slim, lissom.

Juliette, poor child, came to know too well the fate in an American community of one of her sex and her beauty who had the taint of Indian blood. In a French-Canadian village, she might have been the heart and soul of her little world, and would, under the guidance of church and school, have developed into as good a woman as any of her white sisters.

One summer, home from college, I was out in the harbor in a rowboat with a flame of that vacation. Our course took us by a trim yacht that harbored several roaring blades from Chicago —and Juliette. There was singing aboard, and we stopped to listen. 'Juliette!' my companion whispered. So it was, and she was singing some of the plaintive little courting songs of our northern Indians, in a low, clear, sweet voice. The songs were simple and short. One was an Indian love charm:

> I am beautiful as wild roses,
> I am as beautiful as they.
> I can charm a man completely,
> I can make a man I love, love me.
> Anywhere on earth, wherever he may be,
> I can make a man I love, love me.

Another was the parting song of Indian maidens when their lovers go forth to war. Juliette sang the song well, repeating it several times, her voice lower and softer with each repetition:

> When you go,
> I will give you,
> Surely,
> What you most wish.
> When you go!

The next day the yacht left our harbor. Juliette was said to have been aboard. No one ever saw her again; no one ever knew what became of her.

An Arctic Winter

TOWARD the end of our second summer in the North, we could see that something was amiss with the weather. Heavy frosts deadened green leaves before they could take on autumn colors and brought them, brittle wafers of leather, to the ground, too ice-filled to rustle as they fell. Wild geese went south early; Joutel said we were in for a long winter.

In November, with every other boy in the village, I went to see the wreck of a schooner a mile up the beach. The day was dull and gloomy, and the earth a sodden waste as we crossed the harbor point to the lake. The surf was piling far up the hard-packed shore; the air was as keen as snuff, and we had to run to keep from freezing. The sun came out for a moment or two, and in its glint the frothy spume of the surf was beautifully iridescent.

The lake that autumn was taking a larger harvest than usual from our shipping. There was one wreck that shocked everybody in our community.

One of our neighbors, white and a newcomer like ourselves, spent all his waking hours in a sailboat, which he hardly knew how to manage, searching the shores for odds and ends of wreckage. He had a son, two years my senior, a playmate, who was a truant from school every few days to go with his father on the water, which this late in the year was so dangerous that even good sailors had long since put their boats up for the winter. One day in mid-November, father and son made a trip up the coast in a Mackinaw boat to see what the sea might be dispensing. They were caught in a sudden gale; and, though the two-masted, double-pointed Mackinaw is as safe as any craft afloat, they were wrecked. The father clung to the boat; half drowned and nearly frozen, he was washed ashore. The poor boy was lost.

Toward noon news came that the body had been found. Soon the searchers came by our door as in a funeral procession, with all of the children in the town straggling behind. The silence of the searchers intensified the tragedy. Charley, the drowned boy, would have loved the spectacle had he been alive. It was strange to me not to hear his whispered comments.

Poor Charley, frozen to the hardness and whiteness of marble, was in a two-wheeled cart, a shaggy Indian pony in the shafts. The cart had no springs, and on the rough road his body bounced up and down, clump, clump, clump. Charley had taken off his shoes; his clothes had been torn to rags by buffetings against the rocky shore, and now his face, feet, and bloodless body were nearly bare. His hair and the few rags on his body were matted with sand; sand filled the sockets of wide-open lusterless eyes; and sand had been ground into his distorted face.

The day before my playmate was drowned, I had been eating a Baldwin apple. Charley had had several out of the barrel that stood in our cellar and had asked for another. I would not give it to him, not even a bite of mine. Now that he was dead, I felt myself the vilest wretch on earth. My brother had quarreled with him, too.

Charley had said: 'My father is the best man in the village in a boat.'

My brother said: 'Everyone knows your father can't sail and that sooner or later you'll both be drowned.'

They nearly came to blows. Now, as the boy lay in his coffin, it seemed to me that my brother's horrid prophecy might have been the cause of his death.

The drowning of Charley was my introduction to death. My childish mind was bewildered by what the preachers said about life after death. For the good there was heaven, a mansion in the skies, Paradise, New Jerusalem. What were these places like? At the funeral the preachers said Charley had gone to live in the bosom of Abraham. How could anyone live in Abraham's bosom?

On the other hand, there was hell, a lake of fire and brimstone, a bottomless pit, an abyss below. To me, hell was a place several miles beneath my feet. One was carried to heaven in Abraham's bosom. How did one make the journey to hell? In Father Zorn's church a picture showed lost souls being pitchforked by devils into hell. Was that the way people were transported to hell?

Into which of these many places had my playmate been launched by the cruel sea? He swore, he lied, he stole. All boys lied, swore, and stole from their mother's cupboards. He was, of course, being pitchforked by devils, rod by rod, to the abyss below to spend eternal life in a lake of fire and brimstone. Terrifying thought!

Death, hitherto far away, was now at hand. Lying awake at night, I could think of nothing but hell, multitudes of lost souls screaming in torture, devils with horns, tails, and claws in which they held red-hot pitchforks. In sleep, I dreamed of strange animals, dragons, and serpents. Do bedposts beget monsters? At this time I was sure they did.

The doctor was called and prescribed laudanum, in big doses. Laudanum, by the way, in my childhood was as common a household remedy as aspirin is today. The dreams continued and the monsters still came, but they were amiable.

This harrowing period of shattered nerves, of which a real sickness of the summer before was the beginning, came to a climax in a personal tragedy. A few weeks after the drowned boy was buried we were reading in our school reader Dickens' tale of the death of Little Nell. I had to read the most heartrending part, and when I came to the line: 'She was dead. Dear, gentle, patient, noble Nell was dead,' the tears that had been gathering came, and I began to boohoo. The hard-hearted teacher cuffed me and called me a crybaby.

The old termagent had boxed my ears many times before and I had taken her smacks with a grin, knowing well they were deserved, but to be thus thumped for a tender heart was too much. The 'crybaby' became a maniac. I screamed at the school-mistress all the oaths I knew and all the names I had heard sailors and lumbermen use. I struck and kicked, scratched and bit. It was in my heart to kill her. Gladly would I have had carved on her tomb the awful things I had said. In this dreadful fit I felt that I was somehow defending Little Nell.

As the tussle went on, my breath came in gasps, and my heart pounded so that its beating sounded in my ears. The teacher had crowded me into a corner and badgered me as a bulldog would a kitten. She had sent for the principal, and now he came. He picked me up and carried me sobbing to the furnace room in the basement, sat down on a pile of wood, and, taking me on his knee, tried to quiet me. But I must talk.

'I want to be whipped and not expelled!' I kept repeating.

'No! You are not to be expelled! You are not to be whipped! You are to come into my room,' he told me time and again.

Thus reassured, I began to get control of my sobbing, and finally the old man asked me what it was all about.

I told him I could never read about Little Nell without crying, and I did not think the teacher should strike me for what I could not help. Looking up, I saw that tears were running down the principal's face.

'Reading about Little Nell always makes me cry, too,' he said.

The old man felt my pulse, listened to my throbbing heart, and then carried me to the coat room, put on my mittens and scarf, and sent for one of the big girls who drove in from the country and asked her to take me home. As a last word, he told me he would come to talk to my father and mother that evening.

Just what took place at the evening's conference I had no way of finding out. The doctor was sent for and put me to bed. The medicine he gave me sent me quickly to sleep with delightful dreams. The next morning I was told that I must stay in bed for a few weeks.

It turned out that Mother could not keep me in bed. The whole world was talking, I was convinced, about my having been expelled from school. The doctor told my parents that the disease of my mind was worse than the disease of my body, and that I should be better off in school. So it was arranged that I should have a seat in the principal's room. The country girl with the cutter came for me every morning and after school left me at our door.

In a corner of the crowded room into which I was promoted because of my misdeeds, there stood at right angles two cases containing the school library. To the right and left against the walls were wooden benches for readers. Above the benches were windows, one looking to the west over the stormy lake and into the sunsets of winter days, the other to the south over the bay to the cheerless wintry hills on its southern shores. The two benches in this library became my schooltime domicile, which the country girl made into a snuggery with blankets from her cutter. This little corner was to me that winter a library, a study, a playhouse, a place to sleep, and a place to receive callers who came for books.

My schooling in the prinpical's room was quite without order. I went to classes when I pleased, stretched out on my bench and slept at times, read a good deal, and listened to the other pupils recite, marveling at their stupidity. The principal called upon me to read or recite when I chose to attend classes; otherwise he paid no attention to me except at recesses, when he would not let me go out to play. Occasionally he felt my pulse, more interested in my bad heart than in my untutored mind.

Everyone who reads can associate a time and a place with a

book that has given him pleasure. I can now name all at my command in the little corner library. Most of them were beyond my years, but I read their titles, dipped into them from time to time, and thus early made them my friends. I already knew Dickens, because my father, whenever he could lay his hands on the great novelist's books, read aloud from them. But I found Scott a little too hard, and out of several volumes only attempted *Ivanhoe*. I read three most admirable books that few youngsters these days know: *Scottish Chiefs*, *Thaddeus of Warsaw*, and, the best of the three, *The Cloister and the Hearth*. *The Pilgrim's Progress* I could not read. Shakespeare was on the shelves, but was quite beyond a boy of my tender years, but I leafed through the volumes time after time to look and wonder at the illustrations and soon knew the titles, at least, by heart.

Much to my liking were the old readers, of which we had Sanders' and McGuffey's, the fourth, fifth, and the sixth of the series being in use in our room. In these readers I became acquainted with Lamb through 'Wang, the Miller'; Hawthorne in 'Pine-tree Shillings'; John G. Saxe in the 'Dapple Mare,' and 'Riding on the Rail'; Hood in the 'Bridge of Sighs'; Tennyson in 'Enoch Arden.'

It is curious how and why one remembers some of the gems of literature by titles, others by lines. By lines I remember best: 'John Gilpin was a citizen Of credit and renown'; 'A soldier of the Legion lay dying in Algiers'; 'When Freedom from her mountain height'; 'And twenty million bless the sire and sword of Bunker Hill'; 'Charge, Chester, charge! On, Stanley, on!'; 'But Douglas round him drew his cloak, Folded his arms, and thus he spoke'; 'At midnight, in his guarded tent, The Turk was dreaming of the hour'; 'It is an ancient Mariner'; 'We buried him darkly at dead of night'; 'Sweet smiling village, loveliest of the lawn'; 'This is the forest primeval.'

Father encouraged me in my reading, as he did all his children. He repeated to me very often a favorite maxim: 'Books make brains.'

I now count it a happy incident that a testy teacher boxed my ears and shook me because I could not read about Little Nell.

The schoolhouse stood in open land high on the bluff back of the village, bared to the gales of every sky. Storms moaned and roared all that winter; quite human they seemed, as if armies were raging in a great war. The wind found the schoolhouse its happiest hunting ground; it clamored for entrance; it threatened to blow windows from their fastenings. Whenever a door was opened, the wind rushed in with terrifying frenzy; it piled layers and cones of snow near cracks and joints in doors and windows.

The worst storm of the winter came in late January. Before the storm, we had a few days of winter sunshine and languid, bickering east winds. Everybody knew that a storm was brewing. Then the awful Canadian *la poudrerie* rode in on a mighty whirlwind and raged for three days and nights. The air was filled with particles of ice-frozen hail, hard as grains of sand, which the wind drove so fiercely that no one dared to expose his unprotected flesh. On the first day of the storm Father was driven in from his work, frozen from surface to core. His nose and cheeks were white as marble, so badly frostbitten that they gave him trouble for weeks afterward. He complained that his lungs and nostrils had been scorched as if by fire, that every tooth was a point of torture, that his brows ached, and that the pain in his eyes was excruciating. He could not eat, but drank a generous glass of hot toddy and went to bed to sleep off his misery.

Returning to school after the storm I was amazed at the change in our little world. From my window to the west, overlooking the lake, there was an indefinite white plain under a cold, gray sky in which the sun was hardly to be seen; we knew of its existence only in late afternoon, when there was a silver belt low in the western sky, which deepened into yellow, the sun suspended like a huge lemon. In the faint sunshine the air was filled with icy particles, like dust in sunbeams filtering into a dark room. Now and again a squall would drive icy pellets over the water, and then, as it struck our bluff, curved upwards to the sweep of the gale.

After the storm, day after day, snow fell steadily. Snow was an element. It covered the earth to a depth of several feet; it made roads impassable, and we could get about only on snowshoes; it covered the small houses in the village. It so filled the air that we could hardly find our way from house to house. Sounds did not carry in the snow-filled air, and echoes were checked so that the earth seemed to be profoundly sleeping. Paths zigzagged from door to door on top of the snow; no one attempted to keep them open by shoveling. A misstep from the path plunged us up to our middles in the untrodden snow to the right or left. In front of the stores, the Star, and Father Zorn's church, pretense was made of keeping an open space into which we slid or went down in steps. The winter's sun gave no warmth to soften the snow. Everyone knew that the village must remain buried until April came with rain and sunshine.

All of us would have starved had it not been for fish. The ice in the harbor was dotted with fishermen, spearing and bobbing a line for perch and an occasional speckled trout. Out in the bay, in the sweep of gales, were little doghouses where fishermen who could stand the cold fished with long lines through the ice in deep waters for the splendid lake trout, often weighing twenty pounds. The fish thrown on the ice quickly froze, and, left in a cold place, kept for weeks, thus anticipating our modern quick-freezing process.

The snow was too deep to permit much hunting, though an occasional deer was brought in. The snowshoe hare furnished much good food. In all swampy land this hare was abundant and easily caught with deadfalls and snares.

Regardless of weather, the grand business of life went on as usual. Mid-morning found the village astir. The colorless winter days were enlivened with interchanges of greetings;

barter and trade were keen; spite and scandal were aired; women gossiped from house to house, from store to store; children played in the snow; young people skated and sledded. Every afternoon, away went the horses up and down the mile course that stretched from Father Zorn's church to the foot of the steep hill that took one out of town. Daisy, the country girl, in taking me home from school, must join in the race whether she liked or not. Her horse was never a winner, because, it seemed to me, he was held in too tightly. What with urging the horse on and calling to Daisy, 'Let him go! Let him go!' I became overexcited, so that after a few races Daisy would run her horse no more. She had had some command from my mother because of my bad heart. It was good sport, however, to drive sedately up and down the course on the sidelines watching the show, especially when I was permitted to hold the reins.

Life was sweet and full of joy whether this lively scene was surveyed, as most often, through fast-falling snow, or in the western peachblow glow of a winter's sun sinking below the horizon, or in the afternoon of a sunny day when the brightly painted sleighs flashed by in sunlight. In the dusk of bright days when the sun had melted the surface snow, the cold of evening hardened and glazed the village street so that the race course shone like a floor of polished marble.

Our village, Little Traverse, was the chief seat of racing in the Land of the Crooked Tree; in the near-by villages of Charlevoix, Bear Creek, Middle Village, and Cross Village there was racing in the main streets much as in our town. Every winter the owners of fast horses got together for a derby. Toward the end of our long winter, word went out that there was to be a grand race in our village.

The horses were of a breed then common in Canada and until the coming of the whites the only horses in our land. They were small, wiry animals, legs short, ankles slim, breasts broad, heads small, tails and manes long. Mostly they were trotters but there were enough pacers so that there was aways a class for each. All races were in harness and the light Canadian cariole, a sledge with so little weight that it skimmed over the snow as easily as skates on ice. The prizes were in money and small, but the bets were many and ran high.

There is much confusion in my mind about the number of horses and their owners, but the names of some heard on all lips still come to my mind. There was Chicago, Papoose, Sable d'Or, Pegasus, Horace Greeley, Jim, Vedette, Petoskey, and Buckskin. Of the owners I can be sure of but three. St. Leger owned Sable d'Or, a trotter, and Pegasus, a pacer; Buckskin belonged to Chief Blackbird; and Petoskey to someone of the family of that name from across the bay at Bear Creek. Chief Blackbird and the driver of Petoskey took every opportunity as they passed each other to give voice to the war whoops of their tribes.

The horses started at scratch, in front of Father Zorn's church, with the dipping of a red flag. There was no scoring. The race-course ended at the foot of the high bluff, making a track about a mile long. There were three heats for each race. Father Zorn, at the finishing-post, was judge. As starter, Father distinguished himself by dipping the red flag.

These horse races were the most exciting events in my early childhood. There could be no greater excitement on any other racecourse; on none could there be more confusion, gayer colors, or more noise.

The most pleasing sight in the race was of the little Indian ponies as they flashed by with outstretched necks, flying feet, pumping nostrils, and heaving sides. Necks, shoulders, and manes were covered with hoarfrost from congealed breath; eyes were so dilated that they seemed to be popping from heads; sides and bellies were spattered with snow and bits of ice from the iron-shod hoofs; long tails were braided and knotted into short, compact clubs.

The drivers in their light, gayly painted carioles crowded

close to the rumps of their ponies, which their excited faces almost touched. Their beards and eyebrows were white and stiff with congealed breath. All the horsemen wore fur gloves and held the reins in one hand and a whip in the other. All wore bright Mackinaws, gay sashes, fur-topped moccasins, and fur caps. Hardly less gay were the onlookers, the males, old and young, attired as nearly as possible like the drivers of their favorite horses; the women, whether white or red, old or young, were wrapped in warm shawls showing the colors of their favorite steeds. Spectators were crowded close to the small weather-beaten buildings.

Noises from horses and humans filled the air. There were tumultuous thudding hoofs, jingling bells, and the crunching runners of the carioles. There were sharp commands to the ponies, shouts, laughter, banter, and an occasional war whoop as one lucky driver passed another. The noises all had a curious, dead, heavy sound, since the ground and the buildings were so covered with snow that there was scarcely an echo. To be sure, there was also much drinking and some fighting. Father Zorn had extra work for some days.

Finally, the winter began to wear itself out. The great icicles that hung on eaves and cornices fell crashing to the earth. The snow quickly vanished except in the deep shade of the woods, where it lingered until June. With prodigious noises, the ice in the bay loosened from the shore and was blown to open water. Wild geese were honking; bluebirds fluttered in naked tree; adventurous youth put chilblained feet on the happy earth; things were getting ready to happen down in the black, snow-covered ground. Usually our springs came headlong, as though there were not a moment to lose before another winter would be on its way, but this one came timidly, pure and fresh as a virgin.

In May ships began coming into our harbor. My copybook was filled with drawings of them in full sail, schooners, sloops,

and three- and four-masters. Whence had the ships come?
Whither bound? What their names? What their cargoes? Who
their captains? As children these days know and talk about
baseball and pitchers, so the boys in our village knew ships and
their captains.

Spring brought me health in mind and body. I began to take
advantage of my standing in the principal's good graces, and
essayed to be a funmaker. All of a sudden, the old man came
down on me. I was moved from my pleasant library corner with
its windows to a little bench near the principal's desk. Here
there were no near neighbors to whom I could whisper. If I
stuffed my mouth with dried apples from my mother's kitchen,
or if I stuck out my tongue at a comely minx near me, the
principal cracked me over the head with a pointer so hard that
I saw stars, and my body tingled from head to foot. He assigned
me to new classes and kept my nose hard against the grindstone
from morning till night. His soft heart had turned to a lump
of flint.

This was the spring that the children in our family long
remembered as the 'sulphur and molasses spring.' 'The long
hard winter,' Mother said, 'had thinned out our blood.' The
remedy for thinned-out blood in children was molasses well
thickened with sulphur. On April Fool's Day Mother prescribed
a tablespoonful of this elixir for each child every morning for a
month.

The mixture was a dreadful dose, and after a week or two
of the after-breakfast uproar when we were taking our medicine,
Father, in sheer defense of his peace of mind, joined in the
protest against sulphur and molasses and we took it no more.
In the years that followed our spring tonics were dandelion
greens, fresh rhubarb, and young onions.

V

Passenger Pigeons

NOT in the forests of North America or in any other part of the world is there now a single live passenger pigeon. In my boyhood, in the Land of the Crooked Tree, in pigeon years there were millions and millions. Their roosting place, in the season of which I am about to write, made a vast city in the air a few miles from my home. To this rookery a small army of pigeon trappers came to ply their vocation. The pigeon trapper, who did so much in the extermination of this bird, is another vanished species. The prey, the hunter, and the industry, all are gone.

My remembrance of pigeons and pigeon trappers can be summarized best by giving an account of a single day spent in a pigeon roost in one of the big pigeon years, just before these birds disappeared.

The spring after the 'Arctic winter,' wild pigeons came in such countless numbers to the Land of the Crooked Tree that ever after we all spoke of that year as the 'great pigeon year.'

Spring, in the land of our adoption, was always a time of scarcity of food, in which the whites were near starvation and the poor Indians were perishing from hunger. Pigeons came this spring as did manna to the Israelites. For six weeks before the young were of a size to eat, our whole population gorged themselves on the dark meat of old pigeons, eagerly waiting for the tender butterballs into which squabs quickly developed.

Besides, there was money to be made in trapping pigeons to supply cities near the Great Lakes with the bountiful food from sky and woods. Adventurous men followed the pigeons that then existed in a few great conclaves. To these pigeon trappers, the hunt was a means of livelihood. To Indians and settlers it was an opportunity to make a little money as well as to supply their larders.

Father was anxious to see a pigeon roost the birds had established that year near the head of Little Traverse Bay, some four or five hours distant by land and water from the harbor village. Joutel was employed to act as boatman and guide on two different days, on one of which my brother was to go and on the second excursion I was to take my turn. A condition of my going was that Juliette, the half-breed girl, should go to take care of me, on the theory that I could not keep pace all day with the men.

On the morning of the day of our expedition I was awakened by the jangling bell of the mission church and by the creaking of doors, opened by Father on his way to survey the morning sky to see what the weather was to be. Then came the call:

'Get up! Get up! All hands get up!'

The cheery voice augured well for the day. There was a hurried breakfast, an argument with Mother, tearful on my part, about a tippet she wished to tie about my neck. This and other details settled, Juliette convoyed me to the beach where Father and Joutel were making ready a sailboat, two-masted, sharp at both ends, the seaworthy Mackinaw boat of the region. At last we were off, Joutel at the tiller, Father amidships, Juliette and I in the bow.

Joutel, like many French Canadians of the woods, was a fountain of song, and now he started to make our voyage pleasant with melody, his first song suggested by a partridge drumming on the bluff along the shore. In after years I came to know

the words and music as the Ottawan song of Clear Skies, a
translation of which is:

> Verily
> The sky clears
> When the partridge sounds for me,
> Ho, ho, ho, ho, ho, ho,
> The sky clears
> When the partridge sounds for me,
> Ho, ho, ho, ho, ho, ho.

There were repetitions and improvisations and a great volume
of sound that bespoke a full heart and a blithe spirit in a happy
man.

The day was perfect. A soft purple haze floated over the
harbor, with too little breeze to carry it away or to move our
boat at more than a snail's pace with all sails set. Clouds of
mayflies hovered over the waters in love flight, prey to hungry
fish that broke the water with resounding slaps. Swallows
skimmed through the air to share the feast with herring, trout,
and perch. The haze, the languid air, the mayflies, the quiet
water, the still forest, the magic of summer, all gave a feeling
of peacefulness in strong contrast to the expectancy of adventure
in our boat.

The morning flight of pigeons from the roost was nearly over,
and I was fearful that they had taken wing to some distant forest
region; or that the birds of prey, which hovered over them and
shadowed the small flocks now in the sky, had destroyed all but
these few. Joutel said that we should see pigeons in plenty
as they returned to their roost in the afternoon, and I was
comforted.

Joutel, his hunter's instinct aroused, repeatedly called attention to the pursuing hawks. Sometimes these maurauders flew
above the pigeons; sometimes abreast the van; again they loitered in the rear; and always there were goings and comings
from the land where their catch was eaten. From the vantage

point of the boat we were thrilled with the evolutions a large flock of pigeons made as they sought to escape from the pirates of the air. When the hawks pressed close upon the rear, they drove the flying multitude into a compact mass like an enormous swarm of bees, a movement accompanied by a noise like thunder from the fluttering wings. The most remarkable evolution was one in which, for some cause or other, the pigeons divided into columns and then ascended in a spiral like the coil of a long snake.

Our little party hurried into the woods. Joutel briskly led the way. The sun was now well up, and there was a delightful play of light and shade in the more open parts of the woods. Birds poured forth floods of delirious music. For more than a mile our trail was through thick underbrush that dripped with dew; every leaf was weighted, and every spider web was strung with sparkling diamonds; wet glossy leaves shone like polished silver. Soon water dripped from our garments. We followed a stream that leaped and roared over many-colored rocks. As we rested on its banks, Joutel showed me fingerling trout darting to and fro under forest wastage, and in some excitement pointed to a full-grown fish, its dim form vibrating in the shadow of a dark pool, not so dark but that we could see the flashing rubies on his sides.

Some three or four miles inland we came to the roost. The birds had chosen for their season's nesting place alluvial lands about a long waterway of lakes and connecting streams. As we passed from the upland forests into these lower lands, we skirted a dreary waste of oozy swamp, on the banks of which were gardens of fern and clumps of whimsical white, yellow, and red toadstools. The red toadstools, Juliette told me, were 'ears of dead men,' and from their shape and texture so they might have been.

As we passed a rush-grown pond Juliette seized my arm and hissed, 'See! A snake!'

At first I saw no snake and then had a thrill of horror. A serpentine form of black and buff arose in erect, rigid attitude, its head even with the tops of the rushes. Juliette kept up the cry, 'A snake! A snake!'

It was a moment before even Joutel's keen eyes saw the creature. He said, 'Huh! Huh! A Wabita.'

It was a bird, a bittern, its body and neck stretched straight up four or five feet, standing in plain sight, not forty feet distant, among flags and rushes scarcely thick enough to hide a blackbird—yet we had all but missed seeing it. A light breeze rocked the flags and rushes. The bittern swayed to their every movement. Thus he stood for some little time in sublime confidence, his glittering eyes returning our gaze; then, unable longer to endure scrutiny, he rose from the shallow water, legs dangling and dripping, leaving a silver wake upon the pond, and circled above the neighboring trees.

A little farther in this valley of vegetable succulence and sanctuary of wild life, we came to the pigeon roost. Pigeon dung covered the ground, looking like a heavy fall of grayish snow; flowers, shrubs, underwood, and small trees were dead as if fire had swept through the woods, and thousands of large trees might as well have been girdled by the ax; great limbs were scattered about as though a tornado had followed the fire. The ground was strewn with bodies of pigeons, killed by accident in the gathering of the great assemblage. Mingled with the dead pigeons were countless numbers of pure white eggs. The smell of dead birds and rotten eggs added to that of the dung, so that all that breathed were threatened with suffocation. The noise was so great that we could speak to one another only by shouting; cooings of pigeons were to my ears moans of pain; whirring wings sounded like the coming of a storm. These continuous noises were punctuated by the fall of limbs overweighted with pigeons.

Most of the pigeon hunters were Indians, armed with axes, poles, and bows. The men slashed down trees loaded with nests from which the young were about to fly. As the squabs fluttered from their cradles, they were caught by women and children, decapitated by a quick jerk, and their quivering bodies tossed to swell the family heap. Nests on low branches of large trees were knocked from the supports with long poles and blunt arrows. The squabs were covered with scalelike feathers, easily removed by rubbing, after which they were drawn and packed in receptacles to be taken to the camp where they were smoked for winter.

Besides the Indians there were professional pigeon trappers. With L'Arbre Croche as a center, the pigeons ranged for food over a radius of a hundred miles. In this vast territory white pigeon hunters, who captured their prey in nets, multiplied the catch of the Indians a thousandfold.

We came now to a road, the main artery of the traffic. It led from the roost some twelve or fifteen miles to a railroad, which recently had been extended to the southern boundary of our country. The road was a comfort to our tired feet, since holes had been filled with wings and feathers from pigeon-packing places, which had made a kind of carpet.

We passed several pigeon nets before coming to one that had been 'struck.' Here we saw hundreds of glittering heads stretched upward through the meshes of the net, the fluttering birds putting forth frantic efforts to escape. Two hairy Esaus, plastered with mud, blood, and feathers, stood in the ooze of the pigeon bed, red-handed from the slaughter of the catch. One with a pair of pincers and the other with thumb and finger gave the necks of the pigeons a remorseless twist. Blood burst from the bird's eyes, the wings fluttered, the body quivered, and the bird was dead.

A helper at one of the nets was a one-armed Civil War veteran, 'Old Joe,' who lived in our parts. What his last name was I never knew. With his one hand Old Joe would pick up a pigeon by a leg, flip it up so that its head went into his mouth that he might crush the head between his teeth, all done so deftly that he threw as many iridescent corpses in the pile as any other worker. What a sight! His face was smeared with blood from ear to ear; his beard dripped gore; his clothes were covered with it.

The pigeon netters chose for their nets low, marshy spots, from which they removed all growth and forest refuse. Pigeons have a liking for salt, and a bed was first saturated with salt; then the further bait of grain was scattered. Some netters added a perfume of sulphur, saltpeter, or anise seed. On this enticing bit of earth a stool pigeon, eyes punched out, was tied on a block, and a cord was so arranged that the fluttering bird could be raised and lowered to attract pigeons passing high overhead. A pigeon net is 8 feet wide and 30 feet long. The trap was set by an adjustment of a spring pole and rope at one edge of the net. Forty feet from an end of the net, the trapper secreted himself in a bough house and awaited the moment to 'strike' when the bed was azure blue with birds. Twenty dozen pigeons was a good catch.

It was then well toward noon, and Father looked for a spring where we might eat and drink. Father had a sense of discrimination in water, like that lovers of wine apply to vintages; but to Joutel, water was only water, and he objected to going out of the way for a drink of so little strength. Finally we found a pleasing spring, the water of which gushed up in quantity sufficient to supply a city and with such force that the sandy bottom boiled. Joutel took the occasion to demonstrate the miracle of magnetism, a phenomenon wholly new to me. His knife blade, held in the water a moment, became a magnet, feeble in power, but still a loadstone that would pick up a pin.

Mother had commissioned Joutel to bring her a supply of spruce gum. All the youngsters in the village chewed spruce gum, the only gum that could be had. The hardened pitch from spruce trees was golden brown as it came from the tree, changing to pink as it was chewed. It had a pleasant aromatic taste that children, and grown-ups as well, liked. At first chewing spruce gum was frowned upon in our house as another bad habit learned from the Indians. Then Mother began to encourage gum-chewing, for Madame Pettier had told her that spruce gum 'stimulated the urinary tract.' And, though Heaven knows we children didn't need to have our urinary tracts stimulated, and Father's and Mother's teeth were too brittle to chew spruce gum, it was added to the lengthy list of our household remedies.

Joutel collected an abundant supply of spruce gum, and he, Juliette, and I vigorously chewed it. Joutel had poor teeth, and, though spruce gum may be good for the urinary tract, it is about the worst thing in the world for decaying teeth. Soon the poor man had a raging toothache. A torrent of oaths poured from his mouth. He called upon: 'Father Joseph! Mother of Jesus! God A'mighty!' to relieve the pain, and said 'goddam' with every breath.

Father said comfortingly, '*Tout passe! Tout passe!*' a favorite phrase of Joutel's.

Finally Joutel told Juliette and me to gather spider webs. I asked why, and Juliette told me that a worm was gnawing at the root of the tooth, and that Joutel would draw the tormenter out with a web. Was the imp lying? I suspect that there was an Indian belief that a worm caused toothache. At any rate, Joutel invoked all the spiders that spin to draw out the intruder; but, on the other hand, he only wadded the webs and stuffed the ball in the cavity. In due time he was relieved.

Luncheon over, Father and Joutel left to see more of the pigeon netters. I was to sleep while Juliette watched over me. Our table had been spread in a pretty clump of birches, shady yet bright with checkered sunlight. In this cosy bower I now slept. After a time I awakened, stiff from my hard couch and fretful with the torment of flies, mosquitoes, and gnats.

When I had fully awakened, Juliette suggested that we go pigeon-nesting, an amusement easily pursued since there were trees all about, small enough to climb, that held from one to a dozen or more nests. The nests were made of a few dry twigs so carelessly put together as scarcely to hold the single egg that each usually contained. According to Joutel, pigeons nested three or four times in a season.

Passing through open beech woods where nuts were very plentiful, we were overtaken by billows of young birds just learning to fly. They fed on nuts buried in leaves and every pigeon wanted to be in front, so that the scrambling multitude appeared to roll through the forest. They took no heed of Juliette and me, and as the birds struck us with body and wings we were forced to fight them off, as one does a swarm of gnats. We were glad when the waves of birds passed on, and we started back to our luncheon place to wait for our elders.

As we sat waiting, we were amused by pompous male pigeons making love to prospective spouses. A cock would spread his tail, trail his wings, puff his throat, and call a tender 'coo, coo, coo.' Now and then he rose for a short flight, and then returned to renew his wooing. The timorous females responded with cooing endearments. All around mated couples were jangling, so that the forest rang with their clamor. As they had filled their crops during the day, it was easy to approach either young or old. Even my child's eyes could distinguish the sexes, the differences being as marked as in chickens. The neck and breast of the males were vividly iridescent with the azure of the back and outer wings. The females were much less gaudy in color and their bodies smaller and trimmer.

The afternoon was beginning to wane, and we made a hurried start for the beach. I was riding pick-a-back on Joutel. His toothache had gone, and he sang or hummed continuously. One doggerel I remember well because I could not make rhyme or reason of it:

> Sometimes, taken in small doses,
> Holy water does no harm.
> Tum-tiddy-um-tum, tum-tum,
> Tum-tiddy-um-tum, tum-tum.

To Father's disgust, Joutel had another commission to carry out for Mother. Tobacco was scarce in this far-northern country and every Indian smoked kinnikinnik, a mixture of bark and leaves, to be had in plenty from various shrubs growing in open forest places. Joutel's brand was supposed to be of the best, though he mixed it with strong, black home-grown tobacco. Kinnikinnik, without the tobacco, made a strong tea that to the Indians was a sovereign remedy for bowel troubles. Mother wanted a jar of it on her medicine shelf. The foundation of Joutel's mixture was the bark of red osier, leaves of sumac, and bearberry, the whole flavored with wintergreen and princess pine. These ingredients were shredded, dried, and mixed. Kinnikinnik was not a bad concoction in a tea or smoked in a clay pipe, as I well know, and I was glad to have Joutel lay in a fresh supply; it made a beautiful blue smoke that blew from a puckered mouth in perfect curls; in nostril-tingling aroma and in quantity of smoke, it far surpassed the corn silks every small boy smokes.

When materials for kinnikinnik were finally gathered, burdens were taken up and we went our way. Father and Joutel each wore a festoon of squabs. Joutel had made these garlands by pulling out the four long tail feathers of cocks, which he knotted in twos. He then stuck the stiff quill ends through the tender lower mandibles of the squabs, and, to complete the festoon, tied together the feather ends of small strings until he had fifteen or twenty squabs in his wreath.

Suddenly the glow of day changed to twilight. The pigeons were returning to the roost after a day of foraging. The sun seemed to have left the heavens. High above the tallest treetops the pigeons flew, rapidly and steadily, several strata deep. The vast cloud of birds extended as far in every direction as the eye could reach. In the two hours it must have taken us to reach the beach there was no diminution in their numbers, nor was there until we had been at camp quite another hour and the sun had set. Now and then the cloud broke in undulations, whether from attacks of hawks or currents of air, I do not know. When they descended they came in a Niagara-like cataract, eventually rising again to the general level of the flight. Black was the prevailing color in the thick cloud of birds, but at times, depending on sunlight or shadow, the numbers of strata, the height, or the angle of flight, the color was grayish white, a shimmering azure, or a rich deep purple.

At sundown we came to our landing-place of the morning. The shore now teemed with life. A dozen Indian families were on the beach. With appetites whetted by exertion and L'Arbre Croche air, Indian families were hurrying preparations for the evening meal. At last food was in sight, and Joutel struck up the hearty dinner *chanson des coureurs de bois,* which sounds the praise of a *pâté de trois pigeons:*

> Qu'apportes-tu dans ton giron?
> Ha, ha, ha, frit à l'huile,
> C'est un pâté de trois pigeons,
> Fritaine, friton, fritou, poilon,
> Ha, ha, ha, frit à l'huile,
> Frit au beurre à l'oignon.
>
> C'est un pâté de trois pigeons,
> Ha, ha, ha, frit à l'huile,
> Assieds-toi et le mangeons,
> Fritaine, friton, fritou, poilon,
> Ha, ha, ha, frit à l'huile,
> Frit au beurre à l'oignon.

The meal over, the men hurriedly prepared the boat for the voyage home. I was loath to leave the gay and picturesque camp. Fires had been built on the hard-packed sand of the shore, about which the men sat on flotsam and smoked while the women cleared away the remains of the supper. In and out of the shallow water a dozen little Indians played the hopping game of 'Man with his Leg Tied Up.' Leg looped to thigh, in and out, up and down, they hopped to the noisy chant:

Man with the leg tied up,
Man with the leg tied up,
Broken leg-legged,
Legged.

Night was well begun when our boat headed into the vast light of the lake. Behind us campfires lighted the shore with crimson radiance and intensified the blackness of the forest background. Running athwart the skies was the broad white road of the heavens. Juliette said this milky way was the path of souls. There was a cool breeze, and Father made me lie down under the cover of his coat. The silence was broken by the calls of night birds from the distant woods. Juliette would have me believe that these noises were supernatural. The sibilant notes of nighthawks were the voices of water sprites, one of which had once cast a spell on her. The cry of the loon, the hoot of the owl, the whoop of the bittern were the hallooings of the ghosts of Indian warriors who had died long ago.

Far out in L'Arbre Croche waters, a steamboat, outlined by starlike lights, moved slowly along the horizon. I dropped to sleep to dream of traveling on a great boat to see the countries of the world.

VI

Our Farm

SEVERAL chapters have gone by and I have not yet come to the farm, the chief concern of our family in these years. This delay gives a wrong impression of what was on our minds. In my own case, from the time we landed from the *Menominee* I awaited with tremulous elation the first visit to the land Father had purchased the autumn before. Yet, as it turned out, the visit was one of the minor tragedies of childhood. Words cannot describe the disappointment I felt when I first saw 'our farm.'

When Father said, 'Boys, this is the farm,' we could not believe him.

His words awakened his sons from beautiful dreams. We had expected fields, fences, buildings, and a pleasant grove of trees in which we might see deer and possibly bears. The woods were to be a playground of perpetual joy. They were to be full of nuts, maple-sugar trees, and berries; the sky would be full of pigeons, geese, ducks, eagles; we should find birds' nests in every tree. Possibly there would be gold. We had worked ourselves up to believe that our farm was a land of pure delight. Father had not checked our imaginations.

The farm before our eyes was a forest black as night. In it no ax had ever been lifted. Except for the rough trail over which we had come, there was no sign that man had ever set foot on our land. The appalling stillness seemed never before to have been broken by human voices. In the middle of the June day, even the birds were songless. The silence was another surprise. Father had told people before coming to this new country that his farm in northern Michigan was a 'howling wilderness.' Somehow I had expected to hear animals howling in the distance, as we had heard prairie wolves from our home in Iowa. I had been accustomed to the warmth and sunshine of a prairie. The deep, cool gloom of the forest depressed me. Our farm lay wholly in a sunless, shadowless murk. Only at high noon could sunshine steal down tree trunks to warm and brighten little patches here and there in this dense growth.

Had Father been cheated? Had he lost his reason? Something was wrong. No man of his own free will and in his right mind would buy a farm such as this! These were very disquieting thoughts to boys who had believed their father unsurpassed in all the affairs of life.

The foundation of the forest was hemlock, maple, beech, and an occasional elm, basswood, and birch. The green spires of the hemlocks towered high above the deciduous trees, and these, in turn, overwhelmed countless numbers of lean saplings struggling for a bit of sunshine. Underneath the saplings were thickets of Canadian yew and a great assortment of ferns and gay June flowers.

To 'get the lay of the land,' as Father said, we tramped two or three hours over our farm of forest trees. The land was gently sloping—no hills, but so covered with hummocks, fallen trees, and windfalls that the general effect was that of a waste of savage forest vegetation entangled over forest debris. In soft-living modern days I do not believe that there are men sufficiently hardy and work-enduring to undertake the task of making a farm out of a forest such as this.

To Father, the luxuriant forest growths bespoke fertility in the soil; his eyes shone as he appraised the great trees; he went down on his knees to dig up a handful of soil that he might see its color and feel its texture; he lovingly selected a site for our house, choosing a bit of level land on the highest elevation. This unbroken forest was to him a land of wealth and adventure.

'Good land!' was Mother's commonest ejaculation. When she had her first look at the farm, out it came:

'Good land! What a farm!'

Although we began in a small way to clear land the first summer and kept doggedly at it month in and month out until the sons grew up and the father grew old, it was three years before we built a house on our land. Mother would not live in an unbroken forest where there were no roads, no water, no near neighbors, and no school for her children.

When, in due course, we came to build, Mother stood out for a frame house. I wanted a log house. I had been born in a log house and my few years in it had been very happy ones; whereas in our frame house in Indiana, much of the time I had been ill with 'growing pains,' 'rheumatic fever,' 'a bad heart,' and 'nerves.' Sitting in Mother's wooden-bottomed rocking chair in this frame house I had rocked and sobbed: 'I want to go back to the log house in I-o-way.' Now, again, I wanted to live in a log house.

The boxlike, two-roomed frame house that Father built was as mean a structure as human beings could live in (we came to better estate after a few years). The framework was of unplaned hemlock boards running up and down; the cracks, for the planks did not overlap, were battened with thin narrow strips. A single thickness of lumber, papered inside with newspapers, was all that stood between our living quarters and the cold and storms of northern winters. Of God's air there was plenty! The house was an improvement over those of most of our neighbors, because it had a shingled roof and a cellar. The total cost for work and material was $100, an enormous sum it seemed to me.

The wilderness closed in our little clearing, in the center of which stood the boxlike house, the trees making an almost solid wall of verdure. The sky was round and big, its center just above our house. On every square rod of the cleared land there were greater and lesser stumps. A narrow road, heavy in sand, wormed its way through the clearing, running close to our front door. There were no enclosing fences, no walks, no shrubs, no flowers, not a tree left for shade or shelter, no other buildings, except a low barn built of small logs. House and grounds, sublime in simplicity!

A great drawback to the farm was that it was impossible to get water. Happy was the homesteader who had a good spring on his place near which he could build. There was no spring on our land and we had to draw water in barrels for all purposes when that from the cistern gave out, as it did time and again every summer. Cistern water is tepid, and Father must have cool spring water to drink. Thus, once or twice a day for several years, from the beginning of spring to the end of autumn, my brother and I brought fresh water from a creek a half mile away.

The path to the creek led through a splendid growth of hardwood trees, mostly beech and maple, as beautiful as any forest I have ever seen. These woods were pleasant enough, but as a small boy it made my flesh creep to go alone for water. The dipping pool was guarded and darkened and closed in with the thick foliage of a grove of hemlocks, through which the sun never penetrated. It was as fearful a place as I can recall ever having been in, darkened, as it was, by the shades of centuries past. Its silence was broken only by the brook. In the humid darkness of the grove the trunks of trees, now long since brought to earth, furnished nourishment for strange fungi, clammy white, orange, and red, and dark green mosses. The brook rushed over tortuous roots with waving tendons, reminding one of the arms and tentacles of sea monsters. Moreover, the creek came from a near-by swamp, a slum of vegetation in which grew deformed trees. Human feet could not make way in the tangles and ooze of this swamp. It was the home of a family of wildcats, whose screeches we occasionally heard at night.

As we grew older, the dipping pool lost its terrors and became a place of pleasure. After leaving 'the spring,' the creek dawdled for several rods out of the hemlock grove and ran down a rock dam into a larger pool in a glade of beeches. In a minute we could be out of the gloom of the hemlocks and into the cheerful sunshine of the beeches. By the time we reached the beeches, we could throw away shirt and overalls and then take a few minutes to sport in the pool. In the few square rods of this pleasant water my brother and I enjoyed ourselves morning after morning, from the last snow in the spring until the first snow of autumn.

Not much could be done in the first few years in the way of clearing land. Father needed the help of his sons, small though we were, in this arduous task. When we could swing light axes, my brother and I cut and piled underbrush, while Father downed small trees. This was work for summer. In winter, the large trees were felled. Brush and trees were piled in neat wind-rows, waiting a dry time in spring for a consuming fire. Father had a helper in the winter, when we were in school. All the winter through, no matter what the weather, on all the farms in the region could be heard the music of saws, as of brass instrument, to which the clack-clack of the ax and beetle kept time, with grand crashes in the forest orchestra of falling trees.

When my brother and I were old enough to be of real help, tree-felling became a fine art in our family. The work was done with beautiful precision. Father sank his ax to the heart of a tree, making a cut as smooth as if it had been planed. My brother and I, bending and swaying, made the crosscut saw ring in high, sibilant notes as it gnawed a thin cut straight to the tree's heart, opposite Father's notch, and so piled up on each side heaps of coarse, fragrant sawdust. If the tree stood straight or if there was a favoring wind, even a monarch of our woods fell of its own accord. If winds were unfavorable, or the tree leaned in the wrong direction, an iron wedge was inserted in the saw-cut and driven in, with a heavy iron-ringed beetle to make the tree crash to earth in the spot planned for its fall.

The ax has been the tool of tools of those who carved the farms of America out of the wilderness that once covered the land from the Mississippi to the Atlantic and the Rockies to the Pacific. No other utensil used by pioneers in forest regions can begin to compare in usefulness with the keen-edged, shining ax, skilfully hung on a helve of hickory or ash, and swung by muscular, callous-handed sons of toil.

Every farm in the Land of the Crooked Tree had an arsenal of axes. On our farm, each male, including the hired men, had his own ax, and woe be to him who used an ax without the permission of its owner. There were axes to cut hardwoods, to cut pine and cedar, to grub out stumps, to split wood. Those who worked in hemlock forests used a double-bitted ax. You wanted a keen-edged bit to cut the clear wood of hemlock; for cutting limbs and knotty parts of the hemlock, the thick, dull bit of a double-bitted ax.

The weight and shape of an ax and its handle are matters of prime concern to woodsmen; so, also, are the curve of the cutting edge, the size of the pole, and the shape of the socket. The best ax handles are made from dry, second-growth hickory, but there were no hickories in our northern woods, and second-growth white ash, well seasoned, was used instead. Every good woodsman is particular about the shape, length, and diameter of the helve of his ax; an ax in the hands of an experienced chopper must have perfect balance. The helve of a double-bitted ax is straight and strong; of a broad-ax, to be used in hewing and squaring timbers, short and heavy.

To anyone who has been a boy in a forest, an ax suggests a grindstone. Oh, the weary, weary hours a forest-bred boy must spend turning a grindstone! A grindstone is a round, solid, flat stone, from two to three feet in diameter, three inches thick. It is mounted on a spindle-like frame and is turned by a winch-handle. Men in our parts who lived alone turned their grind-stones with a treadle, but I never knew a man who would use a treadle if there was a boy around. The approved time to use the grindstone, the world over, is during the noon hour.

The stone out of which these instruments to torture boys are made is fine standstone. This stone must be geologically common, for our hardware stores sold grindstones made in several states. Our Canadian neighbors swore by sandstone that came from far-off Nova Scotia. A near-by Canadian had a grindstone that, he bragged, came from England. (It was as hard to turn as any stone quarried in America.)

Underneath the revolving stone was a trough filled with water, for the stone must be kept wet. To prevent over-wetting the stone, a mean man made a boy pour on water drop by drop, a practice that ruined the man's chances of hiring any boy in the neighborhood to turn his grindstone at the current price of ten cents an hour.

A boy alternately sits and stands when he turns a grindstone, under the mistaken notion that by so doing he can rest his back and arms; the task is just as hard, monotonous, and unbearably long whether he sits, stands, or changes from one position to the other. The only moment of rest comes when the man holding the ax wants a little respite and takes time to test the edge on a calloused thumb.

After all was done that could be done in sharpening an ax on a grindstone, it was given a still keener edge with a whetstone. A whetstone is a small, smooth stone, six inches long and two wide, kept wet with oil, water or, very commonly, saliva. A scythestone is much too coarse in texture to make a good whetstone. I was always fascinated as I watched John Wilson, one of our hired men, whet an ax, which he did with lightning speed. He was the kind that bore all his weight on a grindstone as I turned, and always, as he finished by whetting, I devoutly prayed that he would cut off a finger or a whole hand.

Using a crosscut saw is hard but pleasant work when the knack of sawing is learned. The stroke must be precisely the same for both sawyers. Each of the pair must pull the same, not too fast, not too slow; each must press down lightly and neither 'ride.' The rhythm in bending and swaying must be perfect; a poor sawyer quickly tires his partner out. When the two men on a crosscut saw co-operate and the sawdust flies in a steady stream, the saw singing the tune of good steel, the work is the most pleasant of any in the woods.

For years we had two hired men, John Wilson and John Johnson, who were perfect woodsmen. They kept our several crosscuts sharp as files could make them, and set the teeth to cut any kind of wood, little set for hard woods and much for soft. They taught my brother and me how to saw, but we never could keep it up more than an hour or two with either of them.

After the ax a crosscut saw is the most used tool on a farm in a forest. A crosscut saw cuts across the grain of timber—hence the name. It is wholly useless in sawing with the grain. The woodman's crosscut, like all saws, is a thin flat tool, made of well-tempered steel, four to five feet long, three to five inches wide at the two ends, straight on the upper side, usually with a more or less pronounced belly on the lower side.

At the two ends of a two-man saw there are round detachable handles, fifteen inches long and a little thicker through than a hoe handle. The cutting edge of this saw has a continuous series of large teeth of various forms and sizes.

There are many makes of crosscut saws, each kind having a trade name. The names that come to mind are Rattler, Diamond Tooth, Champion, Great American, and Electric. Father liked the Rattler best; my brother and I chose the Great American; the hired men thought they had to have a Diamond Tooth. Each kind of crosscut had its own sibilant sound as it cut through a log; each had its individual ring when thumped with a snap of the finger. Expert sawyers liked to hear the ring of the different saws hanging in any hardware store.

Joutel was not much good with a saw, and our hired men quickly tired the old man out, all the while berating him for his poor work. He hated them and always spoke of them as 'Zose goddams.'

To my brother and me he bragged: 'Ba golly! I'll lose zose goddams z'roo de bush. . . . Bi'me by I'm larn zose goddams to run and jomp. . . God A'mity! I'm mak' de canoe walk away from zose goddams.'

In spring Father was desperately energetic. He had the males of our household, sons and hired men, in the woods early in the morning, as soon as birds began to chirp and chipmunks stuck their heads out of their burrows. I was sent for water when only the creek was wide awake and the damp fresh forest was but dimly lighted by dawn.

After a few days of summer sun had dried the fallen timber, burning began. Dark spires of smoke arose from the burning piles of crackling, sizzling forest growths. Our little clearing was filled with fires that shimmered and quivered with hazy smoke and the pleasant smell of burning wood. The workers were creatures from Hades who had strayed into a land of green growth and blue sky. No one would have guessed that we had anything to do with fruits and grains; that we were making sacrificial offerings of forests that hearths might be established. When the preachers preached about hell fire, as they often did in my boyhood, farm boys knew pretty well what they were talking about. Had we not cast thousands of brands in hell fire?

When our clearing was small and I was too young to take part in the work, I would stand near the house and watch. The fires were a lovely sight. The whole opening in the woods where our house stood glowed from flames, which threw a red glare upon dark caverns in the forest and a wavering light to the tops of the tallest trees. When I became old enough to take an active part in burning fallen timber, the beauty of the scene went unnoticed. I could think only of the toil.

Of all the weary hours in the work of clearing land, those spent in burning brush heaps gave me the most torturing discomfort. Smoke filled the nostrils, lungs, and eyes; my body, grimy from head to foot, was wet with sweat; hands and face were scorched; red-hot coals burned through the soles of my shoes. Before the end of the burning season, existence became a nightmare. Every day ended with muscles and bones sore with the pain of toil; legs, shoulders, back, and sides ached with every movement.

When the windrows of fallen timber had been burned and the fires had cooled, logging began, work that called for extra men and a team of oxen. Tools for logging, in addition to men and oxen, are chains, cant hooks, handspikes, saws, axes, skids, a drawboat, and, most in evidence, a jargon of expressive and emphatic words that the workers shout to each other and at the oxen. It requires not a little art to make good log heaps, though when finished they are just a pile of logs, each sixteen to twenty feet long, the largest on the bottom, and from six to ten in the pile. In my day, on our farm my brother and I had a hand in cutting the timber and rolling the logs on some eighty acres of heavy timberland, and became, as youths, masters in the art of logging, most difficult of the several tasks in clearing land.

If there were only two or three acres to be logged, Frank Chandler, with his oxen, and two hired men with Father and his sons could put all the logs in heaps and burn them in two days. Usually there were five or six acres, and Father had two teams of oxen and ten men to get the nasty job over with as quickly as possible. Twice we had ten acres to log and had logging bees with four pairs of oxen and a dozen or twenty extra men. Weary weeks were spent in getting the logs ready for logging, in which all the parts of the fallen timber that could be carried were chunked up about larger logs and burned; long trunks were sawed in lengths of sixteen or eighteen feet.

In logging, one man drove the oxen; a chain boy fastened and unfastened the chain; another boy handled the skids and helped with a handspike; two men used handspikes and a third rolled the logs with a cant hook.

The oxen put the full weight of their bodies in a yoke in 'snaking' the logs to the log heap being put up. This yoke was made of a heavy piece of white ash, six or seven inches square and six feet long. The lower side of the timber was hollowed at the ends to fit over the necks of the oxen. The yoke was kept on the necks of the oxen by two bows passing through the timber and fastened with pins above. In the middle of the yoke was a ring made of half-inch iron to which a thick chain twenty-five or thirty feet long was attached by a clevis, a U-shaped piece of iron with the ends perforated to receive a pin. The other end of the chain was linked to a heavy hook, to hold the chain in place in a single loop about a log; or, it might be attached by a clevis to a drawboat on which one end of a log might be loaded.

A drawboat is a homemade farm tool used in snaking logs considerable distances. It is an A-shaped contrivance made of rounded timbers eight inches in diameter, with the pointed end of the A gently turned up. The end of the log being drawn rests on the heavy crossbar to which it is fastened with a chain.

Father called a drawboat a 'toad,' which Joutel translated into *crapo*. In the first years we were on the farm Joutel was an occasional helper in the logging field, and, too old to do hard work, was chain boy. He hated the toad and always called it 'dat goddam *crapo*.' The name stuck, and behind Father's back his sons called a drawboat the 'goddam *crapo*.'

When the word 'handspike' first came to my ears, Father told me it was a tool with which logs were moved. To my youthful imagination it was a wonderful machine, like the handcar of railroads. It turned out to be a round wooden bar used as a lever to roll logs. Ours were made of young ironwood trees, ten feet long and three inches in diameter, from which the bark had been removed, and one end sharpened poker fashion. Several were used in every logging field.

A cant hook, another indispensable tool in logging, is a factory turned handspike, seven feet long, on the lower end of which is a stout iron hook fifteen inches long, used in turning logs. A peavey is a cant hook shod at the lower end with a heavy spike; it is a tool much used by lumbermen, who sometimes brought it in the logging field.

There were always some big logs that had to be rolled up on a second or third layer. To build a log heap of more than one tier, skids had to be provided. These were trunks of stout young ash trees cut to various lengths. One end rested on the ground, the other on the tier of logs highest up. The log to go up was rolled with handspikes and cant hooks up the skids to its resting place. If the log was very large, the oxen were backed to the opposite side of the log heap and the chain was given two or three rolls around the middle of the log, after which the oxen were started. Up went the log with a bang.

There were often accidents in logging. The skids might slip; one end of a log might slew when the oxen were hauling a log either on the ground, or, more often, on the skids in topping a log heap. Crushed feet and broken legs were the most usual major accidents. Strained or wrenched backs, feet trampled by oxen, and hands caught in chains were minor mishaps common in every day of logging. In a logging bee there was great rivalry between the several crews to see which could put up the most heaps. Everything was done with a whoop, and it was considered a lucky bee when the day ended without someone's getting seriously hurt.

Every spring my brother and I begged Father to have a logging bee. It was great fun to have twenty or thirty men and a house full of women about. The men shouted, swore, told obscene stories; and always some man, usually one of our Canadian neighbors, sang ditties. The women gossiped from morning to night. Mother liked a logging bee because it gave her a chance to display the two arts in which she thought she was most proficient, cooking and doctoring. She knew she must cook, and rather hoped, I suspect, that someone would be hurt and her services as a doctor be required.

At night after a logging bee there was a square dance. The

fiddlers, two or three of them, did not come until supper, since
no one could log all day and have hands in shape to fiddle at
night. The Canadians were the best dancers and amazed us all
with the capers they cut, the ditties they sang in calling off, and
the kisses they stole from their partners. The small fry at the
bee were sent to bed about midnight; most of the men went to
the barn and 'hit the hay' for an hour or two between darkness
and dawn.

Going to bed toward midnight, after chunking log heaps for
three or four hours, was a trying ordeal. You would think a
logger could go to sleep the instant his head touched the pillow.
Not so; the aches and pains would not quiet down; images
flickered before his eyes; and when sleep did come the images
still remained.

As the work of burning brush and logs progressed, time
dragged to eternity. Saturday was like Monday; all days were
alike and all days to come would be. The work of clearing land
is drudgery and monotony unsurpassed by any other labor of
woodsmen. When a man has slashed and piled the underbrush;
felled, limbed, and cut the trunks of trees; burned, logged, and
burned again to the last coal the growth of a forest; grubbed
out the stumps and roots; he has truly taken possession of the
land. No other tiller of the soil is so intimate with his land as
he who has taken it from a forest.

To the children in our family the farm we had worked so
hard to take from the forest was the hub of the universe. We
saw the world from our own doorstep. After a few years we had
the feeling that we had always lived there and that we should
go on living there forever. Five miles from home was far afield
for us. At first, there were only eighty acres of our land, the
'north forty' and the 'south forty,' but often, as a small boy, I
was lost in our own woods. Always there was the great beyond
of two white and two Indian neighbors, whose lands completed
the 640 acres in the section of which Father had bought a part.

The few acres in this square mile of forest were never without new interests; the woods of our township were full of opportunities for adventures.

While our feet did not carry us far from home, our minds were often in distant lands. After several Arctic winters Father began to talk about moving to a warmer climate. He spent the evenings of one winter poring over maps of Florida, Texas, California, Oregon, and Washington Territory. Not only the cold but the quiet and peace of our half-civilization had become tiresome to him. At last he quite made up his mind that he wanted to 'take up land' in the territory of Washington. For several years he had worked in a sort of wild happiness in northern Michigan, but now that his land was pretty well under the plow he wanted to go to Washington Territory where the trees were bigger and the land richer.

My brother and I were with Father in wanting to go to Washington. Who wouldn't want to live near a town with as grand a name as Olympia and in a state with the name of the Father of our Country? We thrilled to the thought of the trip across the plains, where wild Indians and buffalo were still to be seen, on to San Francisco, up the Pacific, down Puget Sound. But Mother would not budge.

'I have moved,' she said, 'for the last time.'

VII

Adventures with Birds

MOST children fear the night, as I did as a small child; but after my eighth or ninth year I came to look upon night as kindly and friendly, and my imagination was stirred by night sounds: the rushing sound of a tree crashing to earth, the calls of the birds, and the echoing woods.

The most doleful night sound is the cry of the mourning dove. Yet one must suppose that this beautiful bird, a miniature passenger pigeon in coloring and shape, expresses his happiness in this dismal voice. When the preacher read from the Psalms: 'Oh! that I had wings like a dove,' it was the iridescent wings of the mourning dove that came to my mind. To me it was the mourning dove that Noah sent out from the Ark. It was the mourning dove that was pure and gentle; the dove in whose shape the Holy Ghost descended must have been a mourning dove.

Another of the birds that lived in solitude was the whippoorwill. In the dusk of May and June evenings we heard in every direction the eerie calls of the whippoorwill, like an earthbound spirit in the forest's depth. Few ever saw the bird. My own infrequent glimpses of whippoorwills were when, in our sugarbush, I stumbled on a nest, never with more than two eggs, creamy and spotted with lilac and brown, laid on dead leaves, with no architecture whatsoever. The same whippoorwills came back to nest under the same tree years in succession, and always the mother feigned lameness to keep me away from her young. In the cry of this bird, whippoorwill, in our forests the middle syllable is slighted, the first and last strongly accented, the notes being repeated time after time in rapid succession.

As dreary as the moan of the mourning dove was the wail of the screech owl, a wail it is rather than a screech, a plaintive, not unmusical wail. We might hear its melancholy voice in our woods in all hours of the night, in all seasons of the year, though not so often in winter. As every boy knows, the screech owl hides in a hollow tree or the thick foliage of evergreens, and is to be seen in daytime only when a squirrel or a blue jay drives it from its hiding-place. A pair of screech owls had their nest in a hollow tree near a path between our house and the house of a neighbor. In the dusk of a May evening as I was returning from a visit to this neighbor, one of these owls attacked me, as I passed the hollow tree. Flying at the crown of my head it was determined to do me harm.

The commonest owl in our northern woods was the barred owl. On moonlight evenings, especially in autumn, he hoots his noisy who-who-too-too until those living in a forest rate him as a nighttime nuisance. Across the road from our house in early years in the North, there was a thick clump of hemlocks in which barred owls lived, as did blue jays. There was no love lost between the two species, and several times I saw the feathers fly, accompanied by bloodcurdling screams of defiance; the nimble, daylight-seeing jays always came out best. We sometimes found a nest in our sugar-bush in late March, always in a hollow tree. There were usually two pure-white eggs as large as those of a Bantam hen. I regret to say that we boys shot the barred owl on sight, though it did more good killing rodents than harm in stealing chickens.

The cry of the loon is a sound unlike that of any other bird. When first you hear it, you think of a wolf or of a pack of wolves. From our inland home, we could seldom hear the call of the loon, but at night and in stormy weather, when chance took us near one of our small lakes, its loud call dominated all other noises. Its hallooing, or laugh, or looning, has a human quality and gave rise to the Indian song, 'A Loon I Thought Was Looning.' I give the original as well as the translation:

Mong-e-do-gwain, in-de-nain-dum
Mong-e-do-gwain, in-de-nain-dum,
Wain-shung-ish-ween, neen-e-mo-shane,
Wain-shung-ish-ween, neen-e-mo-shane,
A-nee-wau-wau-sau-bo-a-zode,
A-nee-wau-wau-sau-bo-a-zode.

A loon, I thought was looning,
A loon, I thought was looning;
Why! It is he, my lover,
Why! It is he, my lover:
His paddle in the waters gleaming,
His paddle in the waters gleaming.

Another bird in our woods was the bittern, though we heard its call but seldom at our house, rather distant from the swampy ponds this bird likes. Still, we knew the call of the bittern very well, a heavy, regular, thumping sound, which gave it the name among woods-people of 'stake-driver,' 'thunder-pump' and 'bog bull.' Whenever we went for an evening's fishing in this or that lake, we could hear bitterns booming in the reedy swamps about us. To the Indians, the bittern was the spirit of swamps, bogs, and pools. Of all the birds I know, the bittern best protects himself by simulating his surroundings.

The last of the birds that I associate with forest nights is the nighthawk, which some call the 'mosquito hawk.' The peculiar call and the whirring sounds of this bird, when the day was done and its heat, labor, and vexations forgotten, must ever be associated with the peace of a dusky summer evening.

On June and July evenings, we could count several pairs of nighthawks zooming about our clearing, winnowing the air for insects. Usually they were to be heard as dusk came on, but sometimes in early morning and sometimes on cloudy days. Their call is a loud nasal *speek-speek*. I recall nighthawks best as coming time and time again in the space of a few minutes from high above the treetops, diving toward the earth with great speed, checking themselves just over our heads, and then sweeping upward. As they checked their downward dive, they made a roaring sound not unlike that produced when you blow with all the power of your lungs in the mouth of a large bottle; it is this noise that I remember.

The night hawk feeds on mosquitoes, but the dozen or two birds about our place could make no impression on the multitudes of mosquitoes that swarmed in our clearing, filling the quiet night with the humming of innumerable wings. There were enough mosquitoes on our land in June to feed a million nighthawks. We could sit out of doors in mosquito time only under the protection of smudges.

In no other part of the world have I seen fireflies so plentiful as in our northern land. Often these little brilliants are solitary or one may count a dozen or two, but in our forest clearing millions might be seen in warm evenings, each flashing its light as regularly as heartbeats. Is it heat, electricity, or phosphorescence? Is its light for noctural protection? Is it a love signal? Or does it switch its light on and off for amusement pure and simple? I believed the last guess as good as any. Fireflies were simply having a good time as they flitted aimlessly about on summer evenings—lights on and off at will.

In warm, wet weather we often saw another light in the darkness of the woods. It came on chunks of decayed wood, caused by light-producing fungi. To us it was 'fox fire,' as it was to the ancients. It did not have the red flame of fire, or the scarlet of a coal, but a soft slumbering white light, not nearly so bright as that of the firefly. It shone continuously, night and day, and was so like fire that one who did not know fox fire would be a little fearful of picking it up. It could be found only in warm, wet weather, always on hardwoods beginning to decay. Occasionally we saw bits of it high up on dead trees, uncanny eyes that might be mistaken for those of a beast. With a chunk of gleaming fox fire in our mouths or plastered under the eyes, in the darkness of night my brother and I would frighten away our playmates.

The period of silence just before dawn in summer is the most enchanting hour of night. At this time the air is as calm and still as before the winds were made. There are no whisperings of leaves, no dropping of fruits, no songs of birds, no fluttering of wings, even if migration is under way. The heavy dews are falling, the damp earth is exhaling its perfumes, the essences of plants are being distilled; clouds float as silently as thistledown. You fancy you can hear the growing of grass and corn. In winter always, and in summer often, boys on a farm are called to get up in the bewitching hour just before daylight.

The birds begin to arrive just as leaves burst from the buds. You first hear them at dawn in the scarcely audible, tentative twitterings and whisperings of mate to mate. Then the early-morning hush is broken by the clear-voiced notes of a robin telling the world 'day is at hand,' and that he has come north for the express purpose of letting us know that winter has gone. The air vibrates for a few marginal minutes with the cheer of the robin, and then there is a gush of song from the white-throated sparrow, the bird of birds in number and in volume of song in northern woods.

VIII

Animals

THE first wild animal in northern Michigan with which our family had experience was the snowshoe rabbit—which is really a hare. Early in our first winter Joutel brought us two, ready to cook, knowing very well he would get a meal in exchange. We had eaten the small cottontails in Indiana and liked them very much, but these hares were better eating and twice as large. Meat could hardly be had that winter, except fish, which we ate so often we loathed it.

The hares were so very welcome in our larder that my brother and I, in common with most of the boys in the village, became trappers. At first we used a figure-four box trap, familiar to every boy bred in the country. Rabbits are the easiest of all wild animals to trap, and we had one in our trap about as soon as we set it. The trouble was to get it out of the box. We had caught cottontails and had had little trouble pulling them out of the box by the hind legs. The snowshoe hare knocked most of the skin off our wrists before we could get him by the hind legs.

This snowshoe hare, by the way, is a creature as large as the domesticated Belgian hare; it is an inhabitant of sub-Arctic regions, so common in our swamps that the Indians would have starved without it. It is sometimes called the 'varying hare,' because in winter it is snow-white; in summer, grayish brown. Its hind legs are abnormally long and powerful, becoming snowshoes in winter. It could, as we quickly found out, strike a nasty blow with these long legs, and we gave up box traps, heavy and cumbersome at best in deep snows, and learned from Joutel how to make a deadfall over a rabbit path in which a small log fell on the rabbit's back pinning him down with a broken back. Or, we hung a wire, tied to a bent-over sapling, over the beasts' path and usually found a hare hanging in the air the next morning.

In the second spring on our farm we became acquainted with the porcupine, an animal that in my first experience with it caused me more pain than words can express. Porcupines were bought by Indians for their quills, used in making moccasins, leggings, birch, and grass ornaments. A porcupine sold for a dollar. None of our Indians ever had that much money, but there were dealers who would buy the porcupines and get their pay out of the squaws who used the quills. My brother and I early resolved to make our fortunes as porcupine hunters.

Our eastern American porcupine is rather larger than the commoner groundhog, of ungainly form, ugly visage, stupid, blundering, and phlegmatic disposition, about the only wild creature that a boy can kill with a club. This slow, clumsy, piglike beast, however, has a means of defense. A thick coat of fur protects him from the coldest weather and covers a second coat of quills. The quills are two inches long, nearly hidden by the hairy fur, yellowish-white tipped with black, and at the end have minute barbs. It is popularly thought that a porcupine can 'throw' or 'shoot' his quills in defense. Scientists say that he cannot. I know porcupines and I agree with the popular notion.

This quilled pig has a broad, flat, blunt tail, thickly studded with quills. As a boy, I should have sworn that his barbed darts could be thrown a full rod; the ground for that distance around a clubbed porcupine was sprinkled with tiny javelins. As a man, I reduce the rod to two feet. When a porcupine is attacked it curls up in a ball and slaps with its tail. The loosely attached quills are flung about for some distance. To be sure, he does not throw those crowded on his back and rump, but he tosses them right and left when he slaps with his flat tail—his quiver of quills.

The first year we were on the farm, coming home from the spring with a pail full of water, I saw my first live porcupine meandering slowly down the road. Flash, our dog, was wild with excitement. So was I. In a few seconds we were both in for the kill. The 'porky' saw no reason for excitement, or for fleeing from his enemies. He curled up on the ground, tucked his head between his hind legs, and began waving his tail, peering with his black beady eyes to see who his assailants might be.

In less than no time Flash was out of the fight, his mouth and nose full of quills. I was in bare feet and soon fought with feet studded with quills. My trouble was in finding a suitable weapon. There were no clubs at hand and I could find only a round stone, too small to use as an instrument of destruction. Finally, however, I thought porky was dead, and sat down on a log to nurse Flash's and my wounds.

Porcupine quills cannot be pulled out of flesh by hand; pincers are needed. Fortunately, my brother was sent to see what was delaying me. Eventually he got me, Flash, the porcupine, and the pail of water home. Then began a terrible ordeal. It turned out that Mother could not use the pincers skilfully enough to pull the quills out of my feet, though my brother did a pretty good job with Flash. John Wilson, our hired man, had had experiences with porcupine quills in human flesh, and took me in hand. After an hour or two of patient work he pronounced me quill-less.

Quills kept coming to the surface for a week to require the aid of John, the 'porcupine surgeon,' and then came an affliction that far surpassed the pain from the quills—a carbuncle came on the bottom of my right heel. This Mother diagnosed as a stone-bruise, an ailment that came within her province. She applied heated bread poultices for a few days 'to keep the swelling soft,' and then lanced it with a razor. This was the first of several stone-bruises that came during the next few years, until the pleasure of going without shoes had to be given up.

In the years that have followed, I have seen many porcupines. Always I let them take their unhurried way. As to stone-bruises, I never see a rotund 'toddy-blossom' nose without a flash in my mind 'it's the beginning of a stone-bruise.'

The most common wild animal in the woods of northern Michigan is the chipmunk, an animal that enjoys the society of humans. He is quite at home about farm buildings, in the woodpile, and under the corn crib—chattering with delight as he scampers along top, bottom, or middle rails of the fences; never so busy in his noisy bustling about that he cannot stop and with a strenuous 'chuck-chuck-chuck' scold an optimistic hunter, whether boy or dog. He hates to be interrupted in his work of storing nuts in his deep underground burrow.

Dogs, and boys between the ages of five and ten, spent most of their time chasing chipmunks in our wooded region. In all the hours my brother, Flash, and I spent in hunting chipmunks we never killed one, and the red squirrels, who kept their black and gray kin in complete subjugation, could never catch his diminutive striped cousin.

No other animals in our woods were as busy as the chipmunks. At first touch of spring, the first whiff of a mellow south wind, chipmunks suddenly began their season's work, and kept at it incessantly, until the cold of autumn had brought every leaf and nut to the ground. Then they went into semi-hiberation in burrows filled with nuts, corn, and seeds. Most of the time during the winter they sleep, but they occasionally rouse to eat a meal from their ample store. Just before sugar-making time, on sunny days, they pop out of their burrows to announce 'sap is running.'

Of the other squirrels in our land there were the red, black, gray, and the curious flying squirrel. All northern squirrels, with the exception of the burrowing chipmunks, lived in hollow trees. Chief Blackbird told us that when he was a boy, gray and black squirrels were very common and an important article of food for his people, and that red squirrels were not known until the whites came; then the red squirrels and the chipmunks, both too small for profitable hunting, took possession of the forests.

Joutel had told us time and again of the *aw-saw-maw-go* of which he said: 'Heem fly wiz hees laigs; heem mak ze long jomp.'

Father surmised that Joutel's strange animal was a flying squirrel. So it turned out. Late one spring Joutel brought in a mother and four little flying squirrels, which he had found in a hollow tree. We kept them in a box for a few days, but the mother gnawed her way out and left her young to die. Late, in clearing our land, we often saw flying squirrels. Truly, as Joutel said, they did 'mak ze long jomp,' volplaning by folds of skin stretched from fore to hind legs. We never saw these graceful acrobats doing their amazing stunts in summer when the leaves were on the trees, but only in spring and autumn when trees were leafless. Curiously enough they make their nests only in beech trees, presumably because the tree tops are open and furnish opportunities for long jumps; also the trunks are often hollow, and in autumn bear a supply of nuts.

The graceful agile gray squirrels we seldom saw, red squirrels and Indian hunters had so depleted their numbers. Of all our wild animals the full-tailed gray squirrel was most beautiful. He, too, was an aerial acrobat and could jump from upper branch to upper branch of beech or maple, ash or birch, nearly as far as the flying squirrel, each jump a ripple of smooth agility. In a contest with a circus performer he would rate higher in balancing; and as he eats a nut the claws of his forepaws are as nimble as the fingers of a sleight-of-hand performer.

Red squirrels were nearly as common in the forests of this northern country as chipmunks. The red squirrel was a nuisance with hardly a redeeming quality. He wasn't worth hunting, for with his skin removed there was little left to eat. He quarreled, fought, and vanquished the larger and much superior gray and black squirrels; he robbed birds' nests; he bullied chipmunks; he shrilly scolded, his voice noisy as he quarreled with the blue jay, who, almost alone, was able to make him seek his quarters. Red squirrels and blue jays began to quarrel and fight in sugar-making time and kept it up all summer, scolding and screeching at the tops of their voices. After a certain amount of name calling, the blue jays would sail in, striking with beaks and wings, and the squirrels would beat a noisy retreat. It was a fight between pirates, for more often than not both were intent on despoiling the nests of some small bird.

Wherever we went in our forest land we might see a red fox trotting along, ears and bushy tail lifted. The foxes were never very common, as trappers had harried them for years. Like every boy, I wanted a foxskin cap, the long tail hanging down my back. In the winter my brother and I set innumerable traps in places where fox tracks were plentiful, following Joutel's directions, for he had caught 'tousans in ze Nor-Wes,' but we never captured so much as a fox hair.

We most often saw foxes in the snappy sunny days of sugar-making, at which time we were strictly limited for leisure to trap. Flash always gave chase when we came across a fox, but his fox-hunting was pathetic. Brother Reynard simply jogged along at a fox trot, looking neither to right nor to left, his purpose in no way changed, making a fool of Flash, who always came back from his chase dead tired, his tongue hanging out, tail down, with a look of utter dejection. The fox has a shady reputation among all farmers as a stealer of poultry, but I do not remember that he ever stole one of our chickens.

One of the earliest adventures on the farm with wild animals was with a wildcat. A few days after we moved into the little cabin on our farm, the forest wall closing in our little clearing on all four sides, Father and my brother were in the village one evening, leaving Mother, my little sister, and me alone. A thunderstorm came up as dusk began to fall and between flashes of lightning and claps of thunder we heard bloodcurdling screams, like those of a human in dire distress. We knew that there was a family of wildcats in the neighborhood and that this unearthly sound came from one of them. The night was stiflingly hot, but Mother closed the doors and pulled down the windows to keep out the cat's screeching; this did not mitigate the horrors of the night. My sister and I held Mother's hand as she tried to reassure us. In an hour the storm was over, the cat left, and Father and my brother came home and laughed at us.

In the years that followed we often heard wildcats screeching in a swamp near us, but no one feared them. I never saw a wildcat until my eighteenth year, when I was teaching a school several miles away. (A thousand times, as a small boy, I saw their glistening eyes in the darkness of roads at night, in our lightless cow stable, and even in the corners in our windowless cellar.) One Friday night in mid-winter I was coming home carrying the frozen carcass of a snowshoe rabbit that one of my schoolboys had given me. Within a mile of our house, with some feeling of being followed, I turned and saw a wildcat a few rods behind me. The beast had not uttered a sound, but as I dropped the rabbit and gave chase, the cat began his terrible screeches. He would not stop and it was useless to follow. Taking up my rabbit, the smell of which, of course, had attracted the wildcat, I went on my way, the beast following until the lights of our house were in sight.

Ruffled grouse, known to all in our land as partridges, were very common in our forests. With the method my brother and I used there was no trouble in getting them for our table. Flash had a good nose for birds. When he scented a covey of partridges and began to yap in a staccato bark, the birds would seek safety in a tree. Thereupon, my brother or I came up with the family two-barreled muzzle-loading shotgun and usually managed to get several of a covey. We never wasted a shot at a bird on the wing.

Mild as such hunting seems, it was a venturesome sport. The old gun was never cleaned and went off like a bomb. In partridge season my shoulder was always lame from the gun's malevolence. Worse still, every few shots the weapon hung fire, and, when lowered, off it went, to the grave danger of other boys who might be near and the great discomfort of the marksman it kicked. We did not shoot much. The cost of powder, shot, and caps was such a drain on our slender purse that a few days of hunting each autumn was as much as we could afford.

During sugar-making, partridges seemed omnipresent. From every direction in this season males were calling females by drumming, the love call echoing all through our awakening springtime world. Of course, we tried to catch the birds in their love-making and often did. Though many times I saw cocks in the act of drumming, I do not know how the thunderlike noise is made. It does not suffice to say, as many observers do, that a cock partridge simply beats the air with his wings. No, he either beats his wings together over his back, or strikes his sides with his wings—in either case, with speed so great no one can say which way the noise is made. Nor is it true that he always chooses a hollow log for a drum; most often I have seen him on solid logs.

However he makes his booming love call, it is effective. A particularly lusty, noisy cock, after a little drumming, has a half-dozen amorous hens awaiting him. There he is, indeed, a handsome swain, a veritable matinée idol. He chooses for his drumming-place a rather open part of the woods, where he can be seen and heard from afar and can keep an eye open for enemies—or, more likely, watch wanton females. The first drum notes are low and his strutting rather slow; then the speed of his short, stubby legs is increased; his chest swells and rounds out, showing the epaulets on his shoulders; his bright, beady eyes are cast hither and yon; he spreads his tail in a large fan, decorated with grayish and reddish-brown fringe and bars, and raises aloft his crested head. Of all the birds in our land, a partridge is the most doughty conqueror of female hearts.

By the end of sugar-making we might expect to find beside a log, or at the foot of a tree, the nest of a partridge, a small hollow lined with dry leaves, containing ten or twelve whitish eggs considerably larger than those of the robin. As soon as the young hatch, the mother teaches them to hide, and so skilfully does she do it that you have difficulty in catching any but the very young. A boy has a bad time with mother partridge. As he approaches, the old bird feigns lameness and tries to lead him away; if these tactics fail, she flies boldly at him striking with beak and wings. You never see the fine gentleman of the drumming log about the young.

In winter we often came across partridges. They selected thickets of dense evergreens in which to roost, well-screened from cold winds. In very cold weather they plunged into deep snow to keep warm. Here, Flash often found them, half starved, crops stuffed with buds and seeds, the flesh so tough and so strongly flavored that it was unfit to eat. In winter partridges wear snowshoes consisting of horny scales fringing the toes; these disappear when the molting season comes.

The only other wild animals of my boyhood were deer and bears, the deer not uncommon but bears rather rare. Often deer came in our grain fields and sometimes we chased them out. In late autumn, bears played havoc with our corn, both before it was cut and after it was in the shock. The glamour of hunting was strong with some of our neighbors, and often enough we had a haunch of venison or the porklike steaks of a bear on our table, but none of our family was fond of either, and emphatically we were not hunters. However, it was through hunting a bear that Flash, the beloved companion of our whole family, came to a sad end.

One June day when my brother and I were hoeing corn, a she-bear with two cubs came ambling slowly across the field. She had been seen before and my brother and I had a plan to kill her and capture the cubs. One of us with Flash was to chase the creature into the woods while the other was to get the gun, which was kept loaded with buckshot for the old bear. We took it for granted that the bear would take to a tree, and that then we might shoot the mother.

Now, at the sight of the bears, off went my brother for the gun (leaving me to put my head in the lion's mouth, as it were, in bringing the bears to bay); off went Flash and I after the bears. The quarry took to the woods as expected, but the old mother did not climb a tree, even with a boy and a dog behind her. Soon Flash stopped barking, and when I came up to him I could see that all was over. The bear had clouted the dog several times on its head and body, laying open ghastly wounds. The shot meant for the bear put poor Flash out of his misery.

When the Railroad Came

TO the south, some five or six miles across Little Traverse Bay, was a roaring little stream called Bear Creek. It was large enough and had fall enough to furnish power for a mill, near which, when we came to the North, there lived a few whites and perhaps a hundred Indians. The hamlet itself was at first called Bear Creek, but about the time we first saw it, Bear Creek became Petoskey, renamed in honor of an Indian chief living in the place.

This village to the south of us set up a claim—absurdly, as we on the northern shore of the bay thought—to be the metropolis of the region, matching its water power against our splendid harbor. Suddenly the balance was changed in favor of the southern town; a branch of the Grand Rapids and Indiana Railroad was to be built nearly as straight as a taut string from Grand Rapids, far to the south, to Petoskey.

Not to be outdone by our rival across the bay, our old trading post of Little Traverse had to have a new name. There was a great difference of opinion among leading citizens about which was the most suitable of the many names suggested. Finally an agreement was reached on 'Harbor Springs': the 'Harbor,' of course, from our splendid haven, and 'Springs,' because along the shore was a chain of sparkling springs, bottoms filled with clean, white sand, up through which boiled clear, cold, magnetic water, trickling in little rills down to the harbor. Though there wasn't the slightest resemblance between squalid little Harbor Springs or Little Traverse Bay to Naples or the Bay of Naples, our two village newspapers called Harbor Springs 'the Naples of the North.'

The children in our family came to think that a railroad was the mainspring of the world. An engine and the cars it pulled, we thought, would bring the grists of the world to our doors. There could be no peace in the family until my brother and I had crossed Little Traverse Bay to see a railroad.

At last a day was appointed, and Father set about preparing our minds for what we should see. The engine was an iron horse that breathed out smoke and steam. We should hear the whistle, the neigh of the iron horse, long before we saw it. No, a car was not like a big wagon box, but like a long room, furnished with seats, lighted by lamps through which ran a rope that rang a bell, the bell cord to be touched only by the conductor.

'Where does the train come from?' we asked.

'The train,' Father said, 'comes from Fort Wayne, through Kalamazoo, Grand Rapids, Big Rapids, Reed City, Cadillac, Kalkaska, and Mancelona.'

Father called the names in the manner of a train announcer.

We had to cross the bay on the little steamboat, *North Star*. Riding on a boat seemed a mean and contemptible way to travel, so slow that we were afraid the train would have come and gone before we landed. At last we were on the wharf, up the bank, through the town, and at the railroad station. The rails shone in the afternoon sun, two glistening tracks of steel. On either side newly thrown banks of sand gleamed like heaps of gold. The arrival of the train was the event of the day in the village, and now a crowd was gathering.

Before the long-drawn, quavering shriek of the engine ended, we saw the monster coming, emitting an enormous smudge of black smoke, a cloud of steam trailing behind, unfolding into wreaths of gold and silver in the hazy afternoon sunlight. I held my breath and could scarcely keep tears of fright from my eyes as, with grinding, whining wheels, clanging bell, and hissing steam, the engine came to a stop.

Father tried to point out the parts of the engine: boiler, steam cylinders, pumps, whistle, headlight, governor, valves; but I was more interested in the engineer and fireman than in the engine. When the train had stopped, two sooty, grimy creatures stepped down from a little boxlike room in the engine and began to pour oil into glistening valves and to rub the outer organs of the iron horse. Were they a part of our world? They spoke to no one, looked neither to right nor left, were concerned only with the monster in their charge.

At last Father succeeded in pulling us away from the engine and led us wonderingly from car to car, explaining as best he could brakes, couplings, and bell ropes. We gazed with amazement at the shining wood, the red plush, the hanging lamps, the big panes of glass, and the brass fittings. To me, coming from a wilderness home, a passenger car seemed like a room in a gorgeous palace; the conductor and brakeman with blue uniforms and brass buttons were high court officials.

A few weeks before, *Uncle Tom's Cabin* had been on the stage in our village. A month of bright sunshine had not erased from my mind the whipping of Uncle Tom. The gray old porter on the Pullman at the end of the train was to me another Uncle Tom, and I wanted to see if his back was scarred with the cruel lash of some Simon Legree. Father, as a Southerner, rather contemptuous of *Uncle Tom's Cabin*, had said that the Uncle Tom in the play was not a 'nigger' but a white man 'made up.' The porter on this train, therefore, was the first Negro I had ever seen.

Long before we had inspected the whole train, the engine, with a series of coughs, snorts, and bell-clangings, started jerkily to back, and my brother and I raced down the track to see a switch work.

It had been a great day. It was marred only by our forgetting to put coppers on the rails.

A few years later the railroad came to Harbor Springs. To children in this little nook before the railroad came, the great world beyond had been 'the outside.' With the coming of the railroad we became part of a world of which we had heard much, but of which very few had firsthand knowledge. For centuries life in the Land of the Crooked Tree had been unhurried; now there was a hurly-burly of activity.

The railroad quickly transformed our whole region. Good roads were built; at every four corners there was a schoolhouse, mill, or shop; the population multiplied apace; frame houses began to take the place of log structures; people dressed better; and a barefooted man with long hair was called a 'mossback.' Everyone talked about railroads, steamboats, mills, stores, town lots. We children in the forest thought there were few places in all America that could offer so many and so great attractions as our town.

Harbor Springs became notable overnight. Stores were built along streets yet without sidewalks. Soon we had a courthouse and a hall. Three hotels and six saloons could not keep the fleshpots filled; much eating and drinking were required to lubricate business. Two newspapers spread knowledge, thus depriving us of the bliss of ignorance; and four new churches were organized to give the town various doctrines.

Nearly every day there was a new excitement. On Saturday afternoons, when everybody was in town, and often in the evenings during the week, quiet, fastidious gentlemen sold goods of many sorts with which came tickets for prizes that ranged from solid gold to diamond ornaments. Counterparts of these merchants, differing perhaps in wearing or not wearing a goatee, were gamblers with wheels of fortune, or 'doctors' selling 'pain-killers' for this or that disease. Thus, the simple-minded villagers of the old regime were induced to part with money, which, however, in these boom times, was easily come by. Joutel, who prided himself on his astuteness, was fleeced by every faker who came to town; one of them once passed off two lead dimes on him.

After each loss he complained: 'Chris', I'm dumb! W'en I'm leve in ze Nor'-Wes' I'm smart. Now I'll tole you I'm dumb as 'ell!'

It was at about this time that a traveling phrenologist stopped at our house, and, Father being away, Mother had her three children's heads mapped at twenty-five cents a head. She thought the man's charts threw considerable light on the intellects and actions of her offspring. Father was a little cross about an expenditure of hard-earned money on such nonsense, but since the maps furnished him amusement for the rest of his life, he must sometime have come to the conclusion that the money was well spent.

The summer after the railroad came, I had an astonishing adventure. I was driving our three cows to the creek for water on a road through the woods. Ambling peacefully around a turn, suddenly the cows turned tail and charged homeward. A few weeks before, a bear and her two cubs had crossed one of our fields; now, as the cows lunged past me to the shelter of the farmyard, I was certain that the bears were behind them. Long practice had made me ready for just such an emergency, and I quickly clambered up a tree. On a branch twelve or fifteen feet up, I came to a safe perch and stopped to look for the bears.

No bears were in sight, but around the turn there emerged a beast of monstrous size and mold. As the big bulk lumbered toward me, I shinnied up another fifteen feet before taking a second look. Then I saw that the great quadruped was accompanied by a man. Seeing the havoc his charge had created with the cows and a very frightened boy in the top of a tree, the man smacked the animal smartly, commanded it to stop, and called to me to come down. With many fears I descended. I realized at first sight, from its bulk, its flapping ears, and its swinging trunk, that the animal was an elephant.

How came this mammoth in our woods? The animal's master so misused his a's and h's that he had great difficulty in making me understand how he came to be there and where he was going, but I finally comprehended that the Englishman and 'Ol' Kite,' as he called the elephant, had come from Grand Rapids to the end of the railroad and that he was bound to the Straits of Mackinaw, where he was to take a boat to far away Duluth, there to join a circus. The man was having many difficulties. He was lost; he was suspicious of Indians; he was afraid of the forest and of everything in it. Moreover, Old Kate's feet were sore and he had to keep them bandaged; and he was having difficulty in getting food for her. Worst of all, Kate fancied she was back in the jungles of her childhood and wanted to browse and loiter. Even as we talked, she squealed with joy as she chewed the twigs and leaves of a yellow birch, with delight in the wintergreen taste.

I was amazed at the beast's huge, fanlike ears, which she flapped like the wings of a bird as the mosquitoes buzzed about them. I had broken off a leafy branch to keep the mosquitoes off my face; and as if in imitation Kate plucked a branch several feet long and gaily switched her head and flank, even though no mosquito could have sucked blood through her thick skin. Her skin, by the way, was so loose and wrinkled, so like that on the face of Granny Woods, that I knew she must be very old.

The elephant's small, shrewd eyes took in everything along the roadside. Her trunk was a wonderful organ to me. She wanted to touch with its tip every new plant we passed, and with it could pull down a stout sapling.

When we came to the watering place for cows, Kate could not be made to go past it, and yet was afraid to wade into the soft-bottomed creek. I told the beast's Jehu that there was a hard bottom to the creek in the woods, and he persuaded his ward to be driven there. The old girl was delighted with this bathing place. She pulled the bandages from her feet and waded in, trumpeting her delight in a voice that must have filled the wild animals in our forest with fear.

Finally, the Englishman said he must go. He invited me to ride a way with him, and I wanted to; but after seeing Kate's snakelike trunk encircle her master's body, lift him high in the air, and set him on her back, none too pleasantly, I turned the invitation down. Old Kate hung back at first but her driver whacked and scolded her and off they went. I followed for a mile or more, fascinated by the elephant's squealings, scoldings, and guttural rumbling sounds, easily translated by anyone who has stood by when a querulous old woman has had to do something she did not want to do.

The railroad brought to our little village a station that we all called the 'dee-po.' Quickly the station became a community center. It was a place where those of us who came from the country could rest at all times and warm up in winter; a place where people came to take the train, and where those who had been 'outside' again reached home; tourists, drummers, land buyers, and businessmen of all descriptions came on the train, preferring to travel by rail rather than by water. The telegraph office was in the railroad station, and the first telephone in town was put in the depot a few years after the railroad came.

This small-town depot was a near relative of the big-town railroad station, but it was as different as a countryman is from his city cousin. It was not a place where people rushed in and out at train times, a driving, bustling place of business. As a news exchange and a village forum it was a rival of the store, the hotel, and the saloon. Without the depot, we should all have been more nearly hermits and introverts.

The depot was a beautiful bit of architecture. It was rectangular in shape, perhaps 25 by 50 feet. It was built of lapped, planed lumber, and the roof overhung the walls on all sides, the overhanging parts being supported by elaborate, heavy cornices. The windows and windowpanes were larger than those of any other building in town. It made very evident that the G. R. & I. had money to burn. The building was painted dark green.

The depot was heated by a large acorn coal stove, a most wonderful heating apparatus. The fuel box was several feet high, its fat belly at least three feet in diameter. This fuel container sat on a highly ornamental base a foot high; the base, in turn, on three curved legs. Around the belly, standing out several inches, was a bright half-round fender on which you could have put your feet had there been chairs. Above the fuel box was a metal canopy that reflected the heat downward, so that the lower half of the room was as warm as the upper. The rectangular door had small panes of isinglass, its edges crimped like a pie crust. The door bore the legend, in big bossed letters, Jewel Stoves & Ranges, Detroit, Mich. Under the door was a projecting iron bar over which you fitted a shaker to shake down the ashes; under this another door opening into the ash pit. My description does not do justice to this depot stove, because from top to bottom it was corrugated up and down and round and round, with much ornamental scroll-work—truly a work of art.

This stove stood in the exact center of the waiting room, and rested on a heavy zinc-covered thickness of hardwood planks to keep the floor from catching fire when the stove was red hot. To me, the most wonderful thing about the stove was that it burned coal, the first I had ever seen. Occasionally I was permitted to shake down the ashes and put coal on the fire, feeling as I did so that I was well on the way to becoming a railroad engineer.

Besides the stove the only other furnishings in the station were heavy board benches, part of the building and immovable. Here one might sit and, if the station master did not object, lie and take a nap. There were a front and back door, and a third one by which the agent and trainmen entered an apartment reserved for them; in it a large case held tickets and on a table were telegraph instruments and eventually a telephone. In this sanctum there were several chairs in which the agent, his assistant, trainmen, and privileged friends sat.

The greatest days for the railroad were in the late 1880's when the excursions came toward the end of summer. Season after season, there were several of these bringing thousands of people from regions far to the south. Friends and relatives came to stay with nearly every white family in the land. Excursion rates to the north were only half the regular rates; but not those to the south; the G. R. & I. wanted the northern country settled. Everyone expecting guests was at the station to meet excursion trains. Hotel runners, hackmen, and the pursers of waiting steamboats were on hand for customers. The boats at neighboring wharves were waiting for excursionists who wanted to go to Charlevoix, Mackinac Island, Beaver Island, points in the Upper Peninsula, or westward to northern Wisconsin.

X

Forepaugh's Circus

THE railroad had brought to our door an elephant, the first foreign animal I had ever seen. The next year it brought a circus to Petoskey, ten miles away. This was the first of the circus days in our land, coming thereafter as regularly as the Fourth of July. What a splendid institution the circus was! To both grown-ups and children in our isolated forest homes, the circus was an opportunity to expand our starved imaginative life. The menagerie brought us strange animals from India, Australia, the Arctic, the Amazon. The acrobats in the ring showed us the skill and beauty of human bodies. The clowns brought songs and jokes that we treasured until the next year brought new ones. The circus was natural history, magic, romance, chivalry, music.

Happily, the first circus to come our way was that of Adam Forepaugh, then the best in the country. My brother and I, twelve and ten, lived, moved and existed in anticipation of 'Forepaugh's.' It was ten miles from our house to the big tent; and we were given money for our admission and an extra sideshow.

For us there was little sleep the night before; by daylight on a perfect June morning, we were on our way to Forepaugh's Great Circus. Our road led us around the bay. When we came to the water we took off our shoes and trod the cool, moist sand of the shore. Twice we stripped and took refreshing dips.

When we came to the road leading into Petoskey we found it filled with wagons and buggies. The wagons were overflowing with mankind. Parents sat in front spring seats, back of them on boards laid from side to side, or, on straw-covered wagon bottoms sat children, blissfully happy, their faces showing the pleasure of their anticipation. In buggies and surreys were sweethearts, dressed in their Sunday best, the tanned faces of the men glowing with pride in horse, buggy, and sweetheart, the faces of the girls, too, beaming with pride of ownership.

Finally we stepped into Bedlam. Petoskey was filled with a noisy, jostling crowd drunk with exhilaration and anticipation. In the main, the augmenting multitudes had had little liquor and were sober and good-natured, but there were many drunks, some of whom constables were dragging to the city cooler.

Joutel, Gasper Quatcheeo, and our two hired men had come over the night before to see the circus unloaded. But when morning came they were so drunk that they did not see anything; and later, their money spent, they could not get inside the Big Tent.

We were in time to see the tents go up, after which, we were told, it would be an hour before the parade would start. We were ravenous for food and went to a grocery store for a nine o'clock breakfast and dinner, consisting of crackers, cheese, bologna, smoked herring, and pop. As we left the store, Joutel and Quatcheeo staggered by and gave us each a handful of peanuts for dessert. Both men were eating theirs unshucked and were quite put out at our daintiness in discarding the shells.

All else was forgotten as from far up Main Street came the cry: 'Here it comes! Here it comes!' We could hear the trumpets, drums, and horns. Then, while pushing to the fore, over the heads of the struggling crowd we saw the wagons with gold and purple banners and gilded crests, each drawn by six pairs of prancing horses with tassseled heads.

A great number of triumphal cars headed the Grand Parade. They were adorned with golden woodwork; on the sides of some were magnificent paintings; on others were bars to keep in all the animals of Noah's Ark. In several of the caged cars were lions and tigers, with trainers commanding them to stand or lie down. One even put his head in a lion's mouth. The teams drawing a car were driven by a helmeted charioteer, behind whom rode kings and queens in gorgeous raiment. On an occasional car, instead of kings and queens, there were musicians tooting fanfares on trumpets, horns, or bagpipes.

Behind the chariots with their prancing steeds came elephants, each carrying a railed, canopied, howdah, in which their drivers sat; behind the elephants were pillioned camels, driven by turbaned Turks; following the camels were giraffes led by coal-black, curly-headed Africans. Then came a score or more clowns, jesting, merrymaking in words, songs, and pantomime.

Circus etiquette seems to demand that a parade be ended with a tooting calliope. So it did with Forepaugh's. The great steam organ played tune after tune as we tagged behind to the circus grounds. No musician, I was pleased to recognize 'Yankee Doodle' and 'The Star-Spangled Banner.'

We could not get in the menagerie for another whole hour, but there were many sights and sounds to claim our attention. The adjuncts and accompaniments were in full swing. The most in evidence of these were the several sideshows, the cries of whose barkers rent the air.

These calls were followed by much fervid oratory, telling what was to be seen inside behind the life-size pictures to which the orator pointed. A woman snake charmer appeared, a snake about her neck; the Wild Man of Borneo came out for a moment; or a group of dancers gave us a show of their skill; these advertising show-offs were led and followed by drummers, cymbalists and bagpipers.

My brother and I had been told by Father to wait until the main show was over before going in a sideshow. Meanwhile we took a look at lesser attractions. There were booths at which you could shoot rifles at moving targets; where swains and sweethearts might be photographed arm in arm; or where you could bet for five cents with a gypsy that he could not guess your weight within a pound; several dark-complectioned vendors were selling toy balloons, the colored bubbles floating above the heads of the crowd. The only merchants that got our trade were those dealing in peanuts, popcorn, and lemonade, hunger and thirst having overtaken us again. We were especially pleased with the ambrosial pink drink whose merits were announced by men with space-filling voices.

'Lemo! Lemo! Ice cold Lemo! Five cents, a Nickel, a half a Dime!'

'Pink Lemo!'

Suddenly we were greeted with a familiar voice: 'Hallo, Olín! Hallo, Ulyssé!'

It was St. Leger, now grown very gray, a little frail, almost feeble. He said he was 'ver' lonsom' and asked if we would 'ke'p company' with him in the 'beeg tent.'

Father had told us not to let anyone take us to the show, thinking, I am sure, of the hired men. St. Leger said we must let him take us to 'Ze 'Ouse of ze Magic,' the only thing he wanted to see. We went with the old man, feeling a little guilty. The program was mostly sleight-of-hand performances, the jugglery not nearly so well done as St. Leger's own tricks.

The old man bought us some candy and then left us to 'atten' to som' beezness.'

It was now time for the Big Show.

From the rear end of an enclosed wagon stood a man behind a counter piled high with bills and half dollars, to whom we passed the exact change, and received precious green tickets. In another minute we had handed these over to a uniformed gateman and were in the animal tent for a closer look at the caged beasts, of which we had caught glimpses in the parade. Somehow they all seemed familiar from pictures we had seen and rather hurriedly we passed to the long-anticipated splendors of what we considered the circus proper.

Forepaugh's was, in the 1880's, but a one-ringed circus. This was as it should be. No boy can see all there is in a three-ringed circus and he comes away from so big a show with regrets that he has missed a great deal.

The show started with a Grand Entrance. The 'largest band ever assembled' began to play; a troop of 'equestrians' followed by another of 'equestriennes' pranced in; performing elephants tramped in, shaking the earth; then came the acrobats, leaping and tumbling; rope walkers and trapeze performers followed; lastly came the clowns, capering to imitate the acrobats; meanwhile the band blared with spirit and gusto that scarcely diminished through the long afternoon.

The paraphernalia and the acts were much the same at my first circus as they were when I took my grandsons to the 'Greatest Show on Earth.' The horsemanship and acrobatic feats on horses were as good then as today, and so were the trained animals. In human acrobatics, the tightropes, trapeze, and pyramids of male and female bodies, the circus of today surpasses that of my boyhood. There were more clowns in my last circus than in Forepaugh's, but they were no more outlandish in costume, no droller in acting. There are many more women actors in the modern shows, and they do their acts better and wear fewer clothes. But Adam Forepaugh was incomparably the best ringmaster I have ever seen.

There was no thought of staying for the Grand Concert after the Main Performance, though we dilly-dallied long enough to see a band of beautiful young women come dancing in, singing to the music of tambourines and cymbals.

After the Big Show we had money enough for only one sideshow. Then came the quarrel of the day. My brother wanted to see 'The Largest Hog Ever Raised by Man.' I wanted to see 'The Only Mermaid in Captivity.' I argued that we saw pigs enough at home. My brother, who had no imagination, said the mermaid was a fraud. We separated, disobeying

Mother's express command, and each went to the sideshow of his choice.

The seamaid had the head and body of a girl, a very pretty face, very large arms and a huge bosom, with a fish tail for her lower half, the only part of her under water. Her hair was black, not golden, as I had pictured, and she did not comb it under the sea as mermaids are supposed to do; neither did she sing. Although this seamaid was not at all in accordance with the specifications in books, I should have thought her genuine had she not given me a smile and a very human wink.

The hog and the mermaid took our last pennies and left us not a cent for supper. Notwithstanding, we stayed to see the big tent struck and the whole show put on its cars. We had planned to ride home on the train; now with our money gone we had to walk the ten long miles.

As we tramped along the shore of the bay, a late moon rose out of the eastern forest and slowly crept above calm and placid Lake Michigan. Two or three times we tried to sleep beside the sand dunes, but the mosquitoes would give us no peace. It was nearly morning before we reached home.

It was the 'altogether' of the circus that had appealed most to me, the glorious hodgepodge of blaring music, lively movement, and brilliant colors. At home I could not for the life of me go into details. I had, in the main, only a rather blurred vision of men and women in costumes of regal purple, gold, and blue; of tumblers somersaulting; tightrope and trapeze performers swinging in the air; ferocious animals loose in the ring doing their trainer's bidding; dwarfs and giants in multicolored garb; a great band in gorgeous colors, with horns blowing, drums beating, and trumpets blaring.

My brother told the family that I had disgraced myself by laughing immoderately at one of the acts of a clown. I did laugh until my sides ached and my eyes filled with tears. Adam Forepaugh, as ringmaster, in scarlet, blue, and white, had cracked his whip about a clown's legs, commanding: 'Speak a piece! Speak a piece!'

The clown was loath to begin and pleaded to be excused, tears running down his cheeks; but, finally, as the whip cracked like a small cannon and the ringmaster roared, 'Speak a piece!' he spoke, gesturing and grimacing the while:

> This morning I rose
>   From sweet repose
> Put on my clothes
>   Out I goes
> Meets one of my foes
>   Whose name was Mose
> I trod on his toes
>   He hit my nose
> Down I goes
>   That's all I knows
> But what I knows
>   I knows I knows.

XI

Father's Garden

FATHER'S garden was wholly utilitarian. In it he grew plants
to furnish food the year around and to add to our small supply
of cash. It was planted with all the vegetables that would grow
in our climate. In his garden, Father was tireless. He worked
from daylight to dark, doing as much as two men, and in a
spurt multiplied himself by three. Just as a soldier likes to die
with a sword in his hand, Father would have chosen to die with
a hoe in his.

In the first lap of spring, with the coming of venturesome
birds and plants, before the ice was out of the bay and when
snow still lingered in the woods, garden-making began. And
so it came about that when the voice of the turtle dove was
heard down our road, when the trout began to bite in the streams,
when the boys in town were shooting marbles, when the woods
were full of the splendors of spring, I had to work with Father
in the garden. The most wistful of all the days in the year
passed with boyish desires unappeased.

While the garden was still in the shadow of the eastern sun,
Father and I began crawling down long rows, our knees in the
cool moist earth, dropping seeds. There were no seed drills.
The only respite came when we got up to cover the seeded row
and change the garden-line. In the morning we felt the gentle
warmth of the sun sift through the tops of trees across our
eastern boundary; at noon, it shone directly above us roasting

our backs; after the midday meal, it sank down at snail's pace behind the western forest wall until the garden was again in shadow.

The first task in our garden was seed-sowing; the second was weeding. It would be difficult to say which was the most wearisome. There was this difference. Father was always with me when there were seeds to be sown, to see that all was done well; I worked alone at the weeding.

Father was a terrible martinet in the matter of keeping his garden cultivated. He would not have a horse cultivator in the garden and didn't like hand cultivators. A hoe was the only tool to stir the soil in his garden, and he was particular beyond all reason about his hoes. For our sandy, garden soil he wanted only lightweight hoes. A hoe, he insisted, should have square corners, so that one could cut close to cabbage, beans, and melons, and use it in thinning lettuce, carrots, and beets. It had to be kept clean, bright, and sharp. His favorite hoe was one made by George Lewis, the blacksmith, out of a square taken from the blade of a crosscut saw.

The garden had to be hoed after every rain and a time or two in droughts. Hoeing, he insisted, should be shallow, extend to the middle of the row, and should leave the topsoil soft and mellow. Clumps of sod and stones as large as hen's egg should be removed. He had a theory that hoeing in the dews of dawn or dusk was best for plants, beans excepted. Woe betide the one who hoed beans when the leaves were wet with dew! It was obligatory for me to get up to hoe in early morning, but not after supper. Yet, I often joined Father for an hour of hoeing in the evening when hermit thrushes were singing, whippoorwills calling, and nighthawks zooming.

Hoes kept the weeds down between the rows, but the rows had to be weeded by hand. Weeds grew apace in the well-manured land, and I had to crawl slowly down the long rows, leanings on the flat of one hand, knees padded with coarse cloth, pulling our superfluous seedlings and handfuls of redroot, pigweed, lamb's quarter, chickweed, quackgrass, and summer grass, piling all in windrows of wilting verdure. Powdery earth and gravel packed under my nails; my fingers, back, legs, and arms ached; there was no shade, and the sun was hotter than at seeding time.

As I worked, chickens cackled, birds sang, grasshoppers shrilled, wagons rumbled along the road, and far away I heard the whistles of steamboats and trains. Soon the whistle of the train did away with Mother's dinner bell. At a quarter to twelve, Number 20 whistled at our station and all hands stopped work and hurried to dinner. None of our family had watches; there was no need, since the whistles of trains told us the precise time of day.

In weeding time, at least twice in the forenoon and afternoon, I went to the house for a dipper of buttermilk and a piece of gingerbread. On these trips, I took a little time out to listen to the catbirds singing in the chokecherry thickets across the road; or to watch the fights always going on between blue jays and red squirrels in the birch trees towering over the wild cherries. Usually Flash, our cocker spaniel, and I took a few minutes off on these trips to chase chipmunks.

The noises of boats and trains transported me to the far-off regions whence they came, and filled me with desires and aspirations. From day to day, dream followed dream; from day to day I resolved that I would not always pull weeds. Sometime I should see the sights of the fabled world outside our forest. Looking back, recalling these dreams of boyhood, the youthful glamour of boats and trains, I can see that gardening had its charms. What better place for daydreams!

Hope thrives on seed catalogues. Father sent for all of the seedsmen's catalogues in the land; he read ever line, from artichoke to water cress. In those days there were no experiment station bulletins (think of trying to make a garden without them!), but in the annual reports of the Patent Office there were articles on gardening. To Father these were added books in the Bible, and he followed the directions 'from Washington' as conscientiously as did any officer in the army or navy.

In winter, when our garden was asleep in snow and Arctic winds blew night and day, the seed catalogues came, perennially heralding the arrival of a vegetable millennium. Evening after evening, Father read aloud the descriptions of varieties, and confided with airy hopefulness, 'I must try that.' His faith in the gaudy pictures was sublime. Exquisitely tantalizing were these catalogues when a gale roared outside and the thermometer was far below zero. With the catalogue in hand, we were as good as ready to harvest in mid-winter.

The day the big order of seeds came was of greater moment at our house than Christmas. For years this event was our closest touch with the outer world. Most of the seeds were necessities, but always there were new varieties that we wanted to try. When the box was opened, each child claimed the packets for which he had saved his pennies. Always the kindly seedsman threw in a dozen or two prize packets of vegetable or floral novelties, which were divided among the gardeners in the family. Sometimes Father tried a new seedsman, but year after year his big order came from an old reliable firm that had sold him seeds since he had first planted a garden.

Soon after the seeds came we were making hotbeds and cold frames. The smell of the redolent, steaming manure in the hotbeds was as musk and myrrh to our noses. By using hotbeds we grew most of the vegetables in the catalogues.

As regularly as he said grace before meals, Father, after meals in growing time, walked in his garden, breathing deep contentment to the full; in the dusk of evening he took a last look at his and Nature's work. One Sunday our preacher took as his text, 'Enoch walked with God three hundred years.' After that we children called Father's route in the garden 'Enoch's Walk.' He did little work on these tours; he went to feast his eyes.

It seemed to matter little whether the things he planted turned out well. His pleasure was seeing and smelling the fragrant soil and in the progress of shoots that came from seeds.

What delightful anticipations our garden gave us! At the first sign of spring our mouths began to water for green peas, new potatoes, and strawberries. (Now that there are no 'spring' vegetables, but all are to be had the year around, why bother to live through the winter?)

In those happy days of agriculture we were little troubled by pests. Insects and diseases had not found their way to our virgin soil. With the rich foods of the forest to sustain them, neither birds nor animals gave us trouble. Joutel was the worst pest we had to combat. I have never known another human being who could swallow and digest uncooked vegetables as could Joutel, always with relish and seemingly without harm to a hard-worked stomach. From the time young onions came until late autumn he had to be chased out of our garden. There was not a vegetable he would not eat raw, including potatoes and turnips. I have known him to devour in a single feast a dozen ears of sweet corn, which he liked better raw than cooked.

The worst real pest was the cutworm, which some seasons played havoc. One can lay hands on cutworms only in the darkness of night, and our garden was 'wormed' several times in May and June by the light of a lantern, the approved hour being just before dawn. Many a white, tremulous daybreak have I seen as I plucked the crawling cutworm at his work and joyfully pulled him in two.

This evil-doer was the only pest of which Indian agriculture took note. The stealthy cutworm turns tail at no cultivated plant and on a June morning the squaw-farmer might find her corn or beans laid low in the morning dew. Against its ravages our Indian neighbors laid a charmed line around their fields over which cutworms could not pass. The line was made by an unclothed squaw dragging her undergarments around the field.

The approved time was in the first heavy darkness of the night, when the squaw slipped out, sought an obscure nook, disrobed, and dragged the proper garments once, twice, thrice around the boundary line.

Longfellow describes this practice in *Hiawatha*. Years after leaving L'Arbre Croche, I found that the Romans in Christ's time used the same charmed line to keep the worms out of their fields. (Probably the Jesuits brought the recipe from the Old World to the New.)

As might be expected, this treatment for cutworms by Indian entomologists brought forth many biological stories and some scandals. If a brood of half-breeds came 'from the wind' to a comely squaw-farmer, it was certain that some near-by bachelor homesteader had employed her to lay a charmed line around his corn field.

It would be hard to say which was Father's favorite vegetable. Onions came earliest, and onions, green or dry, we had almost the year round; ten bushels of dry onions were put in the cellar every winter. For early onions we planted small sets, but our main crop came from seed. Father liked best the two Wethersfields, long-keepers and very strong in flavor. A third variety, Early Red, was mild and delicate, but did not keep—a favorite, however, for green onions.

Lettuce, which we grew as a field crop, was next most commonly served on our table, excepting potatoes. We called it by its seed catalogue name, 'lettuce,' for the term 'salad' had not yet come to our ears. Lettuce, so Mother said, was a good nerve tonic and the milky juice, like that of the poppy, was a strong sedative. Father tried all the varieties that came out, but nothing quite came up to Black Seeded Simpson and Big Boston. Black Seeded Simpson formed large loose-leaved bunches of curled, crisp, tender leaves edged with russet red. It grew quickly and in the hotbed the thinnings were ready to eat in three weeks after sowing. Big Boston surpassed all other butter-head varieties. As soon as snow was off the ground we sowed Big Boston, following with seedings until August, thinned to six inches between heads; every plant made a big, fine, firm head.

It is remarkable how few cooks know how to serve lettuce. The best way, without any question whatsoever, is to dress cool crisp dry leaves with vinegar and olive oil. Unfortunately in our backwoods home we never had olive oil, and Mother brought out the honest flavor of lettuce by putting it in a big butter bowl, salting it lightly, sweetening it with sugar, and putting on a little cider vinegar. So made it was a delightful and refreshing salad. Mother made, also, a dressing with thick cream, salt, sugar, and vinegar.

Some of our New England neighbors cooked lettuce—an awful dish. We often had it wilted with bacon grease, a dish fit for a king. Only loose-leaf lettuce was used, and the leaves had to be young and tender, picked in the dew of early morning. The bacon was fried until crisp, and while the fat still sizzled it was poured over the dry cool lettuce. It was then salted and peppered and given a tang of cider vinegar. Most cooks ruin the dish by dousing with vinegar.

Father specialized in green peas. No better peas are grown in the whole world than in the sandy lands of the northern parts of Michigan. Our peas literally melted in the mouth and were sweet and tasty as well as tender.

When tourists began to come in large numbers, the demand for green peas could hardly be satisfied, and peas became the best money-making crop we grew. Father discovered that he could have a monopoly in pea-growing in our parts if he sold shelled peas. All afternoon the family picked peas; all evening, until midnight, we shelled peas. Everyone who came our way was pressed into pea-shelling. Father gave his children in Indiana pressing invitations to visit us during the pea season. They were glad to come. Joutel was of no account in picking and shelling peas; he ate pounds of them, pods and all. When the Indiana relatives visited us we often had him at shelling-time as an entertainer; he could eat and sing at the same time.

At first we grew the early smooth-seeded varieties, but soon discarded these, one and all, for the wrinkle-seeded peas, which were larger in pod and peas and therefore easier to pick and shell. Besides, they were far better in texture and flavor. We grew only dwarf and semi-dwarf varieties; there was no time for staking tall vines. New varieties mostly came from England, and several seasons Father sent to England to Laxton's or Sutton's for a start of a new pea. We grew our own pea seed.

String beans, which Father and Mother called by their Virginia name 'snaps,' grew well with us. Our season was too short for the lima beans of that period and we grew them but sparingly. The markets called for yellow wax beans, but for home use we greatly preferred green pods, growing, of course, only stringless kinds. American plant breeders have so greatly improved the string bean that the kinds we grew cannot now be had from seedsmen.

Mother did not can snap beans as farmer's wives do now. When the pods got tough and stringy, Nature was permitted to take its course and the beans were hulled as they began to ripen. We were not very keen about dried dwarf beans, but pole beans were planted in such abundance that part of the crop could be let ripen to pick for winter. In soup, or boiled, or baked, pole beans in winter had a more pleasing tang and a richer flavor than any field beans. If you knew how, pole beans were an easy and cheap crop to grow, especially a generation ago when there were no Mexican bean beetles to take heavy toll.

We grew Kentucky Wonder, Lazy Wife, and Dutch Case Knife. These were all very good as string beans or shelled. We knew succotash only as made with shelled pole beans and sweet corn, the combination northern Indians used centuries before lima beans were grown in the North.

Father was very proud of his pole beans, especially when he compared them with those of our neighbors, most of whom came from New England, New York, and Canada. These Northerners planted them in rows, seeds a few inches apart, and staked them with brush. Father planted them as they grew in the South, in hills four feet apart, rows the same distance. Before planting, he dug into the rich virgin soil of each hill a forkful of well-rotted stable manure. In the center of the hills he set tall poles, with rough bark and the spurs of the branches. The poles were set in the ground two feet, and three strong cords, at heights of three feet, looped them together. Around each pole he planted six beans.

When planted late in May the beans quickly climbed to the top of the poles, and clambered along the cords until the row of hills made a solid wall of foliage, flowers, and beans. In picking, one could grab a handful of tender succulent 'snaps' for autumn eating. We saved pole-bean seeds year after year.

All through the cucumber season, Father and I wanted cucumbers twice a day. My brother and sister were not fond of them, and Mother thought they were 'not fit for the human stomach.' They came to the table with salt, pepper, and vinegar. Father insisted that cucumbers be picked in the dewy morning and kept cool and fresh for noon and night of the same day, half grown and sliced thin. Joutel preferred them old and nearly ripe; these he ate as he would an apple.

Father wanted a dill pickle every day in the year that he could not have a cucumber. Mother's recipe for making dill pickles was very simple, the resulting product being a firm, green pickle with a full dill flavor, perhaps a little salty for most palates. In a ten-gallon crock she placed a layer of dill with stems, leaves, and nearly ripened seed. It mattered not at all whether the dill plants were freshly cut or dried. Then came three or four layers of cucumbers well salted; then dill and cucumber again to the top of the crock. The contents of the crock were weighted down with a round cover on which was a gallon jug filled with water. Fermentation went on in a warm corner of the woodshed for two or three weeks, giving off a redolent smell of dill, after which the pickles were put safely away in quart jars—which we called cans.

High quality depended very much upon the kind of cucumbers used. Some time in the 1880's Father began growing the Evergreen White Spine cucumber; from then on he would plant no other variety. These 'Evergreens,' as Father called them, were long, straight, cylindrical, dark green from tip to stem, sprinkled with inconspicuous white spines—perfect for either slicing or pickles. For dill pickles Mother wanted a cucumber five or six inches long, an inch or more in diameter, straight and uniform; she loved to present a friend with a jar of her 'Evergreen' dill pickles.

For some years Mother put a tablespoonful of powdered alum in her dills to keep them firm and green. Then word came in a government publication that alum was very unwholesome; it was never again used in food produced in our household.

Father was too experienced a gardener to plant and harvest 'according to the moon.' For some reason, however, he always looked at the almanac before planting cucumbers. Every year he told us: 'In Virginia they plant crops that fruit aboveground in the full of the moon; those whose edible parts are below ground in the dark of the moon.'

All vegetables except cucumbers he planted when the land was warm, moist, and in good tilth. In Virginia, he told us, the day of days for planting cucumbers was Good Friday, which, of course, was much too early in our northern land. He could not tell us why Good Friday was the day to plant cucumbers, except that everybody thought they were more healthful and less bitter when planted on this sacred day.

Every year Father planted a good-sized field of sweet corn; some of the produce went to market and some was dried for

home use. Sweet corn was a comparatively new garden crop
and there were not many varieties; we grew only three. A large
part of the field was Early Minnesota, which came in season
while tourists were still in the land. Country Gentleman came
next, and Stowell's Evergreen filled out the season. We all
loved sweet corn and fattened on it every autumn. Mother
cooked three dozen ears for our family of five, and very little
was left for the pigs.

Dried corn was a winter staple. The corn was cut from the
cob, given a brief turn in the oven, and then spread for a day in
bright sunshine. If it rained, the whole house was filled with
drying corn. In winter, the finished product was soaked over
night, much as navy beans are, and then cooked with milk,
flavored with butter and salt. It was even better than when fresh.
Corn chowder was a delicious dish we had through the autumn
and winter, of which there will be more to say in another chapter.

We paid little attention to etiquette when eating corn in our
family. We did not break the ear in two and hold a half in one
hand, daintily eating two rows; we held an ear of corn in both
hands and covered rows in accordance with the sizes of our
mouths. The introduction of several varieties with small ears
brought a different technique in eating corn than that followed
when we grew only the robust Country Gentleman and Stowell's
Evergreen.

The chief glory of Father's garden was his cabbage patch,
though, to be sure, he grew so much cabbage that it was a farm
rather than a garden crop. An unexpected attribute in so lowly
a plant is beauty; there is no farm crop quite so attractive as a
field of common smooth-leaved green, wrinkled-leaf Savoy,
or purple-red Danish cabbage.

Just as some men are rosarians, Father was a cabbagarian. A
patch of cabbage in which no plant was missing; in which the
leaves covered the ground so that no spot of earth could be seen;
in which every head was perfect and of largest size, no plants

infested with worms or aphids—this gave Father as much pleasure as ever a prize rose-garden gave any man.

Father grew cabbage for home use, for the market, and to feed the cows, though, to be sure, it had to be doled out to the cows in small quantities, since liberal feedings give milk and butter a bad taste. We had cabbage for home use and some for the cows all winter. A long trench two feet deep was dug back of the barn and carpeted with a foot of dry oat straw. In this trench, four rows of cabbages were put, heads down, covered with a foot of straw, then with a few inches of earth, sloped up to the middle, so that the finished storage place looked like a long grave. The cabbages, a few at a time, could be taken out any time in the winter until spring thaws.

Sometimes the cabbage was put in the pit in the mellow warmth of Indian summer, but more often it had to wait until black frosts threatened and rain and wind were lashing the land. When the cabbage was safely in its pit, we were ready for the icebound months ahead.

Late in the fall a barrel of sauerkraut was made. Firm, well-ripened heads were allowed to wilt for a day; they were then trimmed down to white leaves, quartered, and the core removed.

The kraut cutter was placed over the barrel and a layer of cut cabbage three inches thick quickly covered the bottom. This was salted to taste and firmly pressed down. In an hour the barrel was filled, juice covering the top. A clean cover that loosely fitted the barrel covered the cabbage, and on this a gallon jug of water was placed. The barrel was kept in the warmest part of the cellar until the two- or three-week fermentation was over, and it was wheeled to a cool place.

All winter long and far into spring we ate kraut, raw or cooked. We liked raw, cold kraut, with spareribs, roast pork, and Thanksgiving turkey. In cooking, it was always well flavored with a ham bone, pig's knuckles, smoked jowl, or spareribs.

At one time or another, we tried all the cabbages the seed catalogues offered, but always came back to the delicious little

cone-shaped Early Jersey Wakefield for the early crop; Large
Flat Dutch for our main crop; Drumhead Savoy for a wrinkled-
leaf variety; and the beautiful Danish Ball head for a red
variety.

Seeds for most of our plantings were started in cold frames,
but Flat Dutch, in particular, was planted in the hills in land
where no other crop had been planted. Never have I seen
larger, firmer heads than those that grew on this newly cleared
land, the plants neither cultivated nor fertilized. On such soil,
Flat Dutch at four feet each way, completely covered the land.
No wonder we all took to cabbage.

Tomatoes grew splendidly in our warm sandy soil. (Peppers
and eggplants, close kin to the tomato, we seldom planted.)
We grew tomatoes in great abundance, and all of us ate them
freely, except Mother, who had a notion that they 'brought on
cancer.' Joutel gobbled them in enormous quantities, he, too,
believing they had a medicinal effect, though not by any means
the one Mother had in mind.

'Zey mak' me lov' sick,' he would say as he stuffed one after
another in his mouth. Somewhere he had heard that they were
called 'love apples.' Ever after he called them by this name.

Everyone in our parts pronounced the name of this vegetable
'tomato' to rhyme with 'potato,' its near of kin. Late in the
century the superfine pronunciation 'tomäto' came out of effete
New England.

Until about this time tomatoes were small, corrugated, and
very juicy; then came Trophy, a large, smooth, meaty, deliciously flavored variety; for all the years Father had a garden,
Trophy was the only tomato he wanted to plant. A neighbor
grew a small, yellow, pear-shaped tomato, which Mother had
read would not cause cancer as would the big reds. Every autumn she saved seeds and the next spring planted a row of
yellows for her own use. Joutel liked them because he could
get a whole one in his mouth. This yellow tomato brought the

word 'salad' into our vocabulary. The article Mother had read said that this yellow, pear-shaped tomato, served with lettuce, made a delicious salad. The dish pleased Mother and she called it 'my salad.' The rest of the family liked big meaty slices of Trophy on lettuce, and, at the risk of being sent from the table my brother and I would say: 'Please pass the cancer salad.'

Out of the garden came the raw material for a number of kinds of pickles. As every cook knows, each food of major importance has a natural companion pickle. Cucumbers, green and ripe, furnish most kinds of pickles, of which dill pickles are far in the lead; then there are straight vinegar pickles, sweet pickles, and ripe cucumber pickles. The tomato is next most important, ripe and green. Mother made picalilli, chili sauce, and catsup in plenty, but not tomato juice, which is a modern invention. Onions, cabbage, beets, corn, muskmelons, and beans all furnished material for pickles, used alone or in some relish. In trying novelties, Father once planted martynia, or unicorn plant, bearing long-beaked pods; it turned out to be easy to grow, and the pods were excellent in a jar of mixed pickles. Pickles must be eaten with all pork products and such hearty foods as baked beans, corn chowder, and oyster soup, so there must be plenty of them in the homes of farmers. Every farmer's wife shows off her pickles and preserves at dinners for threshers, at dime socials, and at picnics.

The crop of crops was the watermelon. It was never grown in the garden, but on a warm, sunny slope of newly cleared land. A red-hearted watermelon, cooled by cold water or by burying in cool earth, is the most sumptuous refreshment that a hot, thirsty boy can put in his mouth. On our farm it was always eaten southern fashion, a great segment of the melon cut lengthwise. The males in our family were experts in telling when a watermelon was ripe. We wanted them dead ripe, a condition we could tell by snapping with the forefinger and by the color of the pig-tail curl at the end opposite the stem.

Watermelons ripened after wheat and oats were in their stacks and before corn was ready to cut. This was the time, for two or three weeks, that we cut underbrush on land to be cleared the coming winter. Joutel was always on hand to help, tempted, we all knew, by the watermelons. He could never tell a ripe melon from a green one in the patch, judging them only by size, but if the flesh was turning red he ate it as avidly as if it were dead ripe.

Father, a trustee in one of the village churches, voiced some objection to his sons' going with Joutel to steal melons. We went just the same, knowing well where the best patches were, and being friends with all the dogs; besides, our going was the only way to get melons when our supply was gone. Father ate the stolen melons with as much relish as if he had grown them himself.

Old Hi Woods always had a melon patch in the center of his corn field. Nothing in the world gave Joutel more pleasure than stealing Hi's melons. One evening at dusk, Hi caught Joutel, my brother, and me in his melon patch. Joutel had a grain bag over each shoulder, four melons in the four ends. My brother and I had a bag each in the ends of which were melons. Joutel and I got safely over the fence that enclosed the field, but my brother, when trying to go between rails, got stuck by the bulging melons. Hi would have trimmed him well, but Joutel, grabbing a rail, came at the old man with an Indian war whoop that could have been heard a mile. Old Hi turned tail and ran.

Father roared with laughter when he heard what had happened. He told my brother it would have served him right if Hi had caught him. However, he ate the melons with great relish.

Asked to name the favorite food from the garden, every member of our family would have voted for the strawberry. Nothing so well graced our table as a dish of mammoth crimson strawberries with a pitcher of cream standing beside it—though, on second thought, the same dish filled with dainty little wild strawberries, with the same pitcher of cream standing sentry, was even better. There is a good deal to be said, also, for strawberry shortcake as a dessert, and for a side dish of canned strawberries, or a spread of preserves of this fruit, when three feet of snow covered the patch where the berries were grown.

The strawberry season began in this far-northern country late in June when wild strawberries began to ripen, to be followed two weeks later by Crescent, then the earliest garden berry. From the middle of June until early August we had strawberries at one meal or another every day. The pitcher of cream was not so certain. We should have run out of butter had strawberries for five been covered with cream even once daily. For shortcake, the pitcher often contained milk sweetened and flavored with cinnamon and nutmeg; or, one got along very well when there was only the juice of the berries to cover and soften the cake. We all liked the Pennsylvania Dutch dish of thick, sweetened clabber covering a dish of strawberries.

Every year is a strawberry year in northern Michigan. The warm sandy soil suits this fruit very well. That is, it does if the planter keeps his strawberry patch on sand made dark with forest mold, for the tiny fibrous rootlets like the feel of unctuous decaying vegetation. Our plantation had no other jacket to keep the plants from freezing than snow, which they got every winter in plenty. Father always chose a piece of new land on the south side of our northern forest wall. Here the sun burst forth first in early spring, and here the berries were full of sunlight, full-flavored richness that, well grown, this queen of fruits always possesses.

The plants were kept in hills for three crops, which would be unorthodox in modern strawberry culture. The strawberry was the only crop we watered, for it would never do to have a shortcake-less season. In dry weather, water was hauled from the creek and poured in generous quantities around every plant.

To give the plants further stimulus just before blossoming-time, Father filled a barrel a third full of fresh, strawless horse manure, put in water to the top, and a day or two later poured a pint around each plant. This liquid repast was repeated just before the berries began to color.

In vegetables, Father liked to try all the novelties, but with the strawberry he stuck to old friends. It was easy to get new vegetable seeds, but getting strawberry plants by mail was an uncertain venture. For early berries, we grew Crescent—very early, easy to grow, and very productive. Wilson was the mid-season variety, followed by Sharpless, the largest strawberry then known; it was delicious in flavor, as compared to the large and beautiful Wilson, the berries of which were a little too acid. When visitors came to the farm in summer, Father did not take them to see a heifer or a prize boar, but invited them to sample his Sharpless strawberries.

The least tended plant in Father's garden, but in its season by far the most pretentious one, was rhubarb, or 'pie-plant' as we called it. The large dark-green leaves held up by long, thick, succulent, pink and green stems made a brave show in a row of perhaps fifty plants at the end of the garden nearest the house. In our warm sandy soil the hooded leaves thrust through the ground almost as soon as the snow had melted.

It was our earliest dessert from out-of-doors. White sugar was scarce on our farm, and Mother sweetened the plain sauce with either brown sugar or maple sugar and placed a tureenful on the table twice a day. At the evening meal there was a deep-dish rhubarb pie, the filling more than an inch thick. It might be sweetened with white, brown, or maple sugar, but never flavored with nutmeg or cinnamon, as at the tables of our New England neighbors. It bubbled with juice, to contain which the lower crust was double thick.

According to Mother, rhubarb was the best of all spring tonics. She often told her daughter that the rhubarb she ate so generously was the beauty cream that gave her her beautiful pink and white complexion.

Father's garden was one of the big things in his life. Its bigness came in perfection rather than size: a garden without weeds; a garden without insects or fungi; a garden with big crops well harvested; a garden in which to take quiet walks; a garden in which to build castles in the air and to carry on happy meditations.

XII

Nature's Gardens

FOR several years we had no orchard on our farm. The land was not ready for an orchard, and Father would not have known what to plant. Jesuit missionaries, who had brought farm crops to this region two centuries before, had planted seeds of all the hardy tree fruits, but only apples had persisted. No two trees of these wild apples were alike. Most of them were very poor, but some were really good. Had there been a nurseryman to select, name, and propagate the best of the wildings, it would have been a great boon to the pioneers of northern Michigan. Within easy walking distance of our farm were several deserted Indian clearings in which grew seedling apples. The fruits belonged to the first who came to the harvest. These trees, gnarled and stunted as only neglected apple trees can be, furnished some apples to our family.

The thick-branched, crooked-limbed little runts, so thickly planted in their mossy carpet that their twigs touched, were mounds of lovely blossoms in May; and in October the apples reddening on the boughs were no less beautiful. The ruins of a log cabin or a weed-grown cellar in these deserted clearings added a note of melancholy not without charm. The fruits had neither the size, color, nor fragrance of the aristocrats in cultivated orchards; but still they were apples, their savage tang good enough on a frosty morning or when tamed down in pies or dumplings. Besides, there was the delight of getting apples for the picking.

Under the apple trees wild strawberries covered the ground, their fruits perfuming the air with sweet fragrance. Even the Indians, almost carnivorous, were fond of wild strawberries, and for centuries had held a Strawberry Festival to celebrate the ripening of this fruit.

In our woods there were many sun-lit openings made by wind or fire. These natural clearings produced red raspberries and blackberries in riotous profusion. No cultivated garden could eclipse these natural ones in vigor and productiveness of plants and size and quality of fruit. Thus, at our doors, were fruits for side dishes, pies, jams, and jellies for every day in the year, since Mother canned and dried many of the berries brought to her kitchen.

The flavor of red raspberries is the most difficult of all fruits to disguise in shrubs and jellies. Mother knew this, and with a base of rhubarb juice, easiest of all fruit juices to obtain, combined with red raspberries, made jellies and drinks to flavor our meals and keep the family in good health. The children in our family looked upon picking red raspberries as a good deal of an adventure, since bears are fond of this fruit, and a mother bear with cubs was a dangerous brute to meet in a patch of raspberries.

Wild raspberries grow best in sun-warmed openings in the forest. They like a little shade, shelter, and moisture, but not too much, and a sandy soil. Wild raspberries were at home in every part of the Land of the Crooked Tree. The brambles were not so tall as those of their cultivated cousins, nor the fruits so large. But the deep red nuggets hung in clusters on the short fruiting branches and were filled with a delicious raspberry juice far better than that from garden varieties.

The berry of berries in our land was the low-bush blueberry. It grew so abundantly in the dry, arid lands of the pine plains near us that men, birds, and beasts never had to go hungry in its season. Its simple, wholesome taste makes it a food fit for the gods. In its pine-plain habitat, summer after summer, the plants were so loaded with berries that one might scoop a large pailful in a few minutes. Families about us often went blueberrying, camping overnight and coming back with a wagonful. The berries could be bought from Indians for a pittance; and since on our busy farm we could seldom find time to go blueberrying, our supply was usually purchased.

When one of the children in our family smacked his lips and said 'blueberries,' the rest of the household saw in the mind's eyes the high-bush blueberries that grew in swamps near our farm. The plants of these moist-land blueberries were very different from those of the low-bush berries, which grew on the pine plains, and you could stand up and pick the berries in a gallon pail, fastened to a belt about the body, rather than into the three-gallon pail that stood before you in a low-bush patch.

It was in appearance and taste that the high-bush fruits surpassed those of the low-bush sister. High-bush blueberries were the dark blue of our northern skies, with so heavy a bloom that they looked like turquoise beads. The high-bush blueberry of our near neighborhood was larger, juicier, sweeter, richer, and more fragrant, either eaten as a side dish with cream or in the most glorious of all pastries, blueberry pie. Two favorite foods in blueberry time in our house were muffins, well seeded with juicy fruits, and a blueberry roly-poly, not surpassed for dessert even by blueberry pie, especially if cream were plentiful.

Most of our neighbors called blueberries 'huckleberries,' a misnomer. The chief difference between the two, to berry-eaters at least, is that the true huckleberry has ten large seeds, objectionable in eating; while the blueberries, whether high-bush or low-bush, have minute seeds hardly noticeable.

Blackberries grew all about us, darkening in the August sun. No other desserts, except those from blueberries, were more acceptable than blackberry pie and blackberry roly-poly. Blackberrying was an innocent and profitable sport. Where else can one get something for nothing so easily? Settled in a clump of blackberry bushes loaded with fruit, one quickly filled a pail with black diamonds. The brother of whom I speak so often, for years after he became a college professor, would not take his summer vacation where he could not have a few days in a blackberry patch. He was also an ardent disciple of Izaak Walton, but preferred berry picking to fishing.

Were I an Izaak Walton, I should write *The Compleat Berry Picker*. In my book there would be many dialogues between berry pickers—observations on the dozen or more species of hardy wild berries. I should tell how to pick and keep the different berries cool and fresh—quite an art. I should tell how to dress and prepare the fruits for the table and for fruit juices, so that their flavors and perfumes might best be brought out. I should make observations about mosquitoes, gnats, and black flies, and tell how they can be circumvented and the berries picked in comfort. There would be remarks about the birds and beasts that share the spoils in wild patches of the different fruits. I should consider the meadows, hillsides, fence rows, pine plains, and swamps in which the different berries grow. I should say something about their plant associates. I should consider the rights of berry pickers to enjoy a berry patch as their own, even though they give it no care and pay no taxes. Were I a genius, such as Izaak Walton, I should find so many pleasant and instructive things to say that berry picking would take its place with fishing as a contemplative man's recreation.

The blackberry patches of my childhood were fine places for chattering, gossiping children. Some made love. There was a Maggie Scott, whom I met in a blackberry patch off and on all one season. She had auburn hair, a freckled face, and red, pouting lips. Several times she dared me to kiss her, but I never could gather the courage to do so, though her red, berry-stained lips were very seductive. I was not afraid of snakes, bears, wildcats, or other boys, and I had fought to the finish with another red-haired, freckled-faced girl from a family of Irish fighters when she had pushed my little sister in a mud puddle; but I was afraid to kiss Maggie.

She would say—'I think it's mean of you not to take my dare.' I never did.

There were few wild plants about that could be used as vegetables, though there were many that could have been eaten had necessity arisen. All but one of these wild plants were pot herbs, and the exception, the wild leek, seldom came to our table, though a Welshman would have found them quite as good in texture and flavor as the cultivated leeks in his garden.

Leeks grew in all our hardwood forests in great abundance. No other vegetable is more odoriferous, especially after it has been eaten, than the American wild leek. Madame Pettier told Mother that the leek was a favorite food of the hunters and trappers in the Hudson's Bay Company when she was a child and that they were very good in soups. Mother could hardly wait until spring came to try 'leek soup.' We children and even Father liked it, but Mother would never have a leek in the house again.

School children often ate leeks with the certainty that they would be sent home; no teacher in the land would allow a child in a schoolroom with a 'leeky' breath. Once in a great while my brother and I ate leeks and invariably were made to stay out of doors, rain or shine, and without meals, until the air purified our atmosphere. One year several 'leek parties' were given in our neighborhood at which leek soup was the chief refreshment. Everybody had to eat leeks. Mother would permit none of our family to go.

It was hard to get away from 'leeky milk' and 'leeky butter.' If the cows got in the woods during the season for leeks, milk and butter were ruined unless leeks were eaten for protection. Cows can smell leeks a quarter-mile away and make for them at the first whiff. Their noses wrinkled with delight as, in lush springtime, they snatched mouthful after mouthful of the broad green leaves and white succulent bottoms as we hurried them through the woods from daytime pastures. Our cows were kept in our own pasture when leeks were plentiful in the woods.

The only other wild plants that came to our table from Nature's gardens were dandelions and cowslips. My parents knew nothing about vitamins, but they knew that plenty of fruits and vegetables the year round kept them and their children in such good health that there was no need of patent medicines. Mother was ever of the opinion that there was, in particular, much virtue in 'greens.' If Mother were now alive, she would know where every vitamin from A to Z could be found in vegetables and fruits. The first greens in the spring were dandelions from the fields; they went into our kettle from the time the leaves were an inch or two long, when there was some nutritious matter in the whitish unexpanded flower buds, until the leaves were six inches long with a good dandelion tang. From the swampy woods we had cowslips, a few messes each spring (not the cowslip of the poets, which is a primrose, but the American cowslip, more properly the marsh marigold, of the Crowfoot family) that we brought in just as the flower buds began to form. Greens were always cooked with a ham bone, a piece of smoked jowl, or slices of bacon.

In our three years' sojourn in northern Indiana we had a great abundance of walnuts, butternuts, and hickory nuts, delicious viands especially for winter evenings with cider and apples. Not one of these grew in the forests about our new home. The beaked American hazelnut grew sparingly, but the nuts were so small and so well protected by burs that we seldom bothered with them except to fill our pockets in autumn for schoolroom consumption.

Beechnuts we had in great abundance. In autumn, in a beechnut year, we children could quickly gather a bushel, so thickly were they spread over the garden carpet of beechnut leaves. We picked beechnuts only after heavy frosts, when the four nutlets, looking like huge grains of buckwheat, dropped from their round spiny burs. The kernels had a rich creamy flavor, very delicious, but slow eating because of difficulty in getting the meats out of the husks. In autumn we competed with frisky, chattering chipmunks and red squirrels in the beechnut harvest; in spring, waves of young pigeons swept us off our feet when we trespassed on what they considered their exclusive food. The nuts began to sprout even under the snow, but we ate their shoots and rootlets, until the sprouts were an inch or two long; no doubt they were full of vitamins.

We never had a flower garden on our farm in the early years. The best gardener in the world could not compete with Nature's gardens in the forest all about us. From the time the slanting April sun melted patches of snow in the woodlands, uncovering deep carpets of leaves, until November snows came again, flowers, ferns, mosses, lichens, or the greenery of seedling trees gleamed, first in open woodlands and then in the deepest thickets of swamps, on every square foot of northern Michigan. Even my prosaic father, when he walked in the woods, kept eyes and nose at attention for the beauty and fragrance of the good earth.

The warm days that started sap in our sugar bush persuaded the dogtooth violet, an Erythronium, pluckiest of all flowers, to thrust up through the thick leaves. The plant is not a violet but a lily, with butter-yellow flowers, an inch in diameter, which thus early reach on long stems upward toward the sun. The six lily-like petals curl backward, showing brown stamens; on them came the earliest bees and butterflies. The purple and white leaves shoot from the ground, the spotted leaves giving the name 'adder's tongue.' The Erythronium is happy only in clear skies; the flowers do not open on cloudy days.

With Erythroniums came a rusty-bristly trailing evergreen plant, a little coarse, shy, and not easily found. It bore exquisite flowers, small and fragile, rivaling lily of the valley in fragrance. We called it 'trailing arbutus,' but all our New England neighbors called it 'Mayflower.' It grew in sandy, rocky woods and in evergreen swamps, always under protecting leaves, its chief desire for environment being an acid soil. It was a splendid flower for bouquets, its small clusters of rose and whitish flowers lasting in a living room several days, distilling fragrance to the very end. The first April outings on Sunday afternoons were to gather trailing arbutus.

A favorite flower in our forests was *Trillium grandiflorum*, the great-flowered white trillium. It was as thick in our woods as quills in a porcupine's tail, this simile coming to mind because the only murder of this animal I ever committed took place in a thicket of trilliums; a bloody murder in a field of snowy white.

In swamps were beds of cypripediums, the large, showy pink moccasin flower, the little two-leaved pink lady, more delicate and modest than its showy sister; there were the two yellow lady's-slippers, lovely splotches in deep woods. Other orchids we might find were the great fringed orchid, six-inch spikes of pale purple flowers; the bearded pink-purple Calopogon; Pogonia, coralroot, lady's-tresses, rattlesnake plaintain, and the charming little arethusa. Here in wild gardens were to be found all these orchids in a setting of freshness and beauty never to be found in a man-made garden.

In our woods were a dozen species of violets; the blue-flowered arrow-leaved, the common blue, the palmata, and the bird-foot; of whites, the sweet-scented, the creamy-white, and the round-leaved; of yellows, the round-leaved, the downy-leaved; of violet-colored, the long-spurred, and the short-spurred. The soil was the same for all; the same rains watered all; and yet with no color box, no perfume bottles, Nature's gardener grew them.

Jack-in-the-pulpit is one of the familiars of every child living in a northern forest. Club-shaped Jack stands in a pulpit, the broad, flat summit of which curves over him; the pulpit, in turn, stands between twin leaves each having three leaflets.

These greenish-white leaves, striped and spotted with purple, with the curious flower formation, make the plant seem the most exotic of northern flowers. The fat, round, starchy corms contain an acid juice, which knowing country boys palm off on their urban cousins as an edible 'Indian turnip,' to the wretched unhappiness of the gullible boy who takes a taste. Dried, roasted, and ground, the Ottawa used the turnips to make a kind of unleavened bread; in our rich, moist woodlands they grew in countless numbers. My brother and I could never get Mother to make bread from Indian turnips.

In Round Lake, a few miles from our farm, was a water-lily garden with which no planted garden of this flower in all the world could compete. The lake, more than a mile in diameter, was completely covered with the pinkish-white richly scented lily-like flowers, three inches in diameter, gloriously beautiful as a breeze rippled the sun-spangled pond. The plant is not a lily but belongs to a distinct family, *Nymphæceae*, far removed from the lily family; the genus *Nymphæa* is appropriately dedicated to the water nymph.

It would be tiresome to name more of the many flowers that grew in the woods about our farm, but I cannot stop this floral catalogue without naming *Clintonia borealis*, more common in our moist northern woods than I have ever found it elsewhere. Its two to seven round, dark blue, glossy berries ripening in June convey the spirit of cool woodland better than the fruits of any other plant I know. The true flowers are small yellowish-green, leaf-like organs; yet the leaves and fruits are beautiful and no lover of flowers would pass them by.

Ferns grew everywhere in uncultivated places in the Land of the Crooked Tree. They were of amazing beauty and delicacy in the lights and shadows of forest grottoes. Alone or mixed with sedges or scouring rushes, brackens grew abundantly in old clearings and along roadsides in the uplands. As we shall see,

Indians found ferns useful, but white settlers seldom used them, or even noted their lacy fronds colored in Nature's most beautiful greens.

As everyone knows, ferns do not have flowers and seeds but grow from one-celled spores. Numerous little cases are borne along the veins and midribs and margins, which contain millions of tiny spores.

Mr. Parmalee, our learned botanist-preacher, early told me that fern plants did not grow immediately from the spores, but came from a delicate, fleeting tissue, on which, in time, male and female organs corresponding to the stamens and pistils of true flowers were borne. From the fertilization of elements in these organs ferns grew. Mystery in growth and great beauty made ferns sacred plants to me.

Young fern plants the world over are called 'fiddlenecks,' because they are curled like the scroll that forms the head of a fiddle. Madame Pettier told Mother that the Indians ate these fiddlenecks as potherbs, not only as good wholesome food, but to make them smell like ferns so that they could sneak up on wild quarry. Some of our New England neighbors ate them freely as greens, but Mother would not cook fiddlenecks.

'Snaky things,' she said when we children brought them in. 'Give them to the pigs!'

Even when I read in a Patent Office Report that Finlanders believed that a diet of fiddlenecks conferred perpetual youth on those who ate them, Mother still would not have them on her table.

'Who are the Finlanders?' she asked.

My brother, the historian of the family, told Mother at great length that French peasants before the Revolution ate bread made from the rootstalks of the bracken, or brake as we called it. Although we could gather bracken rhizomes on our own farms by the ton, Mother would not make bracken bread.

'We are not that near starvation,' she said.

In one of the forest stretches near our farm was a bit of land of three or four acres, half open, half covered with a new growth of trees. Level spaces and regular ridges made it plain that man had once had something to do with this piece of soil. There were many such places in northern Michigan, known as 'Indian gardens,' the *grands jardins* of the early French. Our generation of Indians disowned them as their handiwork, nor had they any legends about their origin.

Whence came the gardeners? Whither did they go? These Indian gardens were among the unfathomed mysteries of my boyhood. When in a contemplative mood, or when the desire came for mild adventure, I would go to this wild garden, usually on a Sunday afternoon when the sun was shining brightly. During these visits my emotions were stirred as if by a mysterious presence. I felt that the garden had been the scene of ancient Indian rites whose spirit still lingered there.

Nature planted this Indian clearing with grasses and evergreens, making it a beautiful spot. The evergreens were junipers, firs, yews, and spruces, and these, on the ridges the old gardeners had laid out, together with a natural terrace on one side, and grass everywhere, gave the plot the aspect of a decadent garden in the Old World.

Corn was the staple article of Indian agriculture, and at the edge of this garden nearest Lake Michigan were three deep, funnel-shaped pits in which were the remains of charred corn. No doubt the old gardeners had cached in these pits charred corn and corncakes, the 'yellow cakes of Mondamin,' as Hiawatha called them, along with maple sugar, the three most nutritious and appetizing foods on which our northern Indians lived. The caches were in the center of a level bit of land so hard packed and so bedded with ashes that one knew at once that here wigwams had stood. Here, probably, was held the Green Corn Festival at which the Indians were wont to spend several days in singing, dancing, and feasting sumptuously on corn and succotash.

Whoever laid out this garden had a taste for fruit as well as for corn, and had planted the wild black cherry, which produces a vinous, bitterish fruit much liked by the Indians. About the garden were perhaps a dozen enormous trees of this cherry not to be found elsewhere in our region. Here, also, was a thicket of wild black plums, which grew nowhere else in our part of the world. Years afterward, studying botany, I found that this was the Canada plum, *Prunus nigra* of the botanist, native of the lower lakes and of the St. Lawrence; whoever had planted these trees had traded with the St. Lawrence Indians.

A trail led from this Indian garden through the *grand bois*, as St. Leger called the unbroken forest, to Little Traverse Bay. It was a short cut from our house to the water, and I knew it well in spring, summer, and autumn. Along the trail was a thick border of aspens and balm-of-Gilead poplars, the leaves of which were never motionless even in the calmest weather, beautiful flashings of green in the sunlight: deep green, light green, yellow green, golden green, brownish green, tremulous from the time the first leaf came until the last one fell.

One autumn a storm uprooted one of the large fir trees, exposing in the soil beneath some bits of crockery. This set me to digging for possible treasure, but my labors brought forth only a little more crockery, a broken copper knife, and the bowl of a pipe.

Mr. Parmalee told me that the crockery and copper knife were the handiwork of the 'mound builders,' but he couldn't tell me who the mound builders were, except that they had been in this region long before the French came and probably before the Ottawa, another race, and that long ago they had vanished from the face of the earth.

I could only conclude at the end of my boyish researches that people had lived here before the Ottawa, and had been driven away in Indian warfare, leaving this garden as a monument.

In spite of the creepy feeling I had about going to the old Indian camping-place alone, it was pleasant to know it was there; to know that I had stumbled upon a ruin in a new land that made it an ancient land; and that even wise men knew little about the people that had once tilled this bit of earth.

XIII

Mother's Poultry

MOTHER took charge of the poultry on our farm, training me, unwillingly at first, as a helper. For three or four years we had only a small flock of twenty or thirty chickens, housed in a mean little lean-to built on the south side of the barn. There was no enclosure for the few fowl and they ran hither and yon, straying far afield where the hawks often got them, or into Father's garden, on which, to keep peace in the family, the whole household had to keep an eye; for neither Father nor Mother could keep their tempers when Mother's chickens scratched in Father's garden.

Eventually the matter was happily settled. When summer resorters came in numbers, the prices of eggs, broilers, and fowl soared. Mother's chickens became nearly as profitable as Father's garden. A hen house was built with a commodious park, so that chicken-raising and gardening could thrive side by side. The two industries went well together. Lettuce, peas, corn, cabbage, and even tomatoes and melons, when too old, or when spoiled and unfit for kitchen or market, made good green food for the chickens. Chicken manure made the best fertilizer Father could get for his garden. Besides, there was a chicken for dinner every Sunday.

Our poultry industry was founded on chickens, though Mother tried year after year to grow turkeys, of which she was very fond. In her childhood in northern Indiana, wild turkeys had been so numerous that the early settlers could feast on them nearly every day in the year. When the wild turkeys became scarce, there was little trouble in raising their domestic kin in the barnyard. In northern Michigan it was almost impossible to raise turkeys. The winters were too cold for a fowl that had its origin in a semitropic climate. Nevertheless, spring after spring Mother had Indiana relatives send her a setting of eggs, which were put under a Rhode Island Red for hatching. Sometimes she brought half a dozen of them to maturity, but she was quite content if she had only a turkey for Thanksgiving and another for Christmas.

As we had no pond or stream on our farm, and as water is indispensable for rearing ducks and geese, we did not try to grow either. We occasionally traded chickens to Granny Woods, a neighbor, for a duck or a goose for New Year's dinner, one or the other being, in Father's estimation, indispensable for the proper celebration of the first day of a new year. In my last years on the farm we had a most interesting time with Muscovy ducks, about which something will be said a little later.

It fell to me to do most of the manual labor in taking care of the poultry, though Mother continued to supervise even after I became an experienced poultryman. When I came into my teens, Mother and I went into partnership in the poultry business. First, the house had to be supplied with eggs and chickens, a pretty tall order. Mother took the money from the sales of eggs and dressed poultry to spend for household necessities. The little that was left came from selling eggs and chickens for breeding purposes, and this was my share of the business.

As so often happens in partnerships, there were disagreements. To Mother an egg was an egg, a chicken a chicken. She would take the eggs out of my breeding nests for the kitchen, and snatch any fowl that came to hand for Sunday dinner. What galled me most was that she exchanged a dozen of my purebred eggs, worth a dollar a dozen, with any woman who came along with a 'settin'' of eggs from dung-hill chickens. In spite of my partner's lack of interest in pure-blooded chickens, we did grow some well-bred fowls, of which we had at least, at one time or another, a dozen breeds.

In the 1880's, the years in which our poultry business was flourishing, there was much interest in chickens. Modern poultry-raising was just beginning and there was much discussion in farm papers of breeds for eggs and table fowl. The use of incubators was becoming general for small poultrymen. There was so much of interest that I was quite sure I wanted to raise chickens as my life's work. First, I had to find out what breeds were best for northern Michigan.

White Leghorns were then becoming popular for eggs and broilers, and we gave them a trial. In our cold climate Leghorns did not thrive, probably because our hen house was poorly constructed. Also, Mother did not like small birds and white eggs, so White Leghorns were discarded. We went to the other extreme and tried several breeds of very large chickens.

Two of the large-birded breeds were tried one spring and discarded because they ate much and produced few eggs. These were Cochins and Brahmas. The last-named breed had a beautiful comb and large feathered drumsticks of enormous size, the cocks weighing twelve or fourteen pounds. Mother liked them for the table, and we raised a few for home use year after year. Then we tried Barred Plymouth Rocks and Rhode Island Reds, breeds of birds a little smaller than the Cochins and Brahmas but still large. A trouble with both breeds was that the hens seemed to want to set all summer. We liked both, however, and finally settled on Rhode Island Reds. Mother liked the large reddish-buff eggs of the Rhode Island Reds, thinking they had a better taste than the small white ones of the White Leghorns.

Meanwhile we had an interesting experience with a curious exotic breed. We read in a poultry paper that the Houdans were very ornamental, having large crests for topknots and the cocks having beards. These characteristics appealed to me.

Furthermore, the paper said that the skins were white and the flesh had the finest flavor of all chickens, and in consequence were 'dear to the hearts of French epicures.' Mother loved the word 'epicure' and professed to be an epicure in chicken flesh, whether roasted, fried, broiled, or stewed. At once we ordered a setting of Houdans at three dollars a dozen. When the eggs hatched I was amazed to discover that the curious little chicks had five toes on each foot, whereas in the other breeds I knew there were only four toes to a foot. In great excitement I wrote to the breeder who sold me the eggs and told him of my discovery. Word came back that all Houdans were five-toed.

Having decided that the Rhode Island Red was the best breed for our purposes, the junior partner in our firm insisted on improving the stock. It was hard to convince the senior partner that we needed better blood; but, finally, reluctantly, she consented to an investment that to her mind was outrageously extravagant. We paid to a noted Rhode Island Red breeder in Kalamazoo ten dollars for a three-months-old cockerel. In the end we were astonished at the prices obtained for eggs from stock with a ten-dollar rooster at the head of the breeding-pen. The young rooster came in April and by July was nearly full grown. One morning I discovered that our high-priced rooster was very sick. A glance told me what the trouble was. The greedy bird had eaten too much green stuff and was 'crop-bound.'

Mother and I decided to 'operate,' a safe procedure, so poultry papers said. I trussed the bird up on a bench outside the wood-shed. Mother plucked away the feathers from the distended crop; and, as chief surgeon, I cut a long gash in the crop with a razor and then removed the undigested food to the last scrap. Mother sewed the wound shut with a strong thread. The operation was 'successful' and almost at once the rooster was up and about. In a few days, however, it was evident that all was

not well with the patient. His crop and neck were as stiff as a
ramrod. Mother had sewed the inner crop to the outer skin.

This cock became the most amusing thing in our barnyard
life, where there was always much to amuse. To see him eat,
fight, mate, or to hear the terrible squawk when he tried to crow,
kept us all convulsed with laughter. The cripple's passions were
in no way lessened. His appetite was good and he grew to enormous size; the hens in his harem were ardently courted and it
was apparent that we should have a fine flock of Rhode Island
Reds the next year. In spite of his stiff neck, the cripple quickly
became lord and master of the poultry yard. He could not use
his beak, but he struck terrible blows with his wings and feet.

About the time of the rooster operation, the Greenbackers
nominated Cock-eyed Ben Butler (he who had stolen spoons
from the women of New Orleans during the War) for the
presidency. Our fat, arrogant Rhode Island Red, with prominent eyes, was the spit and image of the famous general, and
Father named the bird Ben Butler. The name took, and all the
neighbors came to laugh at the bird and the name. A few weeks
before election the real Ben Butler came to a grand barbecue in
Petoskey, across the bay from where we lived. Some of our
Republican neighbors wanted to put our Ben Butler in a cage
and drive in a light wagon in the procession at the barbecue.
Father, however, would not give Republicans political comfort.

By the next summer our fine rooster became very ill-tempered.
In particular he disliked children and would come flopping and
squawking at all that came in our yard, putting the fear of death
in them. In the middle of the summer, my eldest sister with her
six-year-old daughter, Alice, came to spend a few weeks with us.
Alice was Father's only grandchild and the only child to call
me 'Uncle.' Our whole family worshiped the little girl. The
first time Alice ventured out, testy old Ben Butler, with a
terrible squawk, came flopping at her and knocked her down.
In less than no time I was on him. I dragged him to a block on

the woodpile and off came his head. The next day we had chicken stew and noodles for dinner.

Modern poultrymen would turn up their noses at the quarters we provided our feathered charges some fifty or sixty hengenerations ago. Our chicken coop was not a two- or three-storied apartment house; there were no incubator brooders, central heating, electricity, ventilating system, running water, feeding troughs, or patent nests, and the floor was mother earth. We gave the setting hens with their clutch of fifteen eggs a small private room in mangers in the stable or odd corners in the barn, with no provisions for air, light, or water. In three weeks the expectant mother came off the nest with a dozen peeping chicks, which, clucking and scratching, she led around the barnyard, keeping a watchful eye for hawks, cats, and rats.

The chicks got a little nursing in the way of milk, mashes, and green food, but the old hens had to put up with wheat, oats, barley, buckwheat, and corn as the several foods came from the granary. It was fun in spring and fall when the chickens were running loose to come out of the barn with a peck measure of grain and scatter it wildly with the call 'Biddy Biddy! Biddy!' at which old and young, cocks and hens came clacking and cackling from all directions to fight for their share. Feeding time was just before breakfast or supper, when males, going to the house for their meals, stopped for a moment to see the cock fights that took place with 'feeding the hens.'

Neither Mother nor I knew anything of balanced rations or vitamins. We did know that our poultry were better off and that we got more eggs when, in winter, we provided fats in milk, green stuff in cabbages, clover hay well chopped, and mashes of chopped grain.

In our poultry-raising, the partners never were able to buy an incubator, and I had the chore of setting hens. A 'settin' hen,' to use the vernacular of the farm, is an interesting illustration of the persistence of animal instinct: the desire to set never leaves the female of this species. My apprenticeship in the chicken business began as a boy of seven or eight in gathering eggs and in hunting biddies that had stolen away to set—or, perhaps, had a brood of chicks far afield in the woods.

The chief adventures of my young boyhood were dealing with the setting hens. To crawl under the barn and drag out a hen that Mother did not want to have set was a common chore. Sometimes the task was to put under the expectant mother more eggs, or take out and give to another hen the two or three chicks hatched in a stolen nest. Sometimes a foolish biddy would not leave her clutch of eggs to eat or drink, and had to be forcibly taken to her meals and kept from going back until she had had a little exercise. Some hens wanted to set in late summer and it became my duty to prevent them from doing so. My means of 'breaking up a settin'' was to substitute stones for the eggs, or cover the nest with boards or a pan of water, or tie the hen's legs and keep her on her back a day or two.

When setting hens were disturbed, the old ladies were belligerent. They struck with their beaks, wings, and feet. When a hen wants to set, she hunts up a dark solitary place where she can sleep the three weeks of her confinement away, resting in privacy in preparation for the busy days ahead of her when she must scratch for her young and keep enemies away. At any time except when they were setting, hens were the most cheerful companions I could have in my boyhood when the family left me alone on the farm. The singing and cackling of hens and the noisy courtship and crowing of cocks were next to human companionship. Hens, in turn, seem glad to have humans about in the 49 weeks free from keeping warm 12 or 15 eggs.

One of the very pleasant sounds on a farm is the 'tuk, tuk, tuk, tuck tu-da-tuk' of a hen that has just laid an egg. She is proud of her accomplishment and wants all the world to know what she has done. In my first days in the poultry business I hurried to the chicken house to gather the newly laid egg while it was still hot and to mark the hen that had laid while she still 'tuk-tuk'ed with joy.

In my early boyhood, a daily task was to 'hunt the eggs.' In winter the hens made their nests in the barn, choosing mangers, haylofts, grain bins, and any dark corner they might find. In spring, summer, and autumn hunting eggs took on the aspect of a real adventure. I crawled under the barn, looked along fence rows, about stone piles, and across the road in tangles of berries, in clumps of bracken, usually stirring up wild life of one kind or another.

Someone about the farm was sure to make note of a hen singing happily before dropping her daily egg, or cackling when her chief business of a day was done, thus giving a clue to the whereabouts of a hidden nest. In the busy summer season for humans, a few hens could always find a hiding-place to brood on a nest of eggs for three weeks and then come clucking forth with a clutch of baby chickens; then the mother and her brood had to be driven and coaxed to a small A-shaped slatted coop in the barnyard.

Once Preacher Cook took as his text Matthew xxiii. 37: 'as a hen gathereth her chickens under her wing.' The children in our family agreed that in his discussion of hens and chickens Preacher Cook was wrong in several details.

I must close this account of Mother's poultry yard with a tale of our experience with Muscovy ducks.

The winter I began high school there was a piece in our poultry paper about Muscovy ducks. The writer of the article said that these ducks with the Russian name (really a corruption of Musk duck) came from the vast treeless plain south of the Amazon, the pampas region of Brazil, on south to Patagonia. These ducks did not quack but made a noise like the hiss of a goose. The bird was described as the handsomest of all domestic fowls, glossy green and brownish black in color, with a crested head, and naked, fleshy, scarlet wattles. The birds, it was said,

were very pugnacious and would keep hawks away from a
poultry yard.

Under the stimulus of high school, my interest in poultry had
dwindled almost to the vanishing point. This account of Muscovy ducks stimulated what I now know was a love of birds
whatever the kind. After reading up on Muscovy ducks, I decided to go back to poultry-raising. Mother's interest in poultry
had begun to lag, too, and it was only by telling her over and
over that all poultry authorities said that the Muscovy duck
was the best of all domesticated fowls for the table that I could
awaken her interest. The Muscovy was an inland bird and did
not need water for his well-being. It took five weeks to hatch
eggs instead of the four for other ducks.

Early that spring I got a dozen Muscovy eggs, from which
a motherly Rhode Island Red biddy hatched ten beautiful
ducklings. They grew apace and were admired by all who saw
them. My sister, just coming into her teens, loved them and soon
was given charge of the little brood; ownership quickly followed.

That autumn we tried them on the table and found broiled
and roast Muscovy duck delicious. Even Muscovy eggs were
better than those of other ducks, which often have a fishy taste.
Mother was delighted and bragged about her 'Muscovites' to
all her friends. There was a fly in the ointment. The ducks,
male and female, were very pugnacious. They drove the chickens
from their food and crowded them off their roosts. Egg pro-
duction sank to an alarmingly low level. A pen was provided,
but the ducks got out and flew into the chicken park. It was
decreed that they must be eaten.

My sister begged that she might keep two, and this Mother
permitted. The two selected to live were cockerels. The gander-
like males were so nearly alike that no one but my sister could
tell them apart. She named them Tweedledum and Tweedledee.
The ducks loved their mistress, would eat out of her hand, come
at her call, and waddle behind her to take the air wherever she
went on the farm. My sister was a strict disciplinarian and taught

her charges to keep out of the house and to live in peace with the dog and the cat.

From the very start, there was war to the knife and the knife to the hilt between Mother and Tweedledum and Tweedledee. Enmity began when the whole brood was alive. The ducklings came into the kitchen and swarmed about the kitchen door for crumbs, and 'always left a muss.' After Mother, time after time, swept them out and away with her broom, they began to get nasty and fight back. As Tweedledum and Tweedledee grew older they became very bellicose. Mother found herself a prisoner in her own house. She could not step out of her kitchen door without being pecked with an enormous duck beak or struck with powerful duck wings. The fastidious birds disliked a washing, and when Mother appeared on Monday morning to hang out her 'wash,' honking and hissing, beak and wing, they went at her.

Tweedledum and Tweedledee loved to waddle behind their mistress on her way to school. Part of the way was through woods, but these descendants of ancestors accustomed to the treeless steppes of South America would not venture into Michigan woods. They would go to the woods and then fly back; for, though not migratory birds, they were strong flyers.

In the autumn of their second year they became a great nuisance. It was impossible to keep them in their pen. When about the yard, they quarreled constantly with Mother, all three sputtering, threatening, and calling names. My sister could no longer take them part of the way to school because they attacked other children. There was only one thing to do. We ate Tweedledee on Christmas; Tweedledum graced the table on New Year's Day. Mother saw to it that my sister was invited out for the day at both these feasts.

XIV

Our Livestock

FATHER loved horses and hated mules; yet he always kept a team of mules. He had been brought up with them in Virginia, and, I suppose, had come to think of them as one of the hardships to be endured in a farmer's life.

When we had been on the farm a few years, an advertisement appeared in a Chicago paper telling of army mules for sale. Father at once bought a pair and had them shipped by water. The day they came, people in the village turned out to see them taken off the boat—a circus had come to town. It was the first span in all the region; the first mules the Indians had ever seen.

No other animals ever on our farm could approach these mules as an influence on the lives of the males of our family. Daily they stirred in us all the human passions—hatred, affection, humor, revenge, and much impiety in the way of profanity. Somewhere I have read, 'He who has not had a mule has had no adventure.' I can vouch for the truth of the saying, be the author who he may.

Long before the mules arrived, the youngsters in our family began to speculate about what service they had seen in the army. Custer's massacre had taken place a short time before, and we knew that Custer had mules in his supply train; could these mules of ours have been in Custer's campaign?

When Jack and Jenny, for so we had named them, were led forth from the steamboat, we realized that they had fought

Indians, for at the sight and smell of the redskins on the dock they laid back their ears, rolled their eyes, and let fly their heels, signs of dislike so unmistakable that every Indian scuttled for safety.

The two mules were beautifully matched. They were of the same size, as large as any I have ever seen, with velvety skins of mouse color. Their hoofs were small, black, polished, their tails trimmed to a flybrush. The two differed in eyes. Jenny's eyes were meek, confiding, pensive, and had a look of sadness. Jack's were roving, shrewd, knowing, and he gave a leering, defiant look at every passer-by. When Jack stood sunk in thought, eyes placid, ears gently moving, one needed to look sharp. In a flash the old rogue would awaken as if suddenly surprised and launch out with heels or teeth at whatever living thing was near him.

Jack's ears were even more expressive than his eyes. Moving backward and forward, laid back, wide apart, or close together at the tips, moving alternately one way and the other, they told when a devilish idea was being born in his brain, and the degree of its malevolence. Jenny's ears, like her eyes, bespoke her patient, sedate, tractable nature, but were quite as expressive of deviltry as Jack's, as when, with furtive agility, she stole a mouthful of some standing crop or a wad of hay from a passing wagon.

Jack had a remarkable stomach. Every now and then he broke loose and took his way to the feed bin to gormandize. If he made a night of it, his belly in the morning would be enormous, indecent. Any other animal would have foundered and died. But when Jack had eaten too much, we just turned him loose in the barnyard and let him roll for an hour or two, and his girth became normal, his appetite as keen as if he had had nothing to eat for a week.

Both the mules were superb work animals, thriving in slavery that a horse could not have endured through a single season. Father would never say how old Jack and Jenny were, but that they were full of years we were sure, Jack in satanic old age, Jenny in the golden age of reflection. They could be kept on so little food that the question was raised whether it was possible to starve a mule.

Jack was a shrewd calculator of how much work he ought to do. When he had done what he considered a day's stint, nothing would induce him to do more; he then became a 'balky mule,' than which there is no stronger term for stubbornness. He would balk in a thunder storm or in a stress of cold weather. In deep snow he would plant his feet, and, with throbbing flanks, nostrils dilated, eyes glazed, ears laid back on his neck, there would he stay as fixed as Plymouth Rock.

Soon we learned a way to make Jack move when he was in a rockbound spell. His love for Jenny (though purely Platonic, since he was a mule) was so intense that he could not be happy with Jenny out of sight. When he was near her, he would kick and bite and otherwise interfere with her bodily comfort, but when she was out of his sight, he was the most wretched beast alive; he would duck his head, swish his whiskbroom tail, astound the silence with his awful voice, and make a dash for Jenny's company.

Jack objected to being ridden, and the instant anyone bestrode him began to walk backward. My brother and I found two ways to make him go the way we wanted. If there was time, we turned his head in the opposite direction and let him back to where we were going. When time pressed, one of us would mount Jenny and with whoop and hurrah ride past Jack. Jack would instantly whirl and follow Jenny.

Sometimes a little could be done through Jack's belly, seat of most of his pleasures. He liked whatever he saw anyone eating. If one stood a little way in front of him, eating anything from a potato to watermelon, and giving Jenny an occasional nibble, Jack could be coaxed into motion. One spring a hen made her nest in Jack's manger, and he learned the taste of eggs, which he ate shell and all. The sight of an egg thereafter became a temptation he could not withstand; thus, a hen's egg could move a load of logs.

Jack's balking brought him to an untimely end. One winter morning my brother and I were told to take a load of wood, on the way to high school, to Preacher Gibson. Before daylight we were on the high hill where the wood was corded, and soon the load was on. The task, the time of day, and the weather had soured all of our tempers. On the brink of the hill Jack set his feet and would not budge. The runners of the sled were encircled with chains to act as brakes. These we took off and Jenny started the load but not Jack, who would not move his legs and went down in front of the heavy, swiftly moving load. At the foot of Crosby's steep hill, we found poor old Jack dead as a door nail. We boys were heartbroken. Life hardly seemed worth living without Jack.

The Saturday after Jack committed suicide my brother and I put him underground. We chose the spot where he had so bravely died for principle, a beautiful place under a wide-spreading beech. He was cold and stiff and hard to move; the ground was frozen, and the roots of the beech were hard to cut. When we had tumbled him into his shallow grave and covered him with earth, we found the shroud woefully skimpy; his four feet stuck up in the air like so many posts, plain to be seen from the main road. What should we do? We could not bring ourselves to undertake the heavy work of reinterring the remains. Must I confess it? We hired an Indian to saw off the legs of the faithful beast and bury them beside the body. Thus, dust to dust for poor old Jack!

Although nearly every farmer in our parts owned a pair of oxen, Father would not have an ox on the place. In Virginia only slaves drove oxen. One of Father's terms of contempt for a neighbor he did not like was, 'common as an ox-driver.' Nevertheless, for certain kinds of work he often hired oxen because of their tractor strength. Oxen were very needful in logging and in plowing newly cleared land.

Deliberate and clumsy as oxen are, a skilful driver can get much more rough work out of them than out of horses. Besides, there was the cost of fuel, a factor always considered in the use of power machinery; it cost less to feed an ox than any other draught animal. The strength of a pair of oxen is amazing. It was a pretty sight to see a pair of oxen stretch their necks, grip the earth with their cloven hoofs, settle their shoulders into a yoke, and pull tight the jangling chain. A yoke, a chain, and five foundation words keep the oxen at work.

The five words are 'Getep!' 'Back!' 'Whoa!' 'Gee!' 'Haw!'

To be sure these words must be shouted loudly and embroidered with a great variety of blackguarding terms.

'Getep, you black limb of Satan!' often came to us from the fields of a neighbor, a churchgoer or there would have been oaths.

A bull is the most vicious farm animal; an ox the most docile. The ox is honest, ever ready to work, and wholly without guile. With these good qualities, we ought to like the ox, but no one does because the beast is content to go through life eating, chewing his cud, and switching flies. I should have liked the ox better had he been less awkward and lighter of foot. In logging operations it was my task to fasten and loosen the chain from logs, and this brought me close to the hoofs of the oxen; between my clumsiness and theirs, my feet were trodden upon almost daily, so that every spring I spent hours in pain.

A distant neighbor of ours, an Englishman, had a beautiful yoke of oxen. He boasted that they were the only purebred Herefords in the region. Both were large, white faced, and had long horns when we first saw them. As two-year-olds, the horns had been cut back, the stubs covered with polished brass tips. Each ox had a large, rectangular, brass bell that gave forth deep, clanging, baritone notes; these were worn the year round. In winter, the proud owner of these matched Herefords encircled their well-stuffed bellies with strings of silver-toned sleigh bells. The music of the bells as the team lumbered down the snow-covered roads and village streets soon made the oxen famous. Every farm boy wanted a yoke of Herefords.

We kept four cows. There were always in our cowshed a Black, a Red, and a Brindle. Topsy was another favorite name. Our cows for the first years had the run of the forest. Bringing home the cows gave me some of the pleasantest hours of childhood. Usually I took my time to follow the slow-tinkling bells, piping on a bark flute of my own making. The homeward way from a distant pasture took me through a forest windfall where trees lay like jackstraws, down a dark ravine of hemlocks thickly set with Canadian yew, which we called 'shin-tangle,' through a thicket of blackberries and choke cherries, across a marshy creek, and, at the edge of our clearing, through a border of fireweed flaunting in season a million racemes of bright red flowers.

If there was some urge to get home quickly, as in the mosquito season, or when one of the cows had a calf, this evening task was quickly over. If I dallied too long and dusk overtook me, or if I lost my way, I took Brindle's tail and let her lead me home. At such times, listening to the *to-whoos* of owls, the calls of whippoorwills, and the shrill cries of tree toads, I was filled with fears, especially if in a distant swamp I heard the screech of a wildcat.

Our cows were never prize-takers. Usually, in the years before we grew feed in abundance, they were thin-bodied, half starved on a forage of underbrush and wild grasses. The milk bags of the poor, insect-worried beasts were small and seldom full. Some seasons, one or two of the little herd, probably because of poor food, were barren. Life goes badly for cows in a forest; still, until the near approach of death, Black, Red, Brindle, and Topsy would chew their cuds in serene contentment.

All our cows were 'grades'; that is, they were not purebred. From their looks, no one on earth could have told what blood ran in their veins. Truth is, for several years after we came to the region there was not a purebred cow or bull in all the square miles of the Land of the Crooked Tree. Then, Mr. Crosby, a near neighbor, a man with more money than we, bought a herd of Jerseys, including a very fine bull. Mr. Crosby expected to get rich selling milk, cream, and butter to the summer resorters who were flocking to the shores of our bay. The Jerseys were elegant fawn-colored creatures, with big udders from which the milk dripped though the cows were milked three times a day. All our family, excepting Father, wanted a herd of Jerseys. Milk, cream, and butter sold at fabulous prices. My brother, who took care of our scrub cows, was sure he could as easily take care of a dozen Jerseys. Mother's fingers itched to skim the milk and pat the butter from ten Jerseys.

To be sure we had no money to buy the cows. What of that? We could mortgage the farm. Father was obstinate. His arguments against the venture were:

'I am not a dairyman, and I hate the smell of cows and cow manure. I have just become a gardener and I like it.'

'We should have to buy feed nine months in the year and sell most of our dairy products in the three months of summer; there is no money in that.'

'Jerseys are too delicate for our cold winters.'

It turned out that Father was right. There was no money in Jerseys in our part of the world. Mr. Crosby had to sell his herd at a great loss.

At any rate, the discussion had a good effect on our family affairs. Father began to replace our runty no-accounts with half-blood Shorthorns, better adapted to our climate than Jerseys. By breeding them to a pure-blooded Shorthorn bull, he had, when I left the farm, very good cows in his little herd.

Father was much more particular about his swine than about his cows. From the very start he had well-bred pigs of the three breeds of his choice. He began with two breeds he knew well from his farming operations in Iowa and Indiana. For salt pork, lard, and as a general-purpose swine, he chose Berkshires. For ham, bacon, and other smoked products he chose Chester-Whites. He thought a long, lean Chester-White sow was ideal for ham and bacon until he found that a Canadian neighbor grew Tamworths, and he tried them. When he fed them on peas and corn, Father was able to produce from Tamworths ham and bacon with plenty of lean as well flavored as Virginia smoked meats.

At butchering time, he wanted two Tamworths, a Chester-White, and a Berkshire, though usually he had two of each, sometimes more, in which case there were pig products for sale. Unlike most raisers of pigs, Father did not go in for great size. Two hundred pounds was quite large enough to satisfy him.

We were all happy when we had a late litter of Tamworths, of which one or two provided roast pig. A six-weeks-old Tamworth, with an apple in mouth, his tail tidily curled, skin well browned to tender crackling, is about as appetizing in appearance and taste as any food in any part of the world.

We had no sheep on our farm, nor were there any in northern Michigan. The French and Canadians brought horses, cows, pigs, and poultry to this part of the world in the 1700's, but not sheep. I do not believe that any of our Indians had ever seen a sheep. Certainly there was no Indian word in the Ottawa or Chippewa languages for this domestic beast. In Father Zorn's church there were pictures of sheep and shepherds, at which the Indians must have looked with wonder. Missionaries must have confounded them with references to the Lamb of God.

It seems incredible, but it is true, that I, born and bred on a farm, never savored the epicurean delights of lamb chops, a leg of lamb, lamb stew, or the tender tidbits of lamb's liver and kidneys. Farmers' families, a generation ago, seldom ate mutton, old or young, and I doubt if my parents had often tasted the flesh of sheep. Mother, had she been accustomed to the delectable dishes that can be served from this admirable source of human food, would have had much to say of the merits of lamb and mutton when properly cooked. I do not remember ever having heard her mention these products, so common to many people the world over, though she often told her children that her mother and grandmother spun and wove—so at least she knew sheep.

The horses that I remember best were a pair of pinto mustangs, small calico-colored, half-wild beasts from the western plains, sold to Father by Frank Chandler, a neighbor, who had been a cowboy and an Indian fighter. About mustangs, as well as about Indians, desperadoes, and cowboys, Frank was an encyclopedia of knowledge. His fancy ran to pinto mustangs, and every year he imported a few, bringing them by rail to Chicago and then by boat to our parts. In the hands of any of his neighbors, Frank's mustangs turned out so badly that he was considered as bad a man as any of the desperadoes he talked about, yet all would buy these unbroken beasts because of their cheapness.

One day Frank came by our house with a new span, small, trim, black and white, and perfectly matched. The males in our family gazed at them with wonder and admiration. According to Frank, each of the pair contained the quintessence of equine virtues. Father bought them for an even hundred.

No male in our family, or all of us working together, could harness the pintos. As soon as one of us came near them, they began to kick and bite. We could handle mules but not mustangs. None of us dared to get on their backs, although Frank bestrode them and stayed on, a feat that brought to all who saw him thus take his life in his hands the hope that he would be thrown and have his neck broken.

Father resold the pintos to Frank, on what terms he would never tell. During the summer we owned them, they were not once stabled, curried, shod, or worked. They had a glorious vacation in our pasture, and we learned much about horses and dealers in horses.

In spite of his crookedness in horse deals, the old Indian fighter was a most remarkable man in my eyes. These were the days of dime novels, and warfare against western Indians was still going on. Frank could give background to any Wild-West thriller that came into my hands; he knew, by name at least, all army officers of high command, the Indian chiefs, gunmen, United States marshals, and buffalo hunters of the Great Plains. He could tell me about old-time trappers. He had seen and fought, so he said, grizzly bears.

Opportunity to hear Frank's tales was not lacking. He was a bachelor, lived alone, and must now and then have a boy to turn his grindstone. Frank was one of the stingiest men that ever lived, so that it was for his tales I worked, not his five cents (ten cents was what most other men paid). My brother said that many of his stories were not true, but to me a tale was a tale.

A more extraordinary man to look at would be hard to find. He was short, spare, legs much bowed, arms long, and powerful. It was because of his abnormal legs and arms, so everybody said, that he could ride his wild horses. His head was elongated, with scarcely any hair, the top as uneven as a pumpkin. In a western blizzard both ears had been frozen and had nearly sloughed off. His head was balanced on a long neck, which bore an enormous Adam's apple over which wrinkled skin hung loose and flapped when he talked.

Like so many men who pioneer in new countries, Frank had a history. His boyhood home had been near Kalamazoo, and he had wanted to enlist with the Michigan Volunteers in the Civil War, but his parents would not consent. At the close of the war he ran away and enlisted in the regular army, being sent West at once to fight Indians. The story of one of his fights with

Indians I am sure I heard a hundred times and I was always spellbound.

Frank had been in the cavalry under Major Forsyth, and it was of Forsyth's famous fight with Roman Nose on the Arickaree River (Frank called it 'the Rickree') that he most loved to talk and I to hear. Frank told the tale in simple ungrammatical words, giving the names of Forsyth's officers and of the Indian chiefs. He told of the part each took, the charges of the Indians, the death of Roman Nose, the scouts sent out, and the arrival of reinforcements. The story gave me greater thrills than any printed pages of warfare had ever given me. He told pathetic stories of the wounded, of the crude surgery practiced, of hunger and thirst, and how they tried to eat horsemeat but could not 'stummick it.' At each telling he added new examples of his courage, heroism, self-sacrifice, and feats of daring.

Skinflint as he was in horseflesh, Frank was to me a hero of the battle between Major Forsyth and Roman Nose on the Arickaree.

Farm Crops

AFTER all, in spite of the big trees on the land, our farm turned out to be nearly worthless for farm crops. Corn, potatoes, wheat, oats, buckwheat, clover, and timothy grew very well in the virgin soil, filled with the decayed humus of centuries. Underneath the rotting foliage of forest trees, however, there was little but sand, in which plant food quickly petered out.

The year after the trees were cut, no plow ever made could have turned the soil, so thick were the stumps and so solid the roots. We planted by the simple expedient of putting a spade in the humus several inches, pressing forward and dropping grains of corn in the hole behind the spade. For potatoes, a hole a foot square and half as deep was dug with a heavy hoe and pieces of potato were covered firmly in the hill.

The only cultivation the two crops received was a few clouts around each hill with a heavy hoe. Our first cultivator was a heavy clumsy tool, pulled by a horse, behind which the driver walked holding straight, stiff handles. Later, corn and potatoes, the only crops cultivated, were sometimes tilled with a crudely made shovel-plow.

Father was delighted with the early yields of corn. In spite of stumps and roots he estimated that he grew forty bushels, on the cob, of the little eight-rowed flint corn. From no other crop could we get so great an abundance as from corn; it was the staff of life for man and beast; it could be more easily utilized as human food than any other grain; it was the cheapest and best food for all our animals. The pioneers in our new land subsisted almost entirely on this admirable grain. Corn stalks provided fodder for a winter's supply of cattle food, the only roughage our cows got. Corn was harvested over a period of a month or more, while other grains had to be garnered in a few days. We grew, in our corn fields, as a sister plant, pumpkins.

Father alternated corn and potatoes for two crops, grubbing out stumps and roots at every opportunity. The third spring we plowed. After a few years of corn and potatoes we could really plow the land with some degree of comfort and not a little pleasure. Plowing a field full of stumps is the hardest kind of work. It is easier to plow a field of stones. When the plow strikes a hidden stone, you know that you must back up and leave the stone in possession. When the plow comes up against a hidden root, you rather hope the plow will win and go through. The first year after a tree has been cut, the stump usually wins.

When the fields were finally freed from stumps, it was a pleasure to plow our sandy loam, especially in fall-plowing of timothy or cover sod. In such a field the plow must have a sharp colter and plowshare, and a bright clean moldboard and landslide. When the colter cuts cleanly through the sward, the moldboard turns a broad, thick ribbon of brownish-black loam, which has a most pleasant odor. The plower walks in the cool, firm furrow behind the plow, reins about his back, fascinated with the steady roll of the earth-ribbon from the moldboard. Every half hour the team must take a few minutes to breathe, and the plower goes to the shady side of a stump to take a drink of water from a jug, which he holds above his head on a crooked arm, letting the water gurgle down his throat. In the spring, crows and robins follow to devour the earthworms and larvae of insects the plow turns up, while in the near-by woods robins warble, crows caw, blue jays scream, and the catbirds sing or scold.

While the land was thickly studded with stumps Frank

Chandler came with his oxen to plow our newly cleared fields, but after a few years horses or mules were used. One can plow with pleasure only if his stride suits that of his horses; if the horses walk too fast, there is great strain on the muscles of the back and arms; if too slow, plowing can be deadly monotonous. The best plow team Father had on our farm were the two mules, Jack and Jenny, who loved to plow and would quickly learn to suit their gait to that of the driver. They balked if there were many stumps. We hitched them to a plow only when the land was nearly stumpless.

Harrowing newly cleared land is strenuous work. Our first harrow was a heavy drag shaped like a capital A. This implement was a leveler, pulverizer, a puller of roots and small stumps, and, I may add, a mankiller. The wooden frame was made of six-inch squared white ash. The teeth were enormous, a foot in length and an inch and a half square, hammered out by George Lewis, our blacksmith; they projected several inches through the frame at intervals of eight inches. This drag bumped between stumps, catching and pulling up roots an inch or two in diameter. Every few rods the driver picked up a corner to let the roots drop out. To do a good job he had to criss-cross the land, following with a 'brush-drag' to cover seed.

The brush-drag was the leafless top of a bushy tree, probably the first harrow used in agriculture. Sometimes it alone was used to give the field a lick and a promise before sowing seed. It had the merits of being easy to manage and of costing only an hour of time in the near-by forest. Later, when the stumps had been pulled, we used a spring-tooth harrow, which we thought a wonderful invention, though I never knew anyone who liked to tramp the soft earth in a cloud of dust behind a harrow of any kind. No one used a wheeled harrow in our part of the country.

My brother and I did all the harrowing. The approved costume for the work was a broad-brimmed straw hat with a conical top; a blue gingham, homemade shirt, buttoned on the shoulder; blue denim pants, coarse socks, and heavy shoes. By night we were caked from top to toes with dust. It was an unwritten law that after harrowing or cultivating, we could, without asking permission, straddle our horses and ride bareback to the bay. Here we stripped, straddled the horses again, and rode into Lake Michigan as centaurs, but came out as horses and boys, the separation having taken place as far out as we dared ride. After the first trip into the water, horses and riders rolled in the sand, the horses snorting with pleasure as they rolled over and over, their legs waving wildly in the air; there had to be a second trip into the deep to wash off the sand.

After harrowing, roots must be picked, the most disagreeable chore on a farm any boy ever has to do. From my eighth to my twelfth year, in early spring, in the northward flight of birds, when pastures were turning green and all the flowers and trees in the woods were in ecstatic blooming, my brother and I 'picked roots.' Deep in our souls we cursed the necessity of roots and the clearing of land.

Not quite so bad but bad enough was 'picking stones.' After a few years, however, roots had turned to ashes and dust, and no more came, but picking stones is a springtime task on a farm as long as land is plowed. Stones are the surest crop of the year, unaffected by pests, heat, drought, wind, or hail. At the end of 'stone picking' each spring, not a stone can be seen, but, during the coming year, aided by frost, stones come up and an abundant crop is in sight when plow and harrow again turn the land.

Our method of picking stones was to toss them in piles several rods apart; then follow with a stone-boat to haul them to fill hollows in roads, to make a fence, or to use for farm masonry.

The lowly stone-boat was the most useful conveyance on our farm. There was scarcely a day in the summer that Father did not say, 'Take the stone-boat.' On it stones and boulders were transported hither and yon for different purposes: it was used to haul off stumps and ends of logs that did not burn; to snake in logs for the wood pile; to haul barrels of water; and to haul odds and ends where the farm wagon could not go.

A stone-boat is a runnerless sled to plow earthly seas, as real boats plow fields of water. Ours were made from tough, strong maple planks sawed in Burt Brainard's mill and put together by George Lewis, who did our blacksmithing and specialized in building stone-boats. The planks were ten feet long, twelve inches wide, and two inches thick, three being used for a boat. Indifferent men had them sawed with an upturned end, but George Lewis soaked them and then bent the ends up to make a graceful prow. The planks were held together by heavy cross-bars bolted through them with the boltheads sunk on the under side so that the bottom was as smooth as that of any boat. A stone-boat has its own clevis, whiffletrees, and drawchain, attached in the middle of the prow so that it takes but a minute to 'hitch up.'

After a few years of growing corn and potatoes, Indian fashion, we began to plant grain crops, rotating them with timothy and clover for hay. Grain farming didn't pay. Twenty bushels of wheat from an acre of ground, even when sown on clover plowed under, was an average crop. All small-seeded crops were sown broadcast by hand, as when men went forth to sow in Biblical times. Pasture crops were cut with a scythe and grains with a cradle. The first few years, all grains were threshed by flailing, afterward with horsepower threshers, a wonderful improvement over flails. To use a scythe, a cradle, and a flail well were arts that gave high standing to a man in our land.

A boy learned to mow with a scythe in a hayfield, and then to cradle in a wheat field. A scythe consists of a handle, or snath, and a long, curved blade with a sharp cutting edge. A mower is as particular about his scythe as a user of fine-gauge instruments is about his tools. As with an ax, a scythe must be 'balanced'; the weight must suit leg and back muscles, and the 'feel' must be 'right.' The blade must be of the best steel, capable of taking and keeping a razor edge.

Eventually we had a number of acres in timothy and Father bought a mower. Mother was strongly opposed to the purchase, as she considered machines to cut hay or grain very dangerous. She could call a roll of a score or more men she had read about who had had arms or legs cut off by mowing machines. A hired man rode on our mower. My brother and I could not ride or even sit in the seat of our mower (as attractive to us as an automobile is to boys of this day) if Mother were about.

A cradle used only in cutting grain is a scythe with long fingers by means of which the grain is cut and laid evenly in a swath convenient for binding in bundles. The cradle proper is a framework of wood holding several long curved fingers that lie parallel to and project a little beyond a broad scythe blade.

In our first years, Perry Nelson, a cooper, made the woodwork of our scythes and cradles. The wood was white ash cut in the winter, seasoned a year, and then made into snaths and fingers. Our blacksmith, George Lewis, made the blades. Eventually, everybody went to the general store for these tools, which were as much poorer than custom-made tools as ready-made clothes are poorer than those made by a tailor.

Mowing and cradling are poetry in motion. Unless one has a sense of timing and balance he can never learn to mow and cradle well. The skilled workman with scythe or cradle moves ahead in short steps, bent a little forward from the hips, swinging his tool with a rhythmic motion, heel of the snath close to the ground. The cradler, above all else, must not leave 'candles,' as tall stubbles cut by the heel of the blade are called.

My brother, at sixteen, was a splendid cradler; even Father bragged about him. My own work with a cradle was never sufficiently satisfactory to warrant my using one, though I handled a scythe very well. Neither did Father cradle well, because one of his legs, owing to a boyhood accident, was slightly shorter than the other. Father, however, was justifiably proud of his ability to rake and bind so well; Father would keep his rake close to the heels of any cradler, driving him to despair, throwing off beautifully bound bundles with clocklike regularity all day long.

Father was a symbolic figure in a field of grain—'the man with a rake.' His wooden rake flashed so regularly that it seemed as if it must be driven by steam or electricity. His sheaves were a foot in diameter, the straws at the butts perfectly even. From each sheaf he took a handful of grain, divided it, and with a dextrous twist of the hands knotted the heads, encircled the sheaf with the band, fastened it with another twist, and the sheaf was made—straight rows of them around the field until there came a time when the last stalk of grain in the field was cut. Before I left the farm, reapers with an attachment to tie the bundles—the 'self-binder'—were coming in. But Father, even in old age, preferred to rake and bind.

We began work in haying and harvesting at daylight when the grass and grain stood straight and stiff with heavy dew. From time to time the reaper stopped, rested the end of the snath in the stubble, the left arm along the back of the blade, pulled a whetstone from a narrow pocket on the outside of the leg of his overalls, and then beat out a melody. With long and short strokes, the whetstone flashed back and forth, ringing against the steel blade; now and again he stopped to touch his thumb to the edge to make sure that it was of razor keenness.

In mid-morning my sister brought refreshments. Mother did not go to much trouble in putting up haying and harvesting 'snacks.' Almost invariably the viands were doughnuts and dried-apple pies, both cold and heavy as lead. From some source or other my brother and I had learned some verses about dried-apple pies. We could not repeat these at the table without being sent away by Mother. Father did not mind in the field.

One of us would begin:

I loathe, abhor, detest, despise,
Abominate, dried-apple pies.
I like good bread, I like good meat,
Or anything that's fit to eat.

It was up to the other of us to continue:

Of all poor grub beneath the skies,
The poorest is dried-apple pies.
Give me a toothache or sore eyes
In pref'rence to such kind of pies.

And then as a sort of amen, we both said: 'Schnitz! Schnitz!'
Schnitz is the Pennsylvania Dutch name for dried apples.

Neither did we fare well in the drinks furnished for these
mid-morning luncheons. If it chanced to be a churning day, we
had delicious, rich buttermilk, of which all the males in our
family were very fond. Or, occasionally, we had thick, sour
clabber. Whey, the watery part of clabber, a by-product of
cottage cheese, was drinkable and fairly good when sweetened
and flavored with lemon.

But a ginger drink, which we called 'switchel,' was the
commonest mid-morning beverage. The main ingredient was
sweetened water, into which was put enough vinegar to give
the drink the sourness of rather strong lemonade; the drink was
then made pungent with ginger. At the house, we children added
a pinch of soda to each glass, to make the liquid effervesce;
switchel in the harvest field did not foam. The only alcoholic
drink we had was spruce beer, which Mother made every
summer. Spruce beer is easily made and has all the alcohol that
can be got from fermentation. What Mother's recipe was I do
not know, other than that it was a decoction of spruce twigs
sweetened with molasses, made to ferment by the addition of
yeast.

The jug of spruce beer was kept in a cock of hay or a shock
of grain. Once my brother drank so much that he was drunk as
a lord and sick as a dog. He was forbidden to drink spruce beer

from then on, a useless ban for the mere sight of it made him sick.

Just as hay was cut by hand so it was raked by hand during our first years. A horse rake could never have been pulled through our fields of stumps. Hay must lie a day or two to dry before it is raked and pitched into cocks to load. A rake for raking hay is made of wood, with a dozen finger-like teeth five inches long.

While not really hard work, raking hay was not a glamorous job for a boy. To begin with, he worked alone hour after hour; there was no snack in mid-morning, and, if he went to the house he got only a drink of water, a doughnut or a piece of *schnitz* pie; everyone he saw impressed upon him an awful sense of urgency. 'Hurry! Hurry! Hurry!' Raking hay is terrifically prosaic; the eyes must be kept on the hay stubble. There are no bird nests, no snakes, no vermin, for the scythe has obliterated all these. The rake's teeth catch on roots and tufts. The weather in haying time is hot and sticky. As a boy, I hated Whittier's

> Maud Muller on a summer's day,
> Raked the meadows sweet with hay.

No Mauds raked the hay in our part of the world.

I call to mind only one good thing about raking hay. I could chew a straw and 'meditate'—one of the best pastimes of humans and bovines. Then for fifty years I forgot the art of contemplation, not to regain it until three-score-years-and-ten.

After the hay was raked it was left in windrows for a day in bright weather to dry further, after which it was hauled to the barn or stack. If rain threatened, it was piled in conical cocks, from which it could be re-spread to dry, and then re-raked.

'Hauling in' was another nightmare for me. As a youngster, I raked after the wagon to see that no hay was left. Later, in my last years on the farm, I 'pitched' while my brother 'loaded.' Loading a long, wide hayrack required more skill than I ever acquired (my elders never let me try). Pitching, at least, was a man's work, and it was a pleasure to crowd my brother with the pitcher's cry, 'Here it comes!' though often enough he did the shouting, 'Come on! Come on!' He, however, was up in the air where he got some breeze and could see all there was to see.

Father usually 'stacked,' a job that required especial skill. Our barn was not large enough to hold the crop and there were always two stacks in the barnyard. My brother unloaded and I helped Father, pitching to him the exact quantity he wanted and to the exact spot. Father's stacks never blew over and the hay never molded with dampness as often happened to those of some haymakers. Occasionally Father and I traded places, and I heard over and over again:

'Keep the center lower than the outer edges.'

The top cap was put on with much care, always left rounded, compact, with a sharp stick driven down in the center.

After cutting a field of timothy we turned the cows in for late summer pasturage, but a second crop of clover was always cut in September. This second cutting was a pleasant task. The scythe swished through the short, succulent growth with surprising ease; the clover was in bloom and the fragrance was delicious, very different but not less pleasing to the nostrils than when, as dry hay, it was hauled to the barnyard to make a small stack of the season's best provender for cows. We could take our time for this second harvest of hay, working in mellow sunlight, hurried only when autumn rains threatened. Whittier must have caught Maud Muller in the hayfield at the second cutting of clover, the rowen time of poets.

Our New England neighbors shocked their sheaves of grain in double rows, eight bundles to a row. Father preferred a conical shock with four sheaves in the center, eight around the outside, butts down, and a cap of four, butts to the center. After two or three weeks in the shock the grain was stacked while we waited for threshers.

Here, again, as in haying, my brother loaded, butts outside, heads to the center crosswise, with three or four rows of sheaves lengthwise in the center at the top. Father and I pitched on, though most of the time I had the miserable boy's job of 'raking-after.' Stacking grain needed little care, since the stack had to last only until threshers came.

Besides corn, potatoes, wheat, oats, and hay, we usually had a small field of beans, another of peas, and always grew an acre or two of buckwheat. Our favorite bean was the Red Kidney, which yielded well and in winter cooked into a rich mellow mass. We liked the White Kidney as well, but it was a little too late to be a certain cropper. The small nutty Navy or Marrowfat bean was well liked but did not yield well. Just before my brother and I left the farm, we grew for two or three years the black turtle soup bean, fit only for making soup, to which it gave a delectable flavor and a color of green-turtle soup, about which we had read but which we had never tasted.

Our Canadian neighbors and hired men were very fond of pea soup; none of our family liked it. We grew a variety for years called Canada field, which made a good soup and was excellent for fattening hogs. Both peas and beans were sown broadcast. Both were pulled with a short-bladed scythe, stacked when very dry near the barn, and threshed in early winter with a flail.

We always planted a small field of buckwheat. It provided provender for humans, swine, and poultry. Besides, the crop was not planted until late in June or early July, and was thus a catch crop for fields in which dought, rain, or birds had destroyed a seeding of some other crop. June-sown buckwheat was ready to cut in our warm, sandy soil before the first frost in late September. The wheat we grew was so poor in quality that we used it chopped with other grains for the farm animals and never had it ground for flour, buying, instead, Minnesota flour. Flour made from northern Michigan buckwheat, however, is as good as that from anywhere in the world. We always had enough ground to provide buckwheat griddle cakes for breakfast from early November until April, by which time we were tired of them, especially as when the weather began to warm up, eaters of buckwheat cakes began to itch all over.

Another minor crop was rutabaga. A rutabaga differs from a common white-fleshed turnip in being larger and in having yellow flesh, which is more nutritious than that of the daintier garden product. The rutabaga was, like buckwheat, sown late and was often a catch crop. It was one of the last crops on our farm to be harvested. Usually we put rutabagas in their winter quarters in late October, when winds blew in icy gales of rain or snow.

Everyone in our family hated rutabagas. In one of our early years, it was about the only vegetable we had for five long winter months; none of us ever wanted to eat or see another rutabaga. We grew them year after year as a cheap, nutritious food for the cows. Only a person who has gone to an icy root cellar in early morning darkness before breakfast to clean, cut, and feed ruta-bagas to cows can know what human hatred of a common or garden variety of vegetable can be.

From the very start, corn and potatoes were main crops. The little eight-rowed, reddish yellow flinty corns yielded little and were poor in quality compared with the large-eared yellow dent corns we had grown in Iowa, but the Indian flint corns of the North were more vauable in our domestic economy than the gorgeous corns of Iowa. Corn was the best crop we could grow to fatten pigs and to feed cows and chickens.

The flint corns ripen early and we could be sure that when crisp, frosty nights came, before a biting hoarfrost, we should be able to cut our corn. In Iowa no one ever thought of cutting and shocking corn, but husked the corn straight from the stalk into the wagon box, the wagon straddling a row while a man on each side husked two rows and a boy took the straddled row. Here in northern Michigan every stalk counted as winter fodder for cows, and was best when allowed to stand until just before a killing frost.

When corn-cutting time came there was the same sense of urgency as in the hot July days when haying and harvesting were approaching; we stretched every sinew to get the whole crop in shocks. We seldom had hired men at this season of the year, and the three males of our family cut in two days the ten acres we grew, using curved hand cutters. shocking armfuls of corn into wigwam-like structures.

There is a bit of fine art in so simple a thing as shocking corn. To begin with, there must be a good tying material. We used strips of the inner bark of basswood. Well before cutting time a trip was made to the woods for the fall supply of basswood bark. Two or three young trees, three or four inches in diameter, were cut and stripped of their outer covering. The inner bark was separated from the outer, and divided into strips several feet long and a half inch wide. These strips were as strong as the stoutest binding twine.

Before going in the field the cutter arranged a handful of these pieces of bast in his belt convenient for use. When an armful of corn is cut, he draws out a piece of basswood and ties a bundle, which he carries to a shock. The foundation of a shock is made by bending over four hills of corn and tying them tightly in a half-recumbent position. Into each of the four quarters of space so partitioned off, three bundles are solidly stacked, the tops of the twelve bundles being tied snugly with long, strong pieces of bast.

A pretty sight these wigwams of corn-yellow made against the background of red, crimson, and yellow autumn foliage of maple, beech, and birch. There they stood through the mellow Indian summer and black frosts of autumn to mature and ripen corn and fodder. Then, in one of the last farming operations of the season, corn was husked.

By the time we were ready to husk, my brother and I were in school. With only Father in the cornfield, with much other work to do, husking went slowly. Sometimes all hands worked after school until dark, and every Saturday found us hard at the husking. Usually, long before we were through, autumn storms were lashing the land and we had to work hard to keep from freezing.

The bundles of corn were taken from the shocks, thrown on the ground, opened up, and the huskers knelt with a few stalks between their knees and the frozen, snow-covered ground. In Iowa Father had become a lively corn husker, and now, husking peg in hand, he took the shucks off as many ears as both his sons could husk. (He loved to twit us about his skill and our lack of it.) He wore a mitten on the left hand made out of grain-bag material and a half mitten on the right hand in which was held a husking peg. A husking peg is a straight hardwood peg, or a metal claw, held in the hand by a leather thong. The peg helped to tear the shucks from the corn. Mittens gave little protection from snow and biting wind, and our hands early in the season became calloused and cracked in spite of being salved morning and night with warm tallow.

When a bundle had been husked, the stalks were put together, re-tied, and re-stacked in the old shock. Our barn never held all the hay, straw, and fodder for the livestock on the place, and the corn fodder was left in the field to be hauled in the leisure of winter.

Between corn cutting and corn husking, potatoes were dug. It is doubtful if anywhere on earth better potatoes can be grown than in the virgin sandy soils of northern Michigan. The tubers were dry, mealy, and so deliciously flavored that they were best boiled or baked, unflavored with butter or gravy.

In the early years of potato growing in this region, tops and tubers were perfect; no blight or other fungi on the tops, no scab or rot on the potatoes. The only pest to contend with was the potato bug, the black and yellow striped beetle that had but recently been introduced, under the name 'Colorado beetle,' from the foothills of the Rocky Mountains. Though it was early known that arsenical powders, Paris green and London purple, would kill the bugs, we could not get these poisons, and had to keep the soft, disgusting larvae from potato tops by knocking them off with a paddle into a pan in which was a little kerosene oil. It was a boy's job and a nasty one. Happily, before we had been growing potatoes long, quick-acting, deadly sprays were obtainable.

Potatoes were our main money crop, and when digging time came in late September sunshine we liked turning out the smooth, beautifully rounded tubers, leaving each hill beside the row to be picked up later, when sun and wind had dried the earth so that when we picked them it fell off, leaving the skin as smooth as that of a baby. It was another story in the rainy, frosty weather of November, when this operation was as disagreeable as late corn husking.

Father made a practice of keeping his potatoes for the spring market, which opened for us in March or April. Usually we had several hundred bushels. These we stored in the field. In the sandy soil, pits two feet deep were dug. On a layer of straw covering the bottom and sides, potatoes were heaped to a height of three or four feet, making a long mound, two or three hundred bushels to a pit. Next came a blanket of dry straw a foot thick, in turn covered with an outside comforter of earth at least a foot thick, nicely mounded and smoothed to shed water. Sooner or later, an additional covering of two or three feet of snow gave protection so thorough that weather 40° below zero did not touch the potatoes.

Every day on a farm is enlivened by some novel, tragic, or amusing incident. Livestock, wild life, freaks of nature, and the behavior of humans furnish some incident of note. One autumn as potato digging came to a close, my brother and I had an adventure with Father—one we dared not talk about for several years.

All his life, Father had a terrible migraine headache every four weeks. One year, on the last day of potato digging, one of these headaches began just before the noontime meal. Father sat down, back to a stump, to rest his aching head. When my brother and I, picking up potatoes, came within a few rods of the stump, my brother said:

'I'll wake Father up.'

Taking a large potato, he threw it at the stump. As my brother threw, Father started to get up. The potato missed the stump and struck Father squarely on the back of his head. Father stood up, unable for a minute to comprehend what had happened. My brother, appalled and horrified, hurriedly began to stammer an explanation. When Father fully realized what had taken place, hand on his unsteady head, he shouted: 'Wilbur, I've a damned good notion to thrash you!'

Thinking better of the thrashing, he turned and stalked to the house, we boys meekly following at a distance. We hated to think of the noon meal; when we came in the house Mother said: 'Father has gone to bed with the worst headache he has ever had.'

She did not know then, or for several years that anything unusual had happened.

My brother and I kept quiet for a week or two; then the humorous side opened our mouths and we roared with laughter. Several years later we began to tell the story of 'how we scared Father,' and he, never having mentioned it to anyone, joined in the laughter.

XVI

Farm Chores

THE daily, light work about the house and barn on our farm made up what we called 'the chores.' My chores were mostly about the house. I built the fires in the morning; kept the wood boxes filled; churned butter three times a week; fed the chickens and cleaned the chicken coop; fed the pigs their rations of corn, grain, and slops; and took care of the snow paths in the winter. My brother's odd jobs were all in the barn. He fed and milked the cows and cleaned the cowshed; nursed the calves for the first few months of their lives; and helped Father care for the horses and clean the stable. My sister washed and wiped the dishes; set the table; helped in the cleaning ('redding the house,' as Mother called it) and in making beds; cleaned the lamps and lanterns and kept them filled with kerosene oil. The first two or three winters 'in the woods' we ran short of matches, and my sister made 'spills' to light fires, lamps, and pipes. A spill is a small, tapered roll of paper, six inches long, made with a peculiar twist that leaves it thick as a lead pencil at one end, a sharp point at the other.

All the matches, by the way, in these years of the eighteen-seventies and eighties were made of a mixture of sulphur and phosphorus. They were expensive, hard to strike, had a villainous odor, and were deadly poison to small children whose curiosity often led them to eat the heads. Mother often cited the case of a woman who poisoned her husband by putting match heads in his coffee.

What remained for Father and Mother in the way of chores? Father repaired the buildings and tools; gave a hand to my brother in taking care of the horses and cows; smoked and salted hams, shoulders, bacon, sidemeat, and sausages in the fall. Mother did the cooking, baking, sewing, knitting, canning, and drying, sewed strips of old cloth for 'carpet rags,' and made quilts and comforters. On Mondays she did the washing, on Wednesdays, the ironing, and on Friday, the baking. She made apple butter and hominy in the fall, a barrel of soft soap in the spring, and every day in the year put away the milk and skimmed the cream, and three times a week made butter.

There was work for all of us the livelong day. That each task was done cheerfully and as well as any of us knew how were the chief factors of our happy lives in our farm and forest environment.

My day began with building fires. At five o'clock every day in the year, Father called:

'Boys! Boys!' to which we were supposed to answer, usually in chorus: 'Yes!'

If a second call was needed, it came as an ominous:

'Wilbur! Ulysses!'

After the second call, I pattered downstairs in bare feet and shirt tails past Father's bedroom door.

Before even putting on socks, I built the kitchen fire.

All was in readiness. The night before, however late I had gone to bed, or however tired I may have been, preparations for the morning fire were made. In front of the stove, a pile of shavings, whittled from a pine stick, were laid out; in another pile were a dozen kindlings of pine; and in a third heap were sticks of dry maple wood. It took less than a minute to put all in the stove, and touch the shavings with a match.

Our kitchen stove was a small furnace. It was big enough to

warm half the house, and had a fire box that burned twenty cords of wood in the course of the year. The oven was commodious enough to bake a small pig. Its back part was a reservoir to heat water. On wash days water was also heated in a washboiler. The stove had three rows of holes, two to a row, over which there were kettles, either on uncovered openings or on the round lids. The lids were removed with a stovehook, a most important implement, which Mother was always losing.

Much of the successes of the coming day depended on my success in making the morning fire. Mother would be down in a minute. Her teakettle and coffeepot were ready to boil on the back of the stove. On the kitchen table was a pan of sliced potatoes ready to fry; a jar of buckwheat batter stood on a small stand near the back of the stove from November to May—from May to November, batter for flour or corn-meal pancakes; eggs, sausage, ham, or bacon were ready to fry. At half-past five work stopped for breakfast. Long before half-past six, we were again at the chores; by seven, all hands must be in the fields.

Before the kitchen stove much of the life of our family was enacted. There the children of the household came after school, from work, and from doing chores in the icy cold and blizzards of winter. Never was the living room so cheery, nor had one the pleasant smells of cooking, or a singing teakettle. There, one of us on each side of the stove rested our stockinged feet on a stick of firewood, to thaw or toast. Behind the stove and the wood box, Flash, the dog, snored, and the cat purred away her nine lives. No gas, or electric, or any other than a wood stove was ever as dependable and comfortable as our kitchen stove.

The kitchen was quite large enough to serve as a living room. Mother did not bother her head about saving steps and would have suffocated in a modern kitchenette. In it were chairs for all the family. After the evening meal we went to the living room, a family group until Father and Mother went to bed.

In the living room, Father and Mother had special chairs

in which we children seldom sat. Father's was a heavy armchair of curly maple; Mother's a low rocking chair, in which she could gently rock back and forth; it, too, was of polished curly maple; both had cushions—once soft. As a tiny child I was permitted to sit in Mother's comfortable rocker. Death had left no vacant chairs in our household, and there were none until my brother and I went to college.

The living-room stove also played its part in the life of the family. By the time supper was ready in winter we had thawed out and toasted our feet, put on our foot wear, and taken our places at the kitchen table. After supper, my brother and I scrambled for the best reading place at the round table in the living room, never taking Father's throne nearest the double-burner kerosene lamp. After the supper dishes were done, Mother and my sister joined us; during winter evenings, we children read or studied. If the kitchen stove was the heart of the family, surely the living-room stove was its brains.

Our living-room stove was an expensive luxury; it cost the enormous sum of $60, as much as our Singer sewing machine. It was in shape a huge acorn and was called the 'Acorn,' made in Dowagiac, Michigan, as we were told by the silver letters on the nickel foot rest. It was roomy enough to hold several chunks of wood, from which, through the square of mica in the door of the stove, we could see flames curling from chunk to chunk. This sturdy stove sat on a heavy square of figured zinc, and, since every winter's night it was red-hot, it must never stand too close to wooden walls. Mother kept the body black and the nickel scrollwork shining. At the top, a brightly gleaming spire pointed heavenward. In early morning, when I shook down the fire, the nestled chunks of maple, beech, or birch burst into bright orange-red flames with bluish curls, popping and shooting sparks, each of the three woods burning a different colored flame.

It was always Mother who wound the one-day clock. Its power was heavy iron weights; its works were brass; it struck the hour with a pleasant musical sound, very comforting to sick children lying awake at night. The clock was made in Waterbury, Connecticut, in 1864, and was encased in beautiful mahogany; under the large, Roman figures was a very good picture of George Washington.

The two stoves called for other chores than building fires. Mother reserved May Day and the first day in October for her sons to move stoves and clean stovepipes. Half of our woodshed, all winter wood having been burned, was turned into a summer kitchen, the other half was kept for storage. Into these rooms the stoves were moved. If the weather was bright and sunny, the stoves were moved and stovepipes cleaned one at a time, just after the midday meal, taking two or three hours for each. If the weather was rainy, an afternoon sufficed to move the two.

Our stoves were heavy. We had to move them on hardwood rollers. First the rollers were properly placed under a stove. Then with strong handspikes, with a chunk of wood to give leverage, the stove, one corner after another, was pried up, the stove legs removed, and the stove lowered gently on the rollers. Then we moved it with tugs, grunts, and as strong words as Mother would let us use, to its new resting place.

Now, of course, was the time to clean stovepipes. Moving the stoves required a little heavy work but was not so bad. Cleaning the stovepipes was a nasty, dirty job. Our stovepipes did not run straight up and down. From the stove the pipe went up to within a foot of the ceiling, then made a right-angle turn to the middle of the room, then passed into the room above into a large drum which held heat. Father's and Mother's room, and the one in which my sister slept were warmed by drums; the room in which my brother and I slept was pretty close to the temperature outside. It was this complicated system of pipes and drums that had to be cleaned.

The first step was to spread newspapers wherever soot might fall or tracks might go. Next the wires that held the horizontal pipes to the ceiling were untied. Then each of us tackled a right-angle turn. Eventually a strong tug brought the pipes apart, there being no way to prevent soot from dropping below. Next the pipe was taken from the short neck of the stove.

Wood for our house fires came from the forest in thick slabs a foot wide and eighteen inches long, and was corded up to dry through the summer for the next winter. Nothing but straight-grained, knot-free beech, maple, and yellow birch went into our stoves, though several cords of knotty chunks were saved to keep fire over night in the sitting-room stove, which Father regularly chunked before going to bed.

The firewood was split into slabs as it was sawed in the woods, and it was my work to split these slabs for the kitchen stove all through the winter. It was a rather pleasant chore to split slabs of wood into pieces small enough for the kitchen stove. A single blow of an ax split a slab; a tough slab went into the chunk pile. Of all the chores I had to do, day in and day out, splitting wood and filling the wood boxes were as agreeable as any.

There were good fat pine kindlings in plenty. In clearing our land we found on every acre several old pine stumps belonging to a century or more before, when a forest fire had burned great pine trees to the ground. These ancient remains had to come out and were cut up for kindling. Every stump was full of pine fat and from them we split the best kindling wood in the world.

One of our luxuries was a commodious woodshed. It was not only a place in which to keep wood, but a carpenter shop, a harness room, a tool room, a storehouse, a lumber room, and what not. To me, the fire-builder, it was always a shed for wood. In it I kept dry beech and maple, redolent pitch pine, and a pile of sweet-smelling corn cobs. From a layer of pungent chips and bark under foot, I could always pick and choose to brighten up the fires in the two stoves.

The worst chore to befall a country-bred boy in his tender nonage is churning. Three times a week I had to churn. Nowadays churning in country homes is not so bad; electricity or gasoline is often used to turn a crank, and the churn goes round and round and butter is quickly made; but ours was a dasher churn, three feet high, nine inches in diameter at the top, ten at the bottom. The important part of this churn was the dasher, made of a circular piece of wood eight inches in diameter, at the lower end of a round broomstick handle five feet in length. The disk at the bottom had a dozen holes an inch in diameter. Cream was put into the churn and my job was to raise and lower the dasher up and down, up and down, until butter came. The handle had free play and this permitted small splashes of gurgling cream to slosh through the top.

I had to do the churning in the morning, after breakfast, before going to school. To protect my clothes, one of Mother's aprons fell from my neck down over my feet. Always the hired men jeered at me as I stood in my apron; always other children on the way to school stopped in and saw me thus arrayed; always I wiped the dasher handle, rich with cream, with a finger, and then put the finger in my mouth, which entailed a punishment if Mother caught me in the act.

There was a saying that butter 'went back' if one stopped churning even for a few seconds. Mother would say: 'Keep churning! The butter is going back!'

It was said, also, that butter 'came' more quickly if a stranger took a hand at the churn. No stranger ever was around when I was churning.

There were preliminaries to churning. When the milk came in from the barn it was strained through a strainer, covered with a thin cotton cloth, into milk pans. These pans were set in a cool place in summer and a warm one in winter. By the next morning a thick top layer of cream had risen; this was skimmed off with a skimmer and put in a tall crock to 'ripen.' Before breakast on churning days the churn was half filled with hot water to warm it up, and the cream was set near the kitchen stove. After breakfast, the water was poured out, the cream put in. When all was propitious, butter came quickly; on some days the cream was stubborn and churning might take an hour.

Eventually, even on bad days, butter 'came' in large golden globules, which were dipped out with the cream skimmer and then worked with a ladle until the milk was squeezed out; the butter was salted, pressed into a round compact cylinder, and stored in a cool place. Some of our neighbors liked unsalted butter; we liked it salted.

Father loved buttermilk and on churning days, if he was not too far away from the house, came in and finished with pleasure the chore I so greatly loathed. Before Mother could take the butter out of the churn, Father had lifted the lid and with a long-handled dipper brought out a full quart of creamy butter-milk with flakes of butter floating in it. He drank the dipperful to the last swallow. 'That's the drink of paradise!' he would say.

My brother had only one chore as unpleasant as churning; he had to teach newly born calves how to drink milk out of a pail—he became a foster mother of young bovines. The first three days in its life, a calf takes its milk from its mother as nature intended; then it must be taught to drink from a bucket so that humans may have the milk. My brother 'broke' a calf into feeding itself, the belligerent mother bawling her emphatic disapproval. The calves were kept in a calfpen adjoining the cowyard. In this pen my brother began the education of his calves.

The newly born calves got only the skimmed milk and this had to be warm. Mother warmed the milk on the kitchen stove and poured it into a wooden bucket, at which point my brother took over, climbed into the messy, ill-smelling enclosure, and began 'breaking-in.' First he chose the cleanest corner and backed the calf tightly into it; he straddled the infant bovine and called for the milk. This having been handed him, he placed it in front of the calf and forced its mouth down into the pail, all the while keeping an eye on the bawling mother. Lastly he stuck two fingers in the youngster's mouth and pushed its head into the milk so that it drank or suffocated. Meanwhile the calf was anything but quiet; it struggled forward, backward, sideways, up and down. Only strong arms and legs kept the juvenile cow from breaking loose or upsetting the bucket. In as few as three or as many as six lessons the calf's education was completed; at least, fingers were no longer inserted in the mouth. In a week, the calf eagerly awaited the coming of the bucket; in two weeks a little corn meal or wheat 'shorts' was added to the milk diet, all this to be followed in a month by a transfer to the pasture.

Before we leave butter and milk, something must be said about two other milk products, ice cream and cottage cheese. Once every two or three weeks, we made ice cream. In our sub-Arctic land, ice was plentiful, summer and winter; with several cows, cream, too, was always on hand. Our freezer was a wooden pail holding three or four gallons, in the middle of which a heavy metal can, holding a gallon, stood upright, supported top and bottom; in this can was a flanged dasher. With the can well covered, an ingenious device permitted a crank to be fastened to the dasher so that it was turned round and round.

First, a smallish cake of ice was brought from the ice house, doused with water to wash off the sawdust, then broken into chunks and put in an old grain bag, in which it was hammered into crushed ice with the woodsman's maul kept in the woodshed. This crushed ice was tamped about the cream container in the freezer with a liberal supply of coarse salt.

Just what Mother's mixture was for ice cream, I cannot say; it may have been pure cream, flavored with coffee, caramel, or vanilla. Chocolate we did not have. I doubt if she used eggs or a custard, as modern cooks do. When a little short of cream,

Mother made an ice cream pie, in which pure cream was frozen and put in a pie crust such as she made for lemon or pumpkin pies. This was a favorite pie in our family the year round.

There was never trouble in getting a boy to turn the crank of an ice-cream freezer, especially if, as sometimes happened, he could stay at home from church to do it. Besides, there was always a reward. Whoever froze the cream could 'lick the dasher.' When the crank of the freezer could no longer be turned, ice and salt were carefully removed from the top of the cream container; the dasher, with its four wooden flanges, was pulled out, always thickly covered with ice cream, very delicious an hour before dinner.

The making of cottage cheese was work wholly for Mother, a product she always called by its Pennsylvania Dutch name, smearcase. When skimmed milk was left over, after feeding calves, Mother made smearcase. A two-gallon crock of sour milk was set in a warm place near or on the back of the stove. In a day or overnight, little curds formed and floated in the whey. The curds were strained out and put in a muslin bag to drip for a few hours—after which they had become smearcase. After being seasoned with salt, a little pepper, and a generous touch of sweet cream, smearcase was ready for the table. Our family ate it mixed with about half as much apple butter. Whey that dripped from the smearcase bag, when flavored with a little lemon juice and sugar, was a frequent drink, as has been said, for workers in the field and for threshers.

My brother gave the cows their hay and grain. Cows gave little milk in winter unless fed some green food; as we had no silo, instead of ensilage our cows were fed carrots, rutabagas, and pumpkins. These had to be cleaned and cut. The pumpkins were easily prepared; we took an ax and cut them in chunks as large as eggs, discarding the seeds, and fed them with a little chopped grain to the animals. But pumpkins lasted only until the middle of December, after which, until spring, the cows had to have carrots and rutabagas.

Cutting these root crops in winter was most disagreeable. The work had to be done in the root cellar, as close and dark as the Black Hole of Calcutta, lighted only with a smoky kerosene lantern. The roots had been cleaned when they were stored, but each one had to be rubbed with a coarse cloth and then cut in pieces small enough to keep the cows from gulping them down and choking. To be sure, we wore grain-bag mittens, but our hands were always cold, always so chapped and cracked that we were ashamed to have them seen in school. This chore had to be done morning after morning all the winter through, before breakfast. What a chore!

Other odd jobs every boy bred in the country had to do before the advent of power machinery were turning a fanning mill, a corn sheller, and a grindstone. There are worse chores than shelling corn and cleaning grain, though few, as I have said in an earlier chapter, worse than turning a grindstone on a farm that is being carved out of a forest. Shelling corn and cleaning grain with a fanning mill are infrequent chores, not to be dreaded day after day, as is turning the grindstone. We shelled corn and cleaned grain only for seed sowing, and when corn and grain were to be taken to the mill to be chopped into coarse meal.

There were special times for cleaning grain. Wheat had to be run through the fanning mill soon after threshing, to provide clean seed for fall seeding. The second and main time came on cold, rainy days in late autumn when the weather prohibited work out of doors. At this time we usually had a hundred or more bushels of wheat and about the same amount of oats, and some years half that quantity of rye. All grain was cleaned preparatory to grinding at the mill for stock food. Turning the crank of a fanning mill hour after hour was terribly monotonous. Because of poor threshing machines, our grain had much chaff and dust, which covered one from head to foot after even a short turn at cleaning it. One man, more often two, handled the grain, which was brought in grain bags just as it had come from the threshing machine; a second man put the grain in bags to go to the mill. Another operation in cleaning grain was to remove, every hour or two, the chaff, weed seeds, dust, and dirt that the mill had separated from the grain. This refuse was kept for poultry.

Shelling corn was much more pleasant than cleaning grain. It was harder to turn the crank of the sheller than to furnish power for the fanning mill, but there was much less dust and no chaff at all. Besides, it was a rather pretty sight to see husked ears of corn, each ear with exactly as many rows as any other, go into the sheller. The brightly colored bushel box that came with the sheller slowly filled with the golden dented kernels of the dent corns or the reddish-yellow smooth flint corns, each kernel a nugget of gold, either kind the most beautiful of all grains. There were always more bushels of corn than of all other grains put together. Some farmers sent it to the mill to be chopped, cob and all, for cows. This the farm papers of that day told us made fat, sleek cattle.

Another farm chore was oiling the harnesses. Late in the autumn, before steady cold weather came, a day was set, usually a Saturday, for this annual event. The real work was done in the woodshed, but water and oil had to be heated in the kitchen. Father superintended the work and the hired men did the greasing. Mother made an awful fuss over 'harness day,' when four or five males tramped into her kitchen with dirty feet and oily hands to borrow her kitchenware; she scolded one and all, and we all took it meekly.

Father made his own harness oil from a formula that called for tallow and unsalted lard, made black as pitch with lampblack. Always the harness oil was made a day or two in advance, and on the day when operations began was warmed up to a temperature as hot as the hands could stand.

The work on 'harness day' started with taking harnesses apart. Woe betide the person who mixed the parts of sets!

What boy, in these days of automobiles, can name the parts of a harness and tell at sight a single from a double harness, a buggy harness from one used in farm operations? Whatever the kind of harness, there were for the head, bridle, blinds, check reins, bit, lines with numerous buckles; the breast harness included breastband, or a collar and harness with yoke straps and traces for a single or tugs for a double harness; the parts of the body harness were the saddle, bellyband, crupper, hip straps, and breeching. In a double harness there was the complicated crossing of the two guiding lines held in the driver's hands to the four ends attached to the two bits in the horses' mouths. It was quite a task to take a harness apart, and there might be much trouble if the parts of each harness were separated.

Mother's wash tubs were brought into service for the first operation in greasing harnesses. They were half-filled with hot water into which a half pound of soda had been added. The leather parts of the harness then went into the tubs and were scrubbed with a stiff brush on a washboard until all the grease and dirt were removed. When the leather had been hung for a few minutes for the water to drip off, the hot harness grease was rubbed in. Meanwhile, my brother and I had been polishing the metal parts, chiefly buckles, to silver brightness. By the end of the long day the half-dozen harnesses for the farm's horses had been washed, greased, repaired, and put together for another year's service.

One naturally passes from greasing harnesses to greasing footgear. All the year, excepting the four or five cold months of winter, the men on our farm wore shoes and boots made of leather. In the rains, snows, and dews of the warmer months, all leather footwear became hard, stiff, and foxy red, unless greased once a week. The same harness oil of tallow, lampblack, and unsalted lard was used, but the routine of greasing was much different. We sat near the warm kitchen stove, oven door open, one hand thrust into a boot or shoe, the other applying the grease. It required quite half an hour to do a good job of greasing a pair of shoes. We rubbed and squeezed the leather as the warm grease was applied, and then held the boot in the oven to 'warm in' a minute or two, repeating the process three or four times until the leather was soft and the inside of the boot moist with grease. The greased shoes were put near the stove to dry overnight. Since greasing boots was a hot, sweaty operation, we waited until bedtime to do the work and at its finish took a rub down with warm water.

Winter footwear of heavy rubbers was spread under the kitchen stove at night, and the next morning found them warm and dry—except when the fire burned low or on a cold night went out. In that case, the next morning the soggy boots were stiff with ice. Until long after breakfast on such mornings, the conversation, too, was frigid.

Another annual autumn chore, about the last before winter set in, was banking the house. Our earliest houses did not have stone foundations. Their framework rested on pillars of sturdy logs down to the bottom of the cellar, and stood perhaps a foot above the surface of the ground. The part aboveground was solidly planked in, but planks, doubled and tripled, could not keep out the searching cold of a northern Michigan winter, and the house had to be 'banked up' to keep frost out of the cellar and from working through into the house to chill feet and legs in spite of red-hot stoves.

For banking some of our neighbors used straw, others manure. We found sawdust cheapest and best. Stakes were driven eighteen inches from the house in sufficient number to support heavy planks a foot wide. When the planks were put in place, and the space so made was filled with sawdust, well tramped down, a second layer of planks was put up and a second filling of sawdust made. With such a covering encircling the house, we could feel comfortable indoors when the days grew short and Arctic gales raged outside.

Until after I felt the farm there were no bedsprings in our house. Our solidly made beds had slats, on which were home-made bedticks. (We did not know, or at least never used, the word mattress.) Mother made her bedticks out of bedticking cloth, which could be purchased at dry-goods stores. The flattish bedtick was filled with oat straw, the tick being closed with a long stout drawstring. For the first few nights the ticks seemed mountain high, but soon flattened down to two feet, and by the end of the year to several inches. An autumn chore for my brother and me was to fill the bedticks.

There were never enough beds in our home for the visitors who came for a night or longer. In winter, when the house was overrun with guests, my brother and I gave up our beds and slept on a 'shakedown.' A 'shakedown,' in our house, was a blanket spread on the floor of the living room or kitchen. In summer the hired men and the two boys in our family slept on 'shakedowns' in the haymow.

Asked to name her most arduous work, I am sure my sister would have said 'cleaning lamp chimneys and lanterns,' a daily task as long as she was in her father's house. We burned kerosene oil and lots of it. Lamps and lanterns had to be filled and their globes cleaned, lamps one day, lanterns the next.

There must have been eight or ten lamps in the house. There were three large double-burner lamps: one in the living room, another on the dining-room table, and a third in the kitchen. There was a single-burner for each bedroom. Common items for Saturday's trading in the village stores were a five-gallon can of kerosene oil, a potato stuck on the spout to keep the oil from spattering, and lamp chimneys and lantern globes. As often as lamps and lanterns were filled with oil, the splotches of black smoke on the inside of chimneys and globes had to be cleaned;

remnants of old dresses, sheets, aprons, and shirts were always saved for this work.

It was amazing how many lanterns were used on our farm. For eight months in the year every male on the place had to have a lantern to do early morning chores and to finish up in the evening. Whoever drove out at night, except when there was a full moon or in the snow whiteness of winter, hung a lantern beneath the front of the vehicle. Each of the two or three persons who worked about a sick animal in the barn needed a lantern. Whoever went to visit a neighbor on a moonless night carried a lantern. Wherever a flashlight would be used now, a lamp or lantern was needed.

Many a time the sight of a light from a lamp or lantern brought cheer to my heart. A gleaming lantern, coming or going, far down a lonely road was a most welcome sight; and a lantern in hand was a most comfortable companion. When I was coming home late on a dark night, especially in a gale in winter, its tiny wick all aglow warmed me all the way through. There was nothing comparable to lamps and lanterns in our isolated home to raise the morale of its inhabitants, whether they were outside or inside the house.

XVII

Our Food

NEARLY all that our family had at table was the product of our own land and the forests and waters about. Our appetites were keyed high by labor and the tonic northern Lake Michigan air, so that every meal was a pleasure. Tasting new foods furnished adventures of high order. What delightful experiences we children had the first time we ate a pineapple, a grapefruit, a banana, an olive, or celery.

In reading accounts of other frontiers, I am always surprised by the scarcity of food. In our new country we had an abundance of good wild flesh from animals, fowl, and fish. There were venison, bear, pigeons, grouse, and the great northern hare for those who would take time to hunt. Of all the delectable, nutritious foods with which the waters of the earth are filled, none surpass the whitefish, trout, perch, herring, and brook trout of our northern lakes. If anyone starved to death in our land, it was a case of committing suicide by inertia. Yet I must not give the impression that our larder was always well stored with game and fish; on the contrary, often, when time and skill were lacking, our table had only the products of our own farm.

There were no hunters of big game in our family, but often venison and bear meat came to our table from some Nimrod in the neighborhood. It might have added spice to life to go out for deer and bear, both of which often did damage to our crops; but there was no gun in our family for big game, and none of us had a taste for the bloody work of cutting throats, skinning, disemboweling, and cutting up. For my brother and me, hunting consisted of trapping the great northern hare in winter, and shooting partridges in the autumn.

Of all the game that came to our table, roasted partridge ranked first. Partridges feed on the quintessence of the forest—beechnuts, birch buds, wintergreens, and partridge berries. Their plump, firm breasts and drumsticks receive virtue from the forest foods, which give them, it seems, their wild woodland flavors. A partridge requires a touch of cold weather to ripen its juices and develop its flavors, and we hunted them only in late autumn, when the cold also gave a fillip to the appetite.

I suppose any wild game is better for hanging a few days, but we liked game to come to table as soon as possible. Our partridges were usually stuffed with a bread and onion dressing and roasted in a hot oven. The birds were supplemented by potatoes, fried corn-meal mush, sausages, sauerkraut, and gravy containing the giblets—as good a combination for this bird as any cook has yet devised. There were no distracting side dishes, nor was the table cluttered up with napkins, glasses, silverware, and finger bowls, among which a hungry man can hardly find his way. Roast partridge was ample for the eye as well as for the palate.

In pigeon years we had pigeons, meal after meal for weeks, fried, broiled, in stews, and in pigeon pies. To prolong the pigeon season, Mother put legs and breasts in a large crock and poured boiling lard over the cut-up birds. Keeping them in this way, she could have fed her family pigeons every day in the year if she had so chosen. We all became sick of pigeons. The only pigeon dish that never failed to please was pigeon pie, a great dough container filled with butterball squabs about three weeks out of the nest.

Mother was a good cook, clever in culinary inventions and in turning what she had to good account. She belonged to the

Virginia-Maryland school of cookery, influenced by the Pennsylvania Dutch, from whom she had several appetizing dishes, such as 'smearcase,' 'kool slaa,' 'panhas,' and apple 'schnitz.' She was little influenced by New England cooks, descendants of the starved Pilgrims, of whom there were many among our neighbors, some coming via 'York State,' where their kitchen accomplishments were little improved. (To Mother, no Northern woman was a good cook.)

A New England dinner we never had. Father did not like 'messes,' and perhaps the name 'New England' did not please my Virginian parents. Nor did we often eat the codfish of New England. (Who would eat codfish when Lake Michigan whitefish could be had?) Baked beans, doughnuts, apple pie, and pumpkin pie were standbys that we had often, and we made no more fuss over them than we did over bread and potatoes. Of the white kidney beans we grew for market we always saved plenty for home use as 'Virginia-baked beans'—not 'Boston-baked beans.' Our baked beans were soaked, boiled, and then baked in a dripping pan with a covering of slices of salt pork. They may have been sweetened with a very little sugar but never with molasses. They solidified in the dripping pan so that, cold, they were served in slices. We liked them covered with catsup.

There was always a jar of doughnuts in the cupboard. Hot off the stove we liked them, but before the jar was emptied we could not look a doughnut in the eye. We knew them best as fried-cakes, fried reddish brown in deep fat. The hired men dunked them in their coffee, but we children were not permitted to dunk, more in the interest of the tablecloth than manners.

We liked apple pie early in the autumn but got tired of it before pumpkin pie took its place as a supper dessert; good tangy cheese stimulated dulled appetites for apple pie, but that came from a grocery store and we didn't have it often. We grew tons of pumpkins for the cows, and the makings of 'punkin' pies were on hand all winter. Mince pie and lemon pie, always reserved for special occasions, we never tired of, and liked best of all the 'ice cream pie' I have already described. I have also spoken of rhubarb pie in another chapter—of this 'pie-plant' pie we never tired.

The many fish that came from our waters were whitefish, Mackinaw trout, brook trout, several kinds of bass, pike, pickerel, perch, and sunfish. Our family liked whitefish best. Father said that northern Michigan whitefish were better than the Chesapeake Bay shad, on which he had been brought up. Whitefish come from a net and all are not equally good. Good whitefish must come from deep, cold water; they must be neither too large nor too small; must have bright red gills, clear eyes, and be clean and bright in scale and skin; they must be cleaned, scaled, salted, and put in cold water at the earliest possible moment to keep the flesh firm.

Whitefish carries its own seasoning. This fish was spoiled for our table if any flavoring other than salt was added. Spices, onions, oil, and a garnish of wild cress might be added to other fish, but the firm, sweet flesh of whitefish needs no flavoring to give it relish. No human being ever wearied of good, fresh northern whitefish; no human being was ever made ill by eating too much of it.

In order of merit, the ways of cooking whitefish in our house were planked, broiled, fried. Broiling and boiling are so simple that careless cooks seldom serve fish well either way. In boiling, the fish should be put in cold water, salted to taste, and boiled very slowly, otherwise the flesh will be soft and flabby. They should be broiled slowly to a delicate brown, never by any chance scorched. Other fish may be dipped in a batter of cornmeal flour—whitefish never. It requires a little more care to plank a whitefish properly. The best plank is a piece of smooth maple an inch thick, a foot wide, eighteen inches long. Our plank had been used long and often, gaining virtue with every planking; it held two medium-sized whitefish cut down the back and pressed firmly on the board. The fish were put in an oven heated with a moderate fire and baked to a rich brown. There were no vegetables piled about our planked fish.

Fresh sea food never came our way, but we often had oyster soup made from oysters that came in tin cans. The cans were eight inches long, six inches wide, and three inches thick, and shiny-bright, without a label of any kind. Father said canned oyster soup was a poor substitute for that made from fresh oysters. He often made our mouths water by telling of the steamed and fried oysters of his early Virginia home. Yet canned oysters were a prized delicacy in our household. We also went to oyster suppers at every opportunity, as oyster soup, served with small square oyster crackers, at the usual charge of 25 cents, was a favorite food for church socials.

The wife of a New England neighbor tantalized Mother by singing loud and often the praises of clam chowder. We could not get clams, fresh or canned, so Mother sometimes made oyster chowder by adding cut-up canned oysters to corn chowder, one of our commonest dishes. Corn chowder was served on our table quite as often as baked beans, boiled ham, or beef stew. In all but spring and early summer, corn chowder was a supper dish about once a week. The addition of oysters was a pleasing variation. Corn-chowder season began soon after roasting ears came, and, made from dried corn, lasted until the next May.

It requires a half day to make good corn chowder. Mother started her chowder in an iron kettle on the back of the stove while doing her dinner dishes. Fried salt pork for dinner preceded corn chowder for supper, slices of crisp fried pork being saved for chowder. The pork was cut in cubes and put with a small amount of pork drippings in the chowder kettle sitting on the back of the stove. Two or three onions and an equal quantity of potatoes were then diced and put to simmer with the pork; then, in a half hour, a quart or two of milk and an equal quantity

of cooked corn, freshly cut from the cob, canned, or dried, were
blended in, the whole to cook, but never boil, until supper. From
the number of times Mother told someone to stir the chowder,
this dish seemed to need a good deal of stirring. The finishing
touches were to salt and pepper, after which it was served
piping hot.

Corn chowder was a meal in itself, served with hot bread,
soda biscuit, or corn bread. Store crackers might be crumbled in
the bowlful of chowder. Uncooked sauerkraut, coleslaw, or
pickled beets were usually served with corn chowder, their tart-
ness making a harmonious blend of flavors. The supper ended
with pie.

There were times in the first few winters when food, other
than salt pork, bread, and potatoes, was 'scanty pickings.' The
year round in pioneer homes the daily meat is pork, pickled in
brine or smoked; for men who work hard, pork is the best of
all foods. America's forests and prairies have been turned into
farms, her railways laid, her canals dug, her ships kept at sea,
on a porcine diet. The pig has been and is the great sustainer of
American muscle and brawn. In our forest home, even when
venison, wild fowl, and fish could be had for the taking, pork
was preferred. When our family came to the last barrel of pork,
the last ham or side of bacon, the wolf was at the door. Pork
was on our table three times a day. For breakfast we had bacon,
ham, or sausage; for dinner, smoked or pickled pork; for
supper, ham, sausage, headcheese, or some other pork delicacy.
Almost daily, in one form or another, pork was boiled with
cabbage, kraut, parsnips, turnips, or one of a dozen potherbs
from the fields or garden. On Sundays chicken took the place
of pork, and for an occasional meal, the meat was fish or,
more rarely, game.

No one, unless he have religious scruples, will keep his nose
in the air in the presence of Virginia ham, Irish bacon, German
sausage, or an English pork pie; but there is another pork dish

of rare distinction. This fifth derivative of the pig is fried salt pork, until as late as the last generation the national dish of America, and as good a one as the mighty roast beef of England.

Of course, to eat with relish so hearty a food, one must begin with a good appetite, plus a good digestive apparatus; and the pork should be homemade by one who knows well the art of curing meats; it must be fried in a cast-iron skillet by one who knows how to use a skillet. Good cooking requires thinnish slices dipped in flour or corn meal and fried medium done, never to dry chips. The best dishes to accompany fried salt pork are baked potatoes, corn pone, and thick milk gravy. When we could add brook trout or perch we had a banquet. This is the midday meal I order now in my old age, when, to use a back-woods colloquialism, I can 'get shet' of my family—only I cannot in these days get good salt pork, the northern fish, or find a cook who can use a skillet.

Our salt pork was kept for winter use in wooden barrels in the cellar. The brine was thick enough to let the slab of pork float when the heavy oaken lid was lifted. At butchering time only slabs of sidemeat, well streaked with lean, went into the pork barrel; fat sow-belly was tried out for lard. Salt pork was freshened over night.

As Father produced, Mother conserved. From wild straw-berries in June to cabbage in October, she canned, dried, pre-served, jellied, and pickled, putting up in some form or other nearly every fruit and vegetable that could not be kept in the cellar. Dried sweet corn, sauerkraut, apple butter, dried apples, bread, pork, corn-meal dishes, and potatoes were the stay and staff of our fare; these, with what Mother preserved and a chicken in the pot on Sundays, made every meal in our house a good one.

When autumn turned to winter, to have her cellar filled with food, plenty of dry wood in the woodshed, and warm garments for her family were all the housekeeper-heart of my mother could wish. Let the winds blow, the snow fall, all life outside freeze, she then had no fear of the long, dreary winter. Those who have plenty of all that money can buy can never experience the pleasure Mother took in her labor to insure comfortable living.

Mother was very proud of the reputation she enjoyed for her threshers' dinners. Threshers, as everyone brought up on a farm knows, must have good food in abundance. Indeed, in my day on a farm, 'good enough for threshers' and 'a dinner fit for threshers' were as flattering terms as one could utter in praise of a meal. Father never had difficulty in getting threshers. At threshing time Mother catered to ten or twelve men and two or three women who came to help in the kitchen. Happily, threshing came at a season very favorable to her arts. Then we had half-grown chickens, sweet corn ('roasting ears' in the parlance of my Virginian father), new potatoes, string beans, tomatoes, lettuce, green apples, and blackberries.

There was a good deal of sameness in Mother's cooking; yet threshers never tired of her meals. At noon they usually sat down to a huge platter of fried chicken, a side platter of cold ham; tureens of mashed potatoes, with little ponds of melted butter in the centers; newly plucked sweet corn on the cob; string beans cooked with a knuckle of ham; a trencher of 'smearcase'; pickles in assortment; plate after plate of soda biscuits; and coffee, hot and strong, by the gallon.

The dessert at the noon meal was a blackberry roly-poly, without which the dinner would have been a failure. This roly-poly was made by putting blackberries on a slab of dough a half-inch thick, which was then rolled into a cylinder two feet long and six inches in diameter, nicely smoothed and rounded at the ends. The rolled dough was put in a cloth and suspended on a grate in a washboiler to be steamed. Out of the cloth, this huge pudding looked like a legless pig stuck full of cloves. The men laboring with grain at the near-by barn knew from the ambrosial odor of the roly-poly when the dinner call was about to be given, and every mouth was watering in anticipation. Nothing tastier ever came to the table of threshers.

Boiled chicken with noodles was the specialty for the evening meal. Noodles were a favorite with Father, and he insisted that they be served year after year to his threshers. I do not know what goes into noodle dough, but I remember that the dough, very stiff, was rolled into a thin sheet and laid out on a cloth to dry; before the drying went too far, the sheet was rolled up and sliced to make shreds as thin as spaghetti. The noodles were boiled in the kettle with the chicken. Another stand-by of the evening bill of fare was corn bread and chicken gravy. Vegetables and desserts for the meal varied. Had the men been consulted, the choice of dessert would have been a blackberry shortcake or apple dumplings. Either of these pastries called for cream, but cream for threshers was not to be thought of, and instead there was sweetened milk spiced with nutmeg and cinnamon to be poured over shortcake or dumplings.

Gravy is quite as essential as butter in farm homes; indeed, gravy was more often on the table of pioneer families. The three fundamentals of gravy are milk, the fat in the skillet after fried ham, bacon, salt pork, sausage, or chicken have been removed, and flour to thicken. This thickening must be done just right. 'Gravy as thin as soup' was about as derogatory a phrase as one farm cook could use of another's cooking. Salt and pepper to taste are important. The final product should be rich and light brown, to obtain which without burning requires much stirring. On our table gravy was found three times a day. At breakfast it was used on bread, soda biscuit, or fried corn-meal mush; at noon and evening on mashed or baked potatoes, and bread. In the winter, there were always pancakes of one kind or another, in which case milk and flour were left out of the gravy; it then consisted of the drippings of whatever meat was served.

It has been written that President Theodore Roosevelt, when he had his meals in a chuck-wagon on a western ranch, put to good use the gravy on his plate by sopping it up with a soda biscuit. This was the daily practice of our hired men. My brother and I also followed the custom, though Mother permitted it, if she saw us, only if we used a fork. There was no better spread for a brown-crusted half of a soda biscuit than gravy piping hot. Hi Woods, Joutel, and the men who threshed our grain preferred a whole biscuit to a half. Mopping the plate by pushing the biscuit around was not efficient enough and they used the spoon from their coffee cups to finish the job, tipping the plate as with soup. Thus taking the gravy straight, they tasted its full flavor. (One doesn't talk when one eats gravy on a farm.)

We had grace in our house when we sat before the fleshpots. Father gave thanks in a devotional sing-song. When Joutel, Hi Woods, or some other half-heathen was at the table, grace was unduly prolonged, not, I am sure, for the good of a visiting sinner's soul, but to tantalize a wretch whose mouth Father knew was watering. At these times my brother and I always kept an eye on Joutel. His beady eyes moved from dish to dish, he licked his chops, and at 'Amen,' with a wolfish look in his eye, he crossed himself.

Never in my life on the farm did we have a loaf of baker's bread in the house, or yeast purchased from a store, or a yeast cake. Mother made her own yeast from wheat flour, corn meal, or potatoes, using a starter from time to time that she kept in a small crock on a shelf back of the kitchen stove. Shiftless housewives sometimes lost their yeast and came to borrow a starter. When I left the farm, Mother could brag that her yeast was twenty years old and as white and sweet smelling as the day she first made it. She often made salt-rising bread as a variation. Yeast bread was 'set' the night before baking and on baking day a few dozen light rolls were made from bread dough.

Once or twice a week we had soda biscuits for supper; Mother did not approve of them, as they were 'bad for the digestion.'

However, the family clamored so loudly for soda biscuits and maple syrup that we usually had them. Mother made soda biscuits white and feather-light inside, and bottom and top crusts firm but crisp and flaky, light, rich brown. These biscuits were served so hot that they steamed when broken in halves. The approved method of eating was to butter them with buttercup-colored butter and let them swim in rich dark-brown maple syrup.

All through the year we ate pancakes and maple syrup for breakfast; from November to April these were made of buckwheat, large and rather thick, grayish white inside, and light, reddish brown outside. The rest of the year flour and corn-meal pancakes came to the breakfast table. Pancakes were fried on a long, heavy cast-iron griddle, which stretched across two lids of the kitchen stove. Flour and corn-meal pancakes were smaller in diameter and thinner and lighter in color than those made from buckwheat. One could eat a dozen of the summer brands, whereas a half-dozen of the heavy buckwheat cakes sufficed for a boy. As with the biscuit, we first covered the cakes with butter and then with maple syrup. Father and I often substituted drippings from ham, bacon, sausage, or salt pork for the butter. The rest of the family did not like meat drippings, nor would I have had them had not Father liked them. Meat drippings and maple syrup on pancakes do not make my mouth water now, but the two seemed a perfectly harmonious blend in my boyhood.

The cheery noise of bubbling pancake batter was as plainly heard as the singing teakettle every morning of the year in our house. I often lifted the cover of the batter crock to look at the bubbles, which reminded me of the eyes of animals.

In our kitchen there was no sink, no plumbing, no washing machine, no can opener, no egg beater, no meat grinder, no aluminum ware. Mother believed that the few foods that could then be bought in tin cans, with the exception of oysters, were potential poisons and would not have them in the house. Had not a family of five in a neighboring town died from eating canned corned beef? Up until 1888, when I left the farm, none of us had tasted artichokes, shrimp, lobster, clams, fresh salt-water fish, hot dogs, a hamburg sandwich, avocados or any but American cheese. Oranges from Florida were a great luxury; but lemons, raisins, figs, dates, prunes, and Corinth currants, all from the Mediterranean, were fairly common. Coconuts from the West Indies were more common than now.

I cannot say much about the food of our Indian, half-breed, and French neighbors. I suspect that, when fish and pigeons were not to be had, the Indians just barely subsisted. I never broke bread in an Indian home, nor in any French home ex-cepting Madame Pettier's, where, as a small boy, I had many generous snacks and once a sumptuous banquet.

St. Leger, our kind friend of the *Menominee*, visited the harbor town once or twice a year before he finally disappeared from our ken forever. He usually stayed with Madame Pettier and always came to our house for a meal. The banquet (I call it a banquet because St. Leger called it so) was in honor of Madame Pettier's birthday. It is worth telling about to show the difference between Mother's Virginian and Madame Pettier's French-Canadian cooking.

All our family were at this birthday banquet. Father Zorn was the only other guest. St. Leger, Father Zorn, and Father were all in brave spirits. Mother was quiet, whether from shyness or because she was put out of countenance by Madame Pettier's fine silver and china I cannot say. We three children had been so lectured on table manners that we were self-conscious and uncomfortable. St. Leger tried to raise our spirits by telling us that this was a birthday, not a burial day.

Finally St. Leger turned juggler and kept knives, forks, and spoons in the air until we wholly mistrusted our sense of sight. He asked Father Zorn to pass him a knife—it turned out to be a spoon; again he called for a knife—it turned out to be a fork.

He accused Father Zorn of having robbed him, and took from the old priest's pockets his missing watch and purse. At this Father Zorn said, 'Chut! Chut! Chut!'

Everybody was now in good humor. Dinner was ready and Madame Pettier commanded us to take our seats. Father Zorn said grace in Latin, Madame Pettier's and St. Leger's lips silently following, and the three Romanists made the sign of the cross. We were now ready to eat, but there was nothing to eat. At a dinner in our house, we sat down to a table groaning with food, but on Madame Pettier's table there was not a mouthful.

Suddenly the dining-room door opened, and a rich odor spread through the room. It came from a huge tureen of onion soup, rich and savory. With it came what I now know would be called *petit pâté*, in this case a small ovate cake of chopped whitefish dipped in a batter and fried to a deep brown. Madame Pettier afterwards told Mother that the Frenchman made the soup (neither of the two women could ever make it so savory). In time to come, the *petits pâtés* often came to our table as 'whitefish balls.'

Mother, who would not have admitted that anyone on earth could make better bread than the loaves that came from her oven, now impatiently awaited the taste and smell of Madame's bread, which she expected to see served like ours in slices heaped on a bread plate. To Mother's disappointment, Madame Pettier's bread appeared as little oval rusks piled in a basket of filigreed china.

All our family were eager to see what the main course was to be. At last it came—planked whitefish. St. Leger was to carve. The onion ambrosia had loosened the springs of his tongue, and he now began to hold forth on the pleasures of the table. He, it seems, had supervised the cooking of the whitefish and now it was his pleasure to tell us how whitefish should be cooked.

Potato chips were served with the fish, the first I had ever tasted, a novelty so surprising that I did not recognize them as being potatoes, even though I was born with a potato rather than a silver spoon in my mouth! There was only one vegetable, green peas. Mother would have had several.

The third course was a salad of fresh, crisp lettuce leaves, which St. Leger mixed at table in a great wooden bowl. The care with which he measured his oil, vinegar, salt, and pepper, and the zeal he displayed in stirring greatly amused Mother. With the salad a cheese filled with green mold was served, which St. Leger said he had brought from Chicago. It had a strong odor and Mother would not taste it; but her children and her husband ate it with great relish. Then came a course of wild raspberries, coral red, served with thick, sour cream. To Mother the sour cream was the height of perverted taste.

The last course rose above all the other dishes as a hemlock towers above a spruce. It was a huge birthday cake, covered with white frosting, colored candies, and small twinkling candles. This masterpiece of the pastryman's art must have come from Chicago—Madame Pettier could never have made it, Mother was sure. With it came a dark, brilliant red, sweet wine, of which we children had a taste in a toast to Madame Pettier, which St. Leger asked Father Zorn to make. The old priest did so unwillingly, and could get no farther than: 'We drink to your health and happiness, Madame Pettier!'

Mother, a teetotaler, was now eager to leave the table, thinking that the men might drink more than was good for them. But St. Leger would have another bottle opened. I now know it was brandy; Father Zorn would not take it, but Father and St. Leger drank several small glasses. Madame Pettier drank a little, wiping her lips and giving little artificial coughs. She saw that Mother did not approve, and said to her, 'It is only a thimbleful I am taking for my stomach's sake.'

The dinner was over, but somehow we could not get away from the table. The wine had warmed the recesses of St. Leger's heart and he must talk. He told of his youth in France, of his life in Montreal. Then he was again in the woods of the North, his canoe sweeping down rivers and across lakes. His tale ended with a boating song, to which he kept time with hands and feet as to the strokes of paddles, so that we were filled with exultation as if we were with him in his canoe.

XVIII

Farm Kettles

WRITERS on pioneer life in American forests say much about the rifle, the ax, and the crosscut saw, but seldom mention the kettle. Kettles of several kinds were indispensable on our farm. The big, black, soot-covered iron kettles of various sizes were always in use for one thing or another, out of doors and indoors. A battery of three of the biggest were stored in the sugar camp eleven months of the year for use in boiling down sap in sugar-making April. A giant kettle hung just outside the pigpen and boiled and sizzled every day in autumn, winter, and spring. Mother sometimes hung a smaller iron kettle back of the woodshed, but for her purposes much preferred a twenty-gallon copper kettle. In the kitchen we had two small ones, also of copper, and there was always a teakettle singing merrily on the kitchen stove.

The 'big kettle,' as we called the giant iron one, had a great variety of uses. All through the summer, it held kitchen slop, which was ladled out twice a day into the near-by pig trough to grunting pigs. This was one of my chores, and I hated it because of the bad odor, the flies, and the great likelihood of my getting spattered by the mouthing pigs. From late September until butchering day, the big kettle, boiling and steaming every morning, contained, beside the kitchen waste, small potatoes, carrots, turnips, or cut-up pumpkins, mixed with chopped grains, peas, or corn meal, a nutritious mixture for the pigs that were to be slaughtered that autumn. Father's formula for stuffing the pigs during the last weeks of their lives varied from year to year, but he became quite convinced that an abundance of corn meal gave him the most meat, and that an equal amount of field peas gave him the best. The eventual solution was to use equal parts of both, with plenty of small, starchy potatoes, the ingredients boiled to a thick, soft, warm mash that the pigs could easily guzzle.

After daily banquets for six weeks the pigs came to their last hour, with the kettle, source of so much of their pleasure, still before their eyes; the great black container was scoured out and water was heated in it to scald the four or five hogs to be slaughtered on butchering day. For the next few months the big kettle might be used for making warm mashes for the cows. In sugar-making time it might be hauled to the sugar camp to supplement the sugar kettles; but when spring came, it again was put in use to hold kitchen wastes for the pigs.

Mother's twenty-gallon copper kettle had even more uses than the big iron kettle; it had, by the way, a rather neat set-up. Trunks of two smooth beech trees, six inches in diameter, ten feet in length, each with strong crotches at the upper ends, were set solidly in the ground eight feet apart. In the crotches rested a sturdy ironwood timber, six inches in diameter. A chain with two hooks hung from the middle of this timber; the upper hook was used to adjust the height of the kettle above the fire; on the lower one the kettle handle was hooked. In hot weather, Mother often used the big copper kettle to heat water for wash day. But to her, this kettle was quite indispensable for making apple butter, soft soap, and whole-corn hominy.

Mother had made apple butter every autumn in Indiana, but in our northern home it was not possible to get apples every year. To make apple butter she wanted fresh, sweet cider and rich, solid-fleshed apples. Cider from Talman Sweet and Baldwin and Rhode Island Greening apples were Mother's choice.

It took an evening and the next day to make twenty gallons of apple butter, the least quantity worth while for a big household.

The whole family took a hand in the evening, with invited guests to help most years. The first step was to peel, core, and quarter the apples. Peeling the apples would have been almost an endless task without an apple-paring machine; usually we had two. This machine, so small that it could easily be put in a box with a cubic foot dimension, consisted of a central shaft with a crank and flywheel at one end and several prongs at the other, long enough to enclose the core of even a large apple. Knives, held in position by springs, turned rather rapidly by a cogwheel, adjusted to be run by the flywheel as the crank was turned, were the essential parts of an apple parer. The machine was attached to the kitchen table and the crank was turned by the smaller members of the family. Father usually placed the apples on the parer, took them off when peeled, and dropped them into receptacles for those who cored and quartered. Usually three bushels were prepared.

A fire was started the next morning, long before breakfast, to put to boil fifteen gallons of cider. After breakfast, Mother took charge, slowly adding the quartered apples. Now came the ticklish part of making apple butter; if the ingredients were allowed to scorch for a single second, the butter was ruined. To prevent scorching, someone must stir the contents of the kettle with a long paddle. Usually the three children in our family took turn about. Always there were two fillings in the big copper kettle to boil down.

In early dawn, Mother could look out of her kitchen window at the red and orange flames, the silhouettes of kettle and boy showing plainly; the deepening dusk of evening also showed a boy and a still brighter flame; occasionally she came out to add more apples and to sniff and taste. Before noon the first lot had boiled down to the right consistency and was ready to store in the stone jars reserved for apple butter. All day long passers-by could smell the delectable odor of boiling apple cider. Some of our neighbors added a pound or two of orange peel; others spiced the butter with cinnamon; some thought they must add sugar. Mother preferred straight apples all the way through.

The most nutritious food cooked in the big copper kettle was whole-corn hominy, although to make this dish there was very little out-of-door cooking. In autumn, after corn husking, a day was set aside for making hominy. The first whites to make hominy were the Jamestown Virginians, who learned the art and took the name from their Indian neighbors. Mother was proud of the fact that she had her recipe from the original source and that it was several hundred years old. Our flint corn did not make nearly so good hominy as the white dent corn of Virginia, but Father found an early white dent that, planted in a warm, sandy spot, usually ripened and made very good hominy.

The corn was shelled by hand so that small and defective grains might be removed. It was then put in a strong solution of warm lye in the copper kettle, and there it soaked for a few hours until the hulls were soft and the 'hearts' of the grains came out, the hearts being embryos to botanists. When hulls and hearts had been sufficiently softened, the corn was dipped out and put in a tub to be washed in warm water until the last trace of lye and bits of hulls and embryos were separated from the starchy grains of corn. The hominy was now made, needing only to be cooked as required for the table.

There was another important use to which the big copper kettle was put. In all my early boyhood Mother made soft soap once a year. To her, soft soap was indispensable for washing dishes, clothes, and cleaning up generally. A certain amount of the homemade soap was hard, to be used by us all in washing our hands and bodies when we were especially dirty. Hard soap was made by putting salt in soft soap as it neared the finishing boiling-down. The materials for making soap are at hand on every farm. At butchering time and whenever meat was cooked, whether pork, beef, or fowl, the excess grease, bones, and rinds were put in the 'soap-grease barrel.' It was amazing how well these fatty substances kept for, of course, they had been well heated by some cooking, and, to be sure, nearly all had some salt. The soap-grease barrel, well covered, stood in a cool corner of the woodshed and even in the heat of summer had little odor.

The other ingredient of soap was lye. Before the Civil War, most of the settlers in forest areas boiled down lye in kettles to make potash, or blackash, or the refined pearlash to bring them ready money. Every settler in our land knew how to make lye.

Mother's method was simplicity itself. All the barrels that came on the farm were saved to hold ashes. These were set in a row behind the woodshed, well covered from rains. Most of the ashes were used to fertilize the garden, but beech, birch, and maple ashes were set aside for making lye. The barrels for making lye had many half-inch holes bored in their bottoms. These, packed full of ashes, were set on small plank platforms, four feet wide, raised two feet from the ground, backs against the woodshed and a little higher than the fronts. Under the fronts troughs were set. Water was poured in the tops of the barrels and soon there was a steady drip of lye.

As the troughs filled, the lye was dipped into the big copper kettle, under which a fire had been built. When the lye began to boil, soap grease was added, and a boy was stationed on the windward side with a long paddle to stir. The smell of boiling apple butter was most agreeable; that of soft soap very unpleasant, as the steam choked us, and the hot lye spattered on our clothes, hands, and feet when soap grease was added. Happily, boiling soap did not take more than an hour or two per kettle, and two kettles supplied the farm for several months.

When the soap was of the proper consistency it was dipped out into a stout oak barrel kept in the woodshed. Half of the last kettle was reserved for hard soap. A few pounds of salt were quickly stirred into the thickening soap, which was then ladled into shallow pans. As this mixture began to cool and 'set,' it was cut in bars four inches long and two inches wide. After a day or two, the bars were hard soap.

The small iron and copper kettles in Mother's kitchen were put to all the culinary uses for which pioneer housewives had need. There were two kettles of each metal, the larger ones of each holding four gallons, the smaller ones half as much. There was, as well, a 'tin' teakettle, which Mother did not like, since in her Father's house there had been a copper teakettle superior to tin for wear and tear. Mother had never been able to purchase such a kettle for her own kitchen. The superior virtue of the copper teakettle was that it never sprang a leak, while its tin counterpart persisted in doing so every few months.

Were there ever more satisfactory odors than those that came from the iron kettles? Was there ever more completely delicious and more satisfying food than came from these black pots? No need to go into details; to name the best-liked dishes cooked in kettles is quite sufficient. Every day in the year, one, two, or three substantials for dinner and supper were cooked in iron kettles on Mother's kitchen range: boiled ham, boiled smoked jowl; all manner of greens and vegetables, including sauerkraut, and beans and peas for soup; meat stews in which might be put potatoes, cabbage, carrots, turnips, rutabagas, or onions, as the garden or cellar allowed; corn chowder and chicken with noodles, or chicken with dumplings for a Sunday dinner. These were the main foods cooked in iron kettles. More prosaic were boiled potatoes, to be eaten whole, or to be mashed. For Sunday-night supper, corn-meal mush was cooked in an iron kettle with enough left over for fried mush on Monday mornings. The children in our family tired of mush-and-milk served every Sunday night for nine months in the year; Father would never eat it, taking instead meat cuts, or cheese, with a pint or two of buttermilk. Mother kept in one of her kettles 'pot liquor.' In winter it was the soluble juices of chicken, ham, fowl, or corned

beef, more properly called stock. In summer it was stock plus
the juices of greens and boiled vegetables, particularly of dandelions, turnip greens, and cabbage, the 'pot lickers' of the
South. These pot liquors of summer contain the quintessence
of several vitamins.

The copper kettles of my boyhood are associated with preserves, jams, and jellies made from berries; we had few tree
fruits and no grapes. The small copper kettle was in use most
often in melting maple sugar into maple syrup and in making
maple confections. Not until my sister became a grown girl did
we know the delights of fudge, usually made by her out of
maple syrup in which milk, butter, nuts, and chocolate in various
proportions were used. The large kitchen copper kettle, tin-
plated inside, as were they all, was used in making pickles,
tomato catsup, and chili sauce.

Pickling began in August when cucumbers were most plentiful. From early August until late September the pungent fragrance of cucumbers, tomatoes, cabbage, peppers, and onions,
spiced with allspice, nutmeg, cinnamon, tumeric, mustard, and
of sharp cider vinegar came from Mother's pickling kettle. The
pickling season ended in September, when red peppers ripened
and green tomatoes were rescued from impending frost. Dill
pickles and sweet cucumber pickles were the family's favorites,
while of the several mixed pickles piccalilli suited best the pork
products with which our larder abounded. Garlic never tainted
Mother's pickling kettle, but onions there were in plenty, small
pickled onions being a prime favorite.

XIX

Maple Sugar

WHEN sap began to stir in April, just before wild geese went honking north, sugar-making fever got into Father's blood. Two seasons out of three it was not profitable, for of all forest industries boiling maple sap is the greatest gamble. Here, as in most of his ventures, Father loved the game beyond the prize, and though the family rebelled, spring after spring we boiled sap.

From time immemorial the Indians in our region had made maple sugar. The discovery of the art of making this delectable product was the golden day of Indian invention. By happy chance, some squaw used sap in cooking, and there came into being maple sugar. It was a wonderful discovery, for the Indian had no other sweet in abundance. He could have had only faint suggestions of sweetness from drops of honey in the comb of the bumblebee, trickling globules of honeydew from aphids, and minims of nectar from flowers.

Ours was a land flowing in maple syrup. Nowhere else on earth have I seen a region where within a square mile a greater number of maples could be made to burst into saccharinity spring after spring. Yet, though there was much cheap, experienced help, we could make no money; we could not compete with sugar and molasses from the cane plantations of the sub-tropics. After several years of losing money in making syrup and sugar for sale, we settled down to sugar-making for home consumption only. Even so, none of the family had much enthusiasm for the work.

Every meal every day in the year, maple syrup was on the table. Its chief use was for pancakes. It was a favorite spread, too, on hot bread, soda biscuits, and fried toast. Sometimes necessity drove us to use maple sugar as sweetening for tea and coffee; none of us liked it for this purpose. We all got tired of maple sugar and we children had to be urged to eat it, being told that it made us strong and was, moreover, a good tonic. No doubt, with its high carbohydrate content, it did supply energy; and since maple sap contains much iron and phosphorus, it was a good tonic.

I read an article that said 'Good maple syrup should have a bright golden color, a delicate flavor, and be perfectly clear; the sugar should be light golden and crystalline in texture.' Bosh! Our syrup, as good as any ever made, was not bright golden but dark brown; the flavor was not delicate but robust; not perfectly clear but a little darkened by smoke and the virtue of forest oddments that the wind blew into the open kettles. Our sugar was not crystalline but had an oily texture, because, to keep the kettles from boiling over, we hung a small chunk of fat pork in each. Lastly, our products had a faint smoky taste, like that of Irish bacon, Scotch whiskey, or Souchong tea.

Northern winters made dormant the life of all vegetation, but the covering of snow kept the ground unfrozen, and the maples only awaited a south wind and a day of sunshine to start the sweet sap that changes a dormant maple into a living one. The prosaic greeting to spring in a forest land was: 'Sap's starting!'

Then, with sugar weather, clear, warm days and freezing nights, sugar-making gets under way.

On our land there were hundreds of sugar maples, and on adjoining lands were hundreds more, which we tapped—no one heeded boundary lines in sugar-making. Nature furnished the raw material; but Father, Southern-born, had had no experience in sugar-making. He looked about for a partner who knew the art. Finally he found Hiram Woods, newly arrived from central New York, who had spent his summers on the Erie Canal and his winters in forest industries. Everybody called him 'Old Hi.'

In our first years of tapping maples, a diagonal incision was cut in the tree; at the lower end of the incision a spile, a small tube or spout, was inserted; at once there was the pleasant sound of sap dripping into a receptacle. Gashing trees was injurious, and after a few years this Indian practice gave way to boring holes with an inch auger. The hole was sunk through the bark into the sapwood, and in it was inserted a wooden spile. These holes were not injurious to the tree, as nature quickly filled the wound with new wood; much smaller trees could be tapped with an auger than with the cut of an ax.

The first year, the receptacles used to collect sap were troughs. The troughs were made from white pines of suitable diameter cut into three-foot lengths, split into halves with a rive, and then hollowed out with an adze. Sap was dipped from the troughs into pails and carried, two pails to a man, with the aid of a shoulder yoke, to barrels drawn on sleds pulled by horses or, much better, by oxen. Gathering sap was a back-breaking, cold, wet task; the first seasons this work was done by Father, Joutel, and an Indian helper, since Old Hi thought his skilled hand and experienced eye were required at the camp to 'Boil down.'

In a cozy, level bit of lowland in the center of our sugar bush a camp was built. Around this rough-planked sugar house stood a few dozen large rough-barked maples—trees never to be cut, though we knew that some were choice bird's-eye and curly maples. It wasn't much of a house. The wind blew through the cracks in the wall; the roof leaked; hinges on the door were of leather straps; hunters came and went the year round at will; a dozen or more cords of wood were piled near by; two or three logs furnished seats for workers and visitors. In this shed barrels, troughs, pails, spiles, augers, funnels, bowls, dishes, axes, saws, jugs for syrup, and Indian *mococks* were stored.

Very pretty, the *mococks* were. They were made from the bark of the white birch in the shape of the lower half of a pyramid, and held from five to twenty pounds of maple sugar. For gift packages, a few were ornamented with porcupine quills.

Father was not given to hospitality in a sugar camp, but Old Hi wanted visitors, who not only delayed work with their gossip but devoured much of the hard-earned maple sugar. Soon our camp became a meeting-place for Hi's New York friends. Father would not be bothered with the old man and his followers, and one evening brought the partnership to an end.

Perhaps the quarrels between Old Hi and Joutel hastened the breaking-up of the partnership. Both loved to quarrel; both would bark, but neither bite. According to Joutel, he had been one of the best fighting men in the Hudson's Bay Fur Company. Old Hi, so he said, had been a champion fighter on the Erie Canal in his youth. From the start, our sugar camp had been soured by quarrels. My brother and I lived in daily hope that there would be a shindy, and that we should see black eyes and bloody noses, but the two fighting cocks got no farther than crowing and strutting.

In our camp there was a battery of three kettles, each holding perhaps a hundred gallons; sap must boil from the time it begins to drip until opening buds bring the season to a close. Each kettle was swung on a heavy ironwood pole supported by two crotched sections of ironwood trunks. Under the kettles a red-hot open fire kept the sap at the boiling point in two of the battery. When the sap in the second kettle became a thin syrup, it was ladled into the third, where once or twice a day it was 'sugared off.'

In April, with fitful spring fever in our veins, work began in the sugar camp. The camp was in a mess every spring. In autumn, leaves blew in and covered the stored equipment. In winter, porcupines, squirrels, and mice got in to add to the dirt and confusion. Always after snow came, one could learn much about the wild life in our woods by going to the sugar bush. On all sides were tracks, at one time or another, of foxes, porcupines, rabbits, and the tiny footprints of birds and mice.

Eventually wooden pails took the place of the troughs of the first years, and these with the barrels must be cleaned every spring and filled with water to 'swell watertight.' Getting the water was a chore of no small magnitude. Either it had to be hauled in, or, more often, the kettles were hung over a slow fire and filled with snow. A few years later we changed to metal buckets, but the syrup, a little brighter, was never quite so good as that made from sap collected in ancient, sap-flavored wooden containers. At no time of the year was there a greater bustle of activity than the few days that preceded sugar-making; Nature and man were at their busiest. Father and Joutel performed the rather nice operation of tapping, leaving the back-breaking work of placing pails to my brother and me. Then came the grueling work of carrying sap from the trees to the roads to fill the barrels on sleds.

There are two or three Currier & Ives prints and many pictures in books showing pleasant groups sitting around picturesque sugar camps watching the several operations. In our camp there was never time for anyone but visitors to sit around. Night and day someone must keep the fires burning. It was all work and very little play in the sugar bush I knew.

Books by early writers on America started the illusions about sugar-making, and a thousand writers, down to today's Sunday newspapers, have kept them up. The first account of which I know was by a French explorer named Joutel (I wonder if he was the founder of the family of our Joutel) in 1687. A picture by Lafitau, 1724, shows nude squaws, beautiful in their hanging tresses, joyfully making maple sugar in a charming grove in which there is no snow, shin-tangle, or underbrush; one of the comely Indian women is luxuriously recumbent on the greensward, feasting on some maple dish. Schoolcraft, the great authority on American Indians, who for many years had charge of Indian affairs in the Land of the Crooked Tree, has a picture in one of his books quite as absurd, except that his squaws are fully dressed; modesty, more likely than accuracy, kept Schoolcraft from reproducing Lafitau's nude women.

None of the writers who sing the praises of sugar-making could ever have tapped a maple tree. Had they served an apprenticeship in a sugar bush, they would have had a different story to tell.

Still, retrospection brings back a few pleasures. There were beautiful sunrises as we went from the house to the sugar bush; the graceful smoke of the fires rose above the maples against a lowering background of dark green hemlocks. There was the pleasant drip-drip of the sap into the pails, the noise of the drops falling as loud in the silence of early morning as the midnight ticking of a clock. My brother and I were always interested in the tracks of wild animals in the snow, and, as time offered, did a little hunting or trapping. In the woods in sugar-making time there was entertainment by birds: at night the lonely hoot of owls in the hemlocks near us; thieving blue jays quarreling about the camp crumbs; woodpeckers of sevaral species hard at work on dead trees; and the chirping of chickadees and nuthatches. I wondered, as a boy, how these birds, especially the delicate little nuthatches, kept their naked toes warm when my heavily clothed feet were freezing.

One spring morning I saw two cock partridges fighting on the hard-crusted snow, several females looking on like ladies at a tournament. What with the strutting, the noises, and the deadly charges, it was a combat between two knights. At the end, a polygamous cock strutted off the field, leading away a harem of admiring hens.

Once every season we gave a party to which old and young among our neighbors were invited. The first sugar product to be served was 'sugar-on-snow,' made by pouring the boiling syrup on snow, which quickly became half-warm, gooey taffy. Next came real taffy. Just before the syrup was ready to make hard sugar, a half-pint was poured into a dish of snow, and as it cooled taffy-makers with greased hands worked the sticky sugar into a ball and began gently to pull. With luck and patience the taffy could be pulled into thick, white ribbons a yard long, from which we made fancy figures or cut into sticks of hard sugar-maple candy. Lastly, syrup and real maple sugar were made.

'Sugaring-off' can be smelled in the air and there are few odors more agreeable. The fragrance comes in the steam rising from the kettles, a little stronger as sap boils down to syrup, and still sweeter and heavier as the thick maple molasses turns into sugar, the big daily event in making maple sugar. Few things on earth taste and smell so good as maple syrup just as it comes hot and steaming from the kettle in a ladle for preliminary sampling.

Modern sugar-makers have an instrument to tell when the boiling syrup is ready for sugaring-off. At a precise point, maple syrup, thick or thin, is gently poured into containers to cool. We dropped a little in a pan of snow and judged from the sugar-on-snow whether the syrup was sufficiently boiled down to make sugar. If cake sugar were to be made, it was then poured into molds and set aside to cool. At the hard-sugar stage, while the syrup was violently boiling, the fire under the kettle was drawn, the syrup was stirred with a heavy wooden paddle; as the mixture cooled it granulated into crumb sugar of the color and texture of brown cane sugar.

Custom dictated that at a sugaring-off party there should be refreshments of hot buttered soda biscuits; these were dunked in thin, hot maple syrup. There might be other food as well, but hot soda biscuits were indispensable. They were baked in an old cookstove in the sugar camp; in fact, much of the food eaten during a busy sugar-making season must be cooked in the camp.

A sugar camp on a pitchy night has many delights. Besides the maple products and foods to enjoy, there are feasts for other senses as well; there are agreeable odors; the roaring fires under the kettles; the lights and shadows of the maple forest standing in deep, pure-white snow; the sounds of cracking forest trees; the *hoo, hoo, hoo,* of owls; and the barking of dogs or perhaps a fox. These and the good cheer of guests at a sugaring-off party make the maple-sugar season one of some pleasure.

By some trick of memory, I associate several jargons with sugar-making. I hear again Joutel's noisy chattering in broken English, French, and Ottawan; Old Hi's obscene and profane phrases from the Erie Canal; the Southern dialect and drawl of Perry Nelson, the cooper who made our pails and barrels; the voices of children pulling taffy, each family having a dialect of its own, depending upon whether its members were New Englanders, New Yorkers, Ohioans, Hoosiers, Canadians, or natives of some foreign country.

Joutel was Father's right bower in the camp. I have already said so much about Joutel that I need only add here that he, as ever, bore the brunt of the work, cheerful, vociferous, impudent, often tiresome, often amusing. At the beginning of every sugar season he filled a barrel with sap half boiled down, put in some yeast, gave it a place near the fire, and in a few days had brewed a beverage about as strong in alcohol as beer. Of this brew he drank such prodigious quantities that it would seem as if he must burst. He was allowed to have his way, for, under the influence of the alcohol, the business of the day proceeded at double its usual pace.

Spring came with a rush in our northern land. Usually a day or two of torrid heat brought bursting buds, and sugar-making was over. As spring began pouring out its favors, Joutel became more and more jovial. I have a vivid memory of him at his morning ablutions, a quart or two of his brew inside him, singing some Indian roundelay, one of which is worthy of a place in any anthology of songs of spring. A rather poor translation, which makes the song much shorter in English than in Ottawan, runs:

> As my eyes
> Search the forest
> I see the Summer
> In the Spring. . .
> See the Summer
> In the Spring.

Joutel sang the words over and over, every note coming straight from the heart, as blithely, noisily and as repetitiously as the chickadees sang their songs.

Spring after spring, an Indian by the name of Gasper Quatcheeo helped in the sugar bush, almost as good a helper as Joutel and not nearly so noisy and troublesome. Quatcheeo was a Chippewa (there were many among the Ottawa), and I do not remember an Indian more typical of those in fiction. He was quite the opposite of Joutel in temperament, being quiet, reserved, and uncommunicative, in spite of which the two were great friends. I would say that Quatcheeo drank as much of Joutel's brew as Joutel himself, if it were possible for any other human to do so, but without the same happy effects. Drink made Quatcheeo more taciturn, and he would down quarts of it without any exhilaration or even a sparkle in his eyes.

To me Quatcheeo was very attractive, and as I followed him about in the woods, I jabbered at him in Ottawan, but seldom got more than 'Oh, God, yes,' or, 'Oh, God, no.' In the woods he would often point to the tracks of a bird or animal and name the creature in a single word. I never saw him laugh or smile except when I tried to use his snowshoes and fell and floundered in the snow until he put me on my feet. Gasper Quatcheeo was the Indian from whom Father had bought our land. He had made sugar there many times and knew every maple in the bush.

After the first season's experience, Father decided that pine troughs were poor receptacles for catching sap and looked about for a man to make him a coopered vessel. Several miles to the north of us was a cooper who had come to our part of the world to make barrels for fishermen; but fish were no longer salted in barrels and the onetime cooper had turned farmer and was slowly starving to death on a homestead he had taken from Uncle Sam. Father went to see the man, who turned out to be a Virginian and a Democrat. He had been a Copperhead, and had at one time made flour barrels for Father's father in Virginia. His name was Commodore Perry Nelson—'Perry' to most people, 'Commodore' to Father.

Having so much in common with this man, Father looked no farther for a cooper, and forthwith we had Perry and his wife Polly on our hands for a meal nearly every week in the year. Mother made a wry face as the Nelsons put in appearance. 'Poor white trash,' she called them. Neither Perry nor Polly could read or write, and a Northerner could hardly understand their jargon. In the summer the old couple went barefoot, though to be sure they did not come to a meal in our house without something on their feet. Often they trudged by bare-footed, shoes in hand, to the harbor for a day of fishing, fish being about the only meat their larder ever held. On the way home, stopping to put on their shoes at the edge of our clearing, they came in to leave us a mess of fish and to eat a snack.

The Nelsons grew their own tobacco, as they had done in Virginia, rank green in the field, black when cured, and so strong that not even a buck Indian could smoke it without a stomach upset. But Perry and Polly preferred their powerful home-grown tobacco to the refined product of the stores, and from morning till night puffed sorrow and care away. The odor of their clay pipes, black from long use, was another cause for Mother's dislike of the Nelsons. She often set forth their short-comings to Father, referring to them as 'those Virginia friends of yours.' I came to know the Nelsons well. As they grew feebler and feebler, Mother often sent me to take them food. Their little log cabin was made of curly maple, beautifully squared and polished inside. It faced the south, and old Perry had made a sun-dial before the south door, their only means of telling the time of day. In winter the cabin was warm and cozy; in summer cool.

Old Hi (Hiram Woods) came into our lives by way of our sugar bush. His farm was but a mile from ours, and in due course we should have known all about him, but a season's partnership in sugar-making quickly gave us a thorough knowl-edge of his qualities, good and bad. Father, with a humor I could not fathom, called him 'Elevated Mutton.' Some six or seven years after I had first heard the nickname, as I sat at the dinner table with Old Hi opposite me, the connection between 'Hiram' and 'Elevated Mutton' popped into my dull brain. I laughed so immoderately for no apparent reason, that Mother, thinking our guest would conclude that I was laughing at him, sent me from the table.

About once a week Old Hi turned up at our house for a meal, and stowed away huge quantities of food, shoveling it down with knife and fork, drinking tea or coffee from his saucer, jabbering in a loud voice (his wife was nearly deaf), winking and smiling, and pouring out gossip and stories as his victuals went down. Old Hi was always on hand at logging bees; he would turn up an hour or two before the midday meal, coming with free and easy grace and a hail: 'Mornin'! Here I be to give you a lift!'

Loquacious 'Elevated Mutton' was a horse trader for other people. He always knew where there were horses to be bought or traded and earned a few dollars by passing on the information, his only source of income except a pension as a Civil War veteran. He came, as he told everybody, from 'the 'arf-way part of the Erie Canal in old York State.' This is David Harum's country, and Old Hi must have engaged that worthy's friendship if they were within driving distance of each other.

A certain sign of spring was the appearance of Old Hi at our house to have his hair cut by one of our hired men. We could see who was coming from afar because of his Santa Claus head, barrel-shaped body, and bandy legs. The 'old moss back' bragged that he never shaved, never combed his hair, and had it cut but once a year.

Hi told our hired men that he hadn't 'washed all over' in forty years. I once heard him say this at an unfortunate time. It was on a summer's evening, just as Mother, who did not like my being with the hired men, called me to wash up for bed. I quoted Hi, adding that he had lived a long time without washing, and was still strong and healthy, whereupon Mother went into an ecstasy of zeal in scrubbing the various parts of my head, sputtering and scolding until she was quite out of breath.

Ill-appearing physically and unregenerate morally though Hi was, the old sinner had genuine charm. With every speech and gesture he overflowed with friendliness. He laughed with his whole body, an infectious laugh to all who were near. Before he made one of his racy remarks, his tongue anointed his lips as if he would taste his words. The truth was not in him; yet all were pleased with his deceits and exaggerations. Young and old, high and low, stopped at his salutation and gave ear, no matter how important the matter in hand was, or what the time of day, and felt a little happier because of his cheerful words.

After I had long been living in another part of the world, I returned one summer to find Old Hi palsy-stricken. His body was a forlorn wreck and his mental faculties nearly gone, but the old rapscallion's eyes still sparkled at hearing a joke or story.

His wife was as slovenly as her husband, but was wholly lacking in his charm. She took no joy in a friendly chat, would neither lend nor borrow, and neither help nor be helped in times of trouble. The old shrew had a fiendish temper and on provocation would pour out a stream of profanity. She was thin and slight, with a thousand wrinkles on her face. In summer she went barefoot, wearing a single garment, a coarse cotton Mother Hubbard that hung straight down so that she seemed to be without breasts, hips, or buttocks, and but for her stooped shoulders would have been as straight as a slab on all sides.

Granny Woods kept a flock of geese; nothing in our woods seemed so formidable to my brother and me. When we must pass the Woods' farm, we armed ourselves with sticks and stones and always had a combat with the hissing geese, headed by a vicious gander whose bill and wings left ugly bruises on our bodies. In the midst of these frays, old Granny would rush out shrieking dreadful oaths ending:

'You little devils! God help you if I get my hands on you!'

XX

Threshers

AT first all our grain was threshed with flails. A flail is an instrument for beating grain out of the heads, or peas and beans out of pods; it consists of a round smooth handstaff five feet long and two inches through, attached to which with a leather thong is a shorter, thicker piece of round wood, called a swingle. The swingle, half as long as the handle, strikes the grain.

There should be three men to flail. One swings the flail, one pitches on and keeps the grain spread, and the third takes care of the grain that is beaten out. Grain is flailed on the barn floor, which means working in a cloud of dust. It takes skill and is hard work to swing a flail, especially if you work at it long. Father would never try, and I was always in danger of knocking my brains out with the flying swingle. My brother, who bragged that he could do anything on a farm that anybody else ever did, could use a flail fairly well, but was always willing to give the job to the hired men. In the early years when we threshed with a flail, Joutel was still around, and once when he came in the barn, the two hired men chased him out swinging the flail about his head, as they often did about mine. Joutel left the place muttering: 'Zose goddams! Zose goddam goddams!'

Nor could he ever be induced to go near the barn again when the noise and dust of flailing were in the air.

Two Canadians worked for Father for several years, and during their stay did all our threshing with flails. They were of English descent and tradition dictated that wielders of flails should wear long, loose duster-like frocks tightly buttoned about the neck; Mother had to make them these uniforms out of blue denim. When threshing machines came, these garments had to be given up, for wheels and belts made tight-fitting garments necessary. The approved uniform for threshers is a close-fitting jacket, overalls, gingham shirt, red handkerchief about the neck, and a slouch hat pulled down to protect the eyes and ears.

Threshers, the world over, are careless of personal appearance. They seldom shave, use little water on face and hands, and in our parts bathed only when a farm lay on the shores of Lake Michigan, when, after supper, all hands went to the lake for a swim. One could always tell threshers and lumbermen by their clothing. Another distinction was that lumberjacks usually smoked pipes, while threshers preferred a quid of tobacco, since smoking about straw stacks was dangerous.

A thresher might be a teetotaler the rest of the year, but in threshing season he went to town Saturday night to 'wet his whistle.' In threshing time at least, he had a mouthful of oaths and spent his evenings telling obscene stories. All had voracious appetites. During the open season for threshers, wives scarcely knew their husbands, or mothers their sons.

Agriculture made great strides in our land when the first threshing machine was brought from Chicago on the steamer *Van Ralte*. The outfit, separator and 'horsepower,' was imported by our next-door neighbor, W. R. Bowser. Everybody went down to see the machinery unloaded from the boat. To a boy's eyes, the machines were magnificent. The separator was painted in brilliant reds, greens, and yellows; the 'horsepower' in black, blue and white.

In threshing, the gaudy separator was drawn between two stacks of grain, while some seventy or eighty feet away stood the 'horsepower' through which the strength of four teams of horses was transmitted by means of a long rod, consisting of lengths of twenty feet, the parts being connected by couplings when in use.

The 'horsepower' was a geared contraption, pegged tightly to the earth with strong stakes. Above the gears was a wooden platform on which the driver stood. Four long, strong sweeps stretched at right angles from the machine, and to these teams were hitched. The driver mounted the platform, cracked his whip, yelled 'Get-ep! Get-ep!' a dozen times, and the horses were off, going round and round in their little circle. All day long the driver cracked his whip, coaxed or scolded his horses, sang amorous ditties, shouted jokes, and squirted tobacco juice.

The whip was a 'black snake' of braided rawhide, very heavy at the butt, tapering gracefully ten or twelve feet to the snapper, where there was a loop to which a foot-long snapper was fastened. A practiced driver became as skilful as an Eskimo sled driver in the use of a black snake; its crack made the noise of a rifle; he could pick a fly off a horse's rump without hurting the horse.

Eight or ten men worked about the separator; two stood at the feeding board in front of the big spiked cylinder that tore out the grain; two pitched sheaves on the feeding board. As fast as they came, a man grabbed the sheaves, which landed butts toward him, slashed the straw bands with a curved knife, and shoved the bundles along to the feeder; with a single motion the feeder grabbed a sheaf, spread it out, pushed the heads on the whirring cylinder, and in a trice grain was pouring out of a spout far below, while chaff and straw were carried on an endless straw carrier to the strawstack, where two men built it into a compact conical stack. A man held open the mouth of a two-bushel grain bag into which the spout man poured the grain. A third man tied the bag, shouldered it, and carried it to the barn. At our farm there was never a lack of men, so that Father could help here and there to keep things running smoothly. My brother was on the feeding platform cutting bands.

About once an hour, work stopped so that the men might catch their breath, clear the dust out of mouth and nostrils, and have a chance to oil machinery. Some of the several women in the house brought out switchel, lemonade, buttermilk, or water. Threshers like an early dinner and at half-past eleven one of the women came to the door with a dishpan on which she would beat a loud tattoo, giving notice that dinner was ready. In an instant work stopped.

The glamour of threshing caught my brother's fancy, and he begged to go with the 'machine' as the official band cutter. Father let him go and soon he was traveling, threshing at every farm in a half-dozen townships. He came home late on Saturday nights, and left Sunday nights riding a big farm horse.

He had wonderful tales to tell of his travels. The machine threshed for all kinds of people. The whites were of a dozen nationalities and came from far distant countries and all the states of the East and the provinces of Canada. He had stayed overnight and eaten in several Indian houses.

Mother thought her eldest son was beginning to look a little tough. He said he never washed his hands and face or combed his hair away from home, because he didn't like to use a wash-pan, a towel, and a comb that others had used. His face was not only dirty and black with machine oil but there was the beginning of a fuzzy beard. He wore a blue flannel shirt, blue denim pants—much too short—no socks, and rough shoes. On the back of his head was an old hat, bandless and full of holes.

After the first trip home, Mother made him leave his clothes out of doors. She wanted to examine his head, but he said, 'No!'

Just before the end of the threshing season, Preacher Cook came to talk to Father. He had been to see the threshing machine at work, and had an awful tale to tell of my brother's behavior. After the first few days with the threshing machine, the boy had changed his work from cutting bands to driving the horsepower. Traditionally the man on the platform of the power machine was a clown; my brother essayed the part. Preacher Cook told Father the boy was chewing tobacco, swearing, singing lewd songs, making vile jokes, and it was said that he was beginning to drink. From the preacher's report, he was on his way to perdition. The family knew it. I had seen him several times, as Father had, standing in the center of his platform, ragged hat on the back of his head, shirt tail out, shouting, cracking his black snake, clowning. It was a terrible contrast to his previous respectable life.

At last the threshing season was over. Late one Saturday night my brother came home, as tough a specimen as one might see in all our land. We were expecting him and had waited up. When we went to bed, Father said, using the name reserved for admonishments:

'Wilbur, I expect you to change your way of living.'

The next morning my brother was up early, bathed, shaved, put on his best clothes, and went with the family to church. In all the years that have followed, I have never seen him with a quid of tobacco in cheek, with a black snake in his hand, or heard him swear or tell a lewd story. In two short months he had sown, reaped, and threshed a generous crop of wild oats.

The next year when threshers came to our farm, my brother cut bands.

XXI

Butchering Day

AFTER all the work in the fields was finished, came butchering day—the grand finale. We never butchered before the middle of November when a little snow had fallen and a skim of ice formed on still water every night. The weather had to be cold so that the meat could chill. Almost always we butchered the week before Thanksgiving. There were days of preparation. Kettles had to be hung; a hogshead mounted on a platform for scalding; a scaffold built on which to hang the hogs after scalding and scraping; knives ground and whetted to razor keenness; and at least a cord of wood provided for the kettles. We butchered only hogs. When we had an occasional beef to kill, it was sold to the butcher in town, and we would take what was wanted.

Father would not stick a pig, nor did we ever have a hired man who could. Someone had to be brought in to kill our pigs. Usually Hi Woods came, and once or twice Perry Nelson did this nasty bit of work. Mother would not have either Granny Woods or Granny Nelson 'puttering around,' and chose two women friends to help try out the lard and make pork products. As a matter of course, their husbands came, so there were plenty to help indoors and out.

In the first years Joutel offered his services as a butcher, always assuring Father: 'I'll kill heem ze pig jus' right.'

And though he never had a chance to kill the pig 'jus' right' he was always on hand. If he came a day or two ahead, he slept in the haymow well covered with horse blankets. He was handy, and while he ate tremendous meals, he earned them. Joutel was Mother's man Friday but she would not have him at the table. While the rest of us ate, she let him finish odds and ends sitting in the warm, odoriferous kitchen. Joutel taught my brother and me to eat boiled pig tails, the tastiest part of a pig. He always asked for the bladders, which, cleaned and dried, made him tobacco pouches to last a year. When we children were small, Joutel made us balloons from pig bladders.

Perry Nelson used a rifle to kill the pigs. Old Hi Woods' technique was to hit a pig on the cranium with the head of an ax, felling the animal to the ground. The trouble with this method was that it required much maneuvering to corner the pig and get him to stand still. In either case a long, sharp knife was run into the jugular vein; in a minute all was over. What with the squealing and the blood, the first hours of butchering day were not pleasant; so repugnant were the sounds and sights that my brother was usually nauseated, and was permitted to go a mile or two away until the noise and carnage were over and the secondary operations had begun.

Long before daybreak a fire was lighted under a large iron kettle, in which water was boiling by the time the pigs were killed. The boiling water, fortified with ashes, was now poured into the hogshead, and then the pigs, one after the other, were soused for a few minutes each. Old Hi believed that all pigs were bewitched (his wife was a witch if there ever was one) and as soon as a pig was stuck and began to squeal he thought it ought to be doused in the cauldron of boiling water, there to die. He said: 'The witches do the squealing. Pork won't keep unless you drive the witches away.'

Father let the pigs squeal it out before scalding.

The scalded pigs were now ready for barbering, tools for which were sharp hoes and knives, leaving the porker as clean and shining as a babe out of its bath. Shaving over, the pigs next went to the scaffold, not head first or with a hangman's halter, but hind heels first on a gambrel (single trees from a wagon make good gambrels) inserted between the strong tendons just above the hind hocks. Here, as the bodies hung, the fat shining bellies were opened for the removal of the 'innards' and the leaf lard. What had been a pig, now made by the butchers into pork, hung for a few hours in the wintry cold to be thoroughly chilled.

At every butchering time we boys got a view of the mysterious insides of a mammal; and so had a very good idea of the vital organs of higher animals, and of their functions. A farm boy who has helped at butchering and has had the care of animals is in a fair way to become a natural surgeon.

It is not to be supposed that the workers stood idly gazing at the cooling meat. The livers, hearts, and brains had to be cleaned, chilled, and dried; the stomachs, intestines, and bladders had to be emptied, scraped, washed, and made ready for use as casings for sausage meat; the fat and lard meat had been removed, and lard was being rendered all the afternoon. Lard was tried out much as whale oil is from whale blubber, though with a difference: in our operation the crisp, brown cracklings, from which the lard had been pressed, were saved for future pork pies and crackling corn bread.

It is amazing how many substantial dishes and savory titbits can be made from a hog, an animal that we begin to like only after it is dead. Next after the body substances of hams, shoulders, and bacon, come several kinds of appetizing sausages. All who have lived on a farm will agree that sausages made in the home are incomparably better than those from the stores. The home butcher, of course, must know what to put in and what to leave out of his sausage meat. You can be sure that our nostrils would tingle with sage and black pepper. Father liked sausage with plenty; Mother did not like sage. Half of our sausage was fragrant with sage and black pepper; the other half, salted and lightly peppered. Father liked link sausage, while Mother preferred patty cakes. Our stuffed sausages were yard-long pieces to be cut in cooking, not constricted by tying as the professionals make links. There could never be any suspicion about the freshness or quality of our sausage. It could not be said of our product, as the Germans say of sausages generally: 'Place little faith in sausages and widows: one doesn't know what their skins hide.'

Homemade sausage required two machines, a grinder and a stuffer, both run by boy-power. After a day at butchering my brother and I took turns running these machines until midnight. Only the thought of what we should eat kept the toil of butchering from becoming unendurably tedious.

Half of the product each season was smoked for summer use. When quantity permitted, a five-gallon jar was filled with link sausage, over which melted lard was poured. This larded sausage could be kept until the next butchering day.

Pigs' hocks and feet were boiled and put in spiced vinegar. Heads, tails, snouts, jowls, lips, ears, tongues, livers, hearts, and skins were cooked to make several delectable dishes. One of our hired men always asked to have the snouts saved separately: he thought a boiled snout was the best of all pork products. Some of these meats and the strained soup were put in flavored vinegar, poured into molds in which the mixture jellied, and thus became white, jelly-like souse, delectable in texture and taste. Other parts were ground, flavored, reheated in the soup, and chilled in milk pans to make headcheese. Still other portions were mixed with corn meal and flavored to become a tasty breakfast dish, scrapple, eaten sliced and fried. When these several dishes had been made, there was left much of the richly flavored water in which the meats had been cooked; into this broth Mother put corn meal, which was cooked into a mush, poured into a shallow pan, and hardened, making the gustful dish the Pennsylvania Dutch call 'panhas.'

The only edible part of the pig that we did not use was the

blood. Mother had a prejudice against blood and would not use it in her cookery, so that gallons of rich swine blood went to waste on butchering days. Our German neighbors liked blood sausages and blood puddings, both of which pleased my palate. These products were made by mixing in the blood small cubes of fat pork and some cereal flour. Blood is rich in iron and albumen and the Germans believed blood pudding to be a sovereign remedy for anemia.

Father had recipes for smoking hams, bacon, sausage, tongues, and jowls. That for hams was:

To preserve color, rub each ham with half a teaspoonful of saltpeter; then rub with a large teaspoonful of fresh black pepper; rub well with blackstrap molasses. Then for ten hams take:

¼ peck coarse salt
¼ pound saltpeter
¼ pint hickory ashes
¼ quart blackstrap molasses
¼ teacupful of red pepper

Mix all together; rub each ham with this mixture and spread the remainder on layers of hams in the barrel; pack skin down and let stand for five weeks. Then smoke in damp, cool weather in a close smokehouse for six weeks, using hickory or sugar-maple chips with now and then a few corn cobs.

Bacon, sausage, tongues, and jowls were smoked with little special preparation, though all were salted down for several weeks before smoking. Father was very fond of smoked jowl. Cooked with any of the cabbage family, greens, string beans, or parsnips, smoked jowl is a splendid dish.

Butchering day ended with a grand feast. All who had helped in any way sat down to the groaning table. Sometimes the preacher and his wife came out from town, though visitors were not encouraged, as they were a hindrance rather than a help in the work that followed, and all who came expected to carry away a helping of fresh meat. Mother wanted only two women to help on butchering day. She liked best to have Melissa Elliot (if Melissa was not having a baby, which happened during several butchering times) and her cousin, Susie Elliot (who had no children), both old friends of Mother's childhood in Indiana.

Three or four kinds of meat were served at the feast. Custom called for tenderloin, cut thin and fried brown and not too crisp. The tenderloin of a pig is the meat of fine texture that lies underneath the backbone. A sample of sausage, its sage fragrance perfuming the house, was always on the table so that the 'professionals' might pronounce upon its flavor. Liver, which didn't keep well, was always served. For an hour or two preceding supper, spareribs had been simmering in the oven; a dish of crisp golden cracklings was passed around.

On butchering day, pork must be offset by a proper assortment of other foods. Mother chose sauerkraut and cooked quartered apples for vegetables at her butchering-day supper. There was usually a variety of relishes, but Mother's specialties for the day were piccalilli, homemade catsup, and preserved watermelon rind. Besides, there were soda biscuit, mashed potatoes, and thick, brown milk gravy. The dessert, year in and year out, was apple pie and tangy cheese. Coffee was the drink. Father always lamented that there was no hard cider, as there had been in Virginia.

XXII

Forest Products

THERE was little pine in our region, but there were thousands of acres of hemlock that furnished bark for the tanner and logs for the lumberman. The only other softwood of value was the American arborvitæ, known by lumbermen as white cedar. This tree grew abundantly in all swamps and was cut for shingles, railroad ties, telegraph poles, and paving blocks. Of the hardwoods we had a plentiful supply of maple, beech, birch, elm, and basswood, which furnished lumber for flooring, furniture, and turned articles, and wood for fuel and charcoal.

The most valuable tree in our woods was the bird's-eye maple. From the outside one could not tell whether a maple was straight grained or curly grained with markings like the eyes of a bird. Since a good log of bird's-eye is worth several times as much as one of straight grain, if the first chip that you took out of a maple disclosed that it was a prize, you got the same thrill that a trapper gets when he snares a silver fox in a region of red foxes.

In low, moist parts of our land, there were not a few red birches, prized greatly by builders for floors and panels. As we cleared our land, red birch logs went to the sawmill. Two or three fine specimens were left along the highway as handsome ornamentals. The ragged, loose-hanging, red-brown bark reminded me of a beggar in rags and tags. We children chewed the slender drooping reddish twigs as a substitute for wintergreen. Red birches were the first trees in our forest to foretell winter by putting on a garment of bright gold foliage.

Our forest flora was much like that of southern New England, differing chiefly in not having many elms. The few on our land were saved for timber to be used on the farm. Eventually most of them were sawed to make runners for bobsleighs, wagon tongues, stoneboats, and similar objects in which great strength was wanted. In one of our fields a group of three elms was left to furnish shade for livestock. They were beautiful trees, each one in summer a tall gracious vase of green foliage, changing to gold in autumn; in winter each was an austere etching silhouetted against the gray sky. When working near by in summer we took time to enjoy their shade as we drank buttermilk or ate watermelons.

The acres my father bought from the Indian, Gasper Quatcheeo, were covered with a good growth of hardwoods on the high lands and groves of towering hemlocks on the low lands. Forest industries were in full blast in our bit of northern Michigan within a few years after our coming, and my father, in common with all of our neighbors, sold timber products for the ready cash he needed.

In the winter on our land, all the work was with the hardwoods, which went into saw logs and fuel. In June and July, when the bark would peel, we cut hemlocks for tanbark.

Hemlock bark is a by-product of land-clearing and lumbering in all northern woods. In our hemlock groves the trees stood thick, two, three, and even four feet in diameter at the butts, with trunks limbless fifty or sixty feet upward. These splendid bodies were surmounted by tops of dark-green foliage, so dense that the presence of the sun in the sky could be known only by a few vertical shafts of light at midday. The deeply creased bark was so thick that, peeled and corded, two cords were often obtained from a single tree, and sold for from three to five dollars a cord.

If you could steel your heart against giving the deathblow to these potentates of the forest, laying them low and stripping them of their rough, fragrant coats was a thrilling game. Usually my father and his two sons played the game alone. Hired men came to help only when the price of bark was high.

The first move in peeling bark was to throw two or three small trees, much as if we were playing jackstraws on a gigantic scale, to make a couch upon which to lay the hemlock chosen for sacrifice. Before cutting began, however, a survey had to be made to see if strumpet winds were blowing in the treetop—not easy, for no breeze short of a gale whispered on the ground. A high wind in the treetop might bring disaster in the placing of the monarch and danger to the bark peelers. The next move was to peel a cylinder four feet long from the base of the trunk to save from the saw and ax a length of the thickest bark. Next, in our gang of three, Father sank a notch with his ax halfway to the heart of the tree on the side where the couch had been prepared. On the opposite side my brother and I, with a cross-cut saw, on the same level as the notch made by the ax, all but severed the trunk from the stump.

The shining saw flashed back and forth through sapwood, oldwood, into the dark heartwood; each woody cylinder giving the sibilant saw a different note, and the sawdust from each having a different color and odor. As soon as the saw was buried in the trunk, an iron wedge was driven in to widen the fissure. As the saw drew near the notch made by the ax, the towering bulk began to tremble, then to crackle, then to sway; then there was a long-drawn sigh, the noise of tearing, splintering wood, and crunching branches, and the hemlock plunged through its neighbors to the earth with a thunderous crash, crushing and maiming trees that stood in its way.

The tree down, my task was to lop off the branches and pile them for future burning. Meanwhile, my brother had ringed the bark through to the wood in four-foot cylinders and opened them at the top the length of the trunk, using as his tool a sharp ax. Father began at once to remove the bark with a sharp spud in whose blade, two inches in width and length, was set a straight handle thirty inches long. Stripped from the tree, the bark was stood against the trunk, smooth side out, that the sun might dry the oozy cambium. After two or three days of sunshine, the bark was piled in cord tiers, smooth side down.

The bark of the hemlock must be stripped in June or July, when it easily parts from the bole. At this season cambium, the formative tissue between bark and wood, is most active. It is of the consistency of thin butter, with the same rich yellow color, and Nature has spread it much as a man greases a pole for Fourth of July games. The gentle crunch of the spud and the soft tearing sound of the bark as it is pulled from the trunk are peculiarly human tones, as if the fallen tree was beseeching man to spare its kin in the ancient grove.

Bark peeling involved several dangers. When the tree was cut, there were falling branches from neighboring trees. Sometimes the hemlock split and kicked back, endangering life and limb. The slippery boles made the use of edged tools dangerous, the cause of accidents every season.

At no other work in the forest did we suffer tortures of so many kinds. We panted for breath in the dead, hot air of the closed-in glades in which hemlocks choose to grow; swarms of mosquitoes found their way to every part of our thinly clad bodies; black flies chewed the flesh and raised great welts; small, tormenting gnats set neck and face on fire. It was work for strength and skill and for surpassing patience and fortitude. We had to keep at it from daylight to dark in the short season, stopping only to take a draught from a jug, lifted high on a crooked arm, from which lukewarm water gurgled into the parched mouth of grimy, insect-bitten faces.

In the cool of early morning and late afternoon, when the swarms of insects were not astir, the work was pleasant, and one who liked the picturesque had compensations. In the dappled shade of the grove, the eyes lighted on the torsos of a score or a hundred lords of the forest stripped of their bark. They lay in scattered confusion, the long boles beautiful in shape and in their clear, rich yellow color. The peeled trunks were marked with curious bulgings, knots, severed limbs, and rings made by the peelers at uniform distances, flickering in the light and shade of uncut trees. Intermingled with the fallen trunks were ramparts of dried bark. The ground was covered with the Canadian yew, mazy gardens of ferns, hummocks carpeted with mosses, and an assortment of fleshy fungi, flowers lingering from spring, red-berried partridge vines, wintergreen, and splashes of red bunchberries.

Morning and evening the air was loaded with the scents of shady woods, of soil and leaf mold, bruised hemlock, fungi, spicy wintergreen, and sweet ferns. In the heat of noon, the smell of hemlock foliage is delightful.

No lovelier view ever greets the human eye than the scene that cheers the peelers of bark as they come into broad daylight from a dark grove of hemlocks. Those who live in the Land of the Crooked Tree know at once the view I mean: white clouds floating serenely in the perfect blue of a June sky.

In the early morning there were the songs of late-singing birds, the voice of the white-throated sparrow sweetest of all. Throughout the day one heard the rat-a-tat of the redheaded woodpecker hammering his way into worm-infested trees. Woodpeckers were very common and, with their red heads and necks and their velvet bodies in the heat of the summer, gave the woods a tropical touch. It was in the bark-peeling season that we most often saw scarlet tanagers, birds of brilliant plumage, with a delightful robinlike song. The tanager was never rare in our beech and maple woods from May till September. More rare, but often seen, was the great black woodpecker, very conspicuous because of his large size, dark brown, almost black color, bright red cap, and the drumlike noise he made in cutting grubs out of dead trees. His usual call was a loud *cack-cack-cack,* not unlike the clack of a barnyard hen.

For some reason, our woodsmen had a high regard for this bird and had several names for him: woodcock, wood hen, woodchuck, log cock, and Johnny cock. Toward evening the delightful songs of the wood thrush, veery, and hermit thrush filled the woods with music. The noises from human throats were not in accord with those of nature. Toilers in forests are seldom men of genteel words. I remember all too well the oaths, obscenity, nasty stories, and amorous ditties of my father's hirelings, always at their worst in the intimate teamwork of peeling hemlock bark. Their oaths, it must be said, were not so much out of place when directed at the torturing insects, the burning heat, and the slippery boles of the peeled hemlock trunks.

Sooner or later the bark was hauled to the shore of our bay to be shipped to the tanning centers of Milwaukee and Racine. The ships anchored a half mile from shore and the bark was taken out on scows by man power, the men, ten or twelve to a scow, pulling hand over hand on a rope that passed from the ship, between the tiers of bark on the scow, to an anchorage on shore. Night and day, calm or wind, rain or snow, a ship's captain demanded his load. In autumn gales, when the wind whistled and screamed and the waves ran high, the spray struck those of us on the scows like hurricane sands in a desert. Often with the wind there came rain, and on front, back, and sides, from crown to sole, our bodies stood the shock of the icy water driven by the gale.

Loading hemlock bark was the most profitable work in our region. Father was paid a dollar an hour for work with his own team of horses, hauling the bark from the corded tiers on the shore to the scows. My brother and I, in our teens, were paid 25 cents an hour, which, as we grew older, was increased, nickel by nickel, to 50 cents. It took fifty men and several teams working twelve to eighteen hours a day, ten days, to load the several hundred cords that we and our neighbors had piled on the sandy beach. Thus our family started the winter with one or two hundred dollars from this work.

The men on the scows led a dangerous life. Often in a storm they were washed off their flat-topped boats and had to cling to pieces of bark until rescued. Sometimes scows were washed ashore and men had to pull and push them on heavy rollers high on the beach to get them out of the way of battering waves.

Peter Clayton, an ex-English seaman, was foreman of bark loading. In an autumn gale, one of the scows came ashore and all hands were pulling and heaving to get it high on the beach out of the way of waves. Peter, coatless and hatless, beard and hair flying, pulling in front, called out to his son Harry, pushing in the rear, waves washing over him: ' 'Arry, you ain't 'eavin' like 'ell.'

Forever after on the farm, when someone was thought to be shirking, the shirker was admonished, ' 'Arry, you ain't 'eavin' like 'ell.'

My work was prosaic enough. To save time, the men were furnished food at noon and evening, and I had to buy and prepare their meals. The railroad ran around the bay and trains would stop on signal. Early in the morning I took the train and went to one of the two towns on the north and south sides of our little sea and bought provender. The menus were always the same: cheese, canned corned beef, drief beef, smoked herring, and bologna sausage, with bread and butter, crackers, cookies, and ginger snaps. Coffee was drunk in enormous quantities. There was a rough shack with a stove on which the coffee was made, and tables on which the food was stacked. Twice a day there was a buffet party in which the chairs were logs or piles of bark on the beach.

Twice in less than an hour I nearly lost my life. We were loading the *Gilbert Knapp;* the last cord of bark was on the scows; the loading season was over; it was mid-October, with the wind blowing a gale, waves too high for safety, and snow coming down. Every man was on the scows pulling for dear life. I had no evening meal to prepare and was told to go on a leaky scow and bail out. The bailing was done with a tin pail through a three-foot square hatchway level with the deck and in the stern of the scow. The going was bad from the start. Near the *Gilbert Knapp,* we met an unloaded scow being pulled to the shore. In a calm sea, passing was not difficult but in this gale it was almost impossible. The line of the empty scow must be dropped, the scow inched along our loaded craft, and the line picked up in our rear. Everyone knew what to do and did his best, but as the line was being picked up, the lee tier of bark was caught and pulled into the lake; the windward side of our scow went down and the tier of bark slid off, carrying me into the waves.

The men on the two scows hung on to the strong rope-line and were safe enough. As for me, I was floating on a piece of the bark in Lake Michigan. With bark all around me, there was little danger of drowning, but in the icy water I should quickly freeze to death. There was no way the men on the scows could help me, but I knew the *Gilbert Knapp's* yawl could pick me up. In a few minutes, the yawl swinging at the stern of the *Gilbert Knapp* was manned and I was soon safely in the captain's cabin being given a hot toddy. The next problem was to get me ashore.

The captain was in a hurry. The storm would blow him on the beach if the ship did not get away while there was sea room. The sails were all set. It only remained to get rid of the several landlubbers and hoist anchor. I was dragged, being a little giddy after the toddy, to the stern. The yawl was alongside the stern, four members of the crew were at the oars, the mate was in the stern with a sculling oar to steer, and Father and two of our neighbors were in the bow. I was to drop, when the captain gave the word, into Father's arms, At a sharp 'Let go!' I dropped. The boat, however, had been heaved away by a wave, and down I went into Lake Michigan a second time. How many times I went under before the sailors could hold the yawl from the *Gilbert Knapp,* I do not know, but finally I came up between yawl and ship and was hauled in, more dead than alive. At once we were off, I making ballast in the bottom of the boat. In short order we were as close as the mate would go to shore, and I was dragged out and pulled to land. After that I only remember being piled on the bottom of a wagon box and covered with horse blankets, and I have a faint recollection of being helped to bed by Mother.

The next day I was in the corn field cutting corn.

Ours was not a notable lumber region, as there were no extensive forests of pine. Many of the younger men, however, worked in winter in the lumber camps in the pine woods to the south, so that the heroic figure of the old-time lumberjack was a familiar one about my boyhood home. We heard much about him in song and story. 'The men are coming home from the woods' was as accurate a herald of spring as wild geese honking northward, or as 'the sap's running in the sugar bush.'

Usually they came home in companies, a dozen or more burly, bearded, devil-may-care, swaggering fellows, with swash-buckling gait. Not a few of the young, unmarried men spent their wages in a week's drunk, and then hired out to some farmer for work in the fields until it was time for another winter in the woods. Most of the lumberjacks, however, were steady homesteaders who had sown their wild oats and now were saving their earnings.

In our neighborhood there were every winter two or three small camps of a dozen or twenty men, getting out railroad ties, telephone poles, paving blocks, or shingle bolts. Two or three times Father took a flyer in such a camp, though never to his profit, and I became quite familiar with swamping (cutting roads), cutting, skidding, loading, hauling, and all the rest of the complicated work of getting these products to market. I served occasionally as a 'tote boy' to take in supplies, or as a 'chore boy' around the camp.

Until I was a well-grown youth, I was not permitted to hang

around a lumber camp. Mother had as great fear of the insect parasites of man as any human ever had of the larger beasts of prey. Whenever I came home from a lumber camp, Mother made me change every garment and take a bath. Sometimes she washed my head with kerosene oil. Always she examined my head for nits. ('Nits' have a respectable tradition, for one reads in the renowned diary of one Pepys that his periwig was at a certain time alive with them.)

In the winter when I turned eighteen I came to know well an old-time lumber camp. The autumn before, I had become a schoolmaster, as is told in a later chapter, and the school at which I taught was near a large swamp. In the center of the swamp was an island of the finest pines that a lumberman ever set eyes on. The trunks were from two to three feet in diameter at the butts, with boles as clean and straight as the barrel of a cannon, without branches for sixty or seventy feet to a little tuft of green top. The pines had stood unmolested for centuries, isolated by the swamp.

In early winter, a timber cruiser spent a few weeks on the island, marking trees to cut, laying our roads, locating the best place for the bunkhouse and stables, and preparing places for skidways. A skidway is a rough log platform on which logs, in this case squared timbers, were to be placed for loading. The timbers were drawn to the skidway on a drawboat. The men who did this work were skidders; the several extra men at the skidways who loaded logs were loaders; those who cut the roads and kept them in condition for hauling were swampers.

First the pines had to be cut and the timbers squared. Snow was dug away from a tree to be cut so that the stumps were as low as possible. The men who brought these forest giants to the ground were choppers and sawyers, of whom the choppers were the giants of the camp, much muscle being needed to make a good ax-man. The best sawyers were the smaller men, quick and active. The timbers were squared by men with a broad ax and an adze.

To haul these long, heavy timbers required bobsleds, as sturdy as could be made, hitched tandem and hauled by two or three teams of the best horses that could be hired. The long journey of the logs began with a winter ride on bobsleds from the island to the head of our bay. In June they were boomed together in rafts for a voyage through Lakes Michigan, Huron, and Erie to Buffalo; thence by canal to Lake Ontario; through that lake and a canal into the St. Lawrence to Montreal. At Montreal the squared timbers were put aboard ship and carried to a much greater island than the little speck on which they had grown, eventually to find places in the hulls of British ships and taken to visit innumerable islands in the all-embracing oceans.

In early autumn, as I tramped morning and evening the several miles from home to my school, I passed swampers widening the road, straightening curves, and leveling ups and downs. When freezing weather came, sprinkling-sleds wetted down the road until it was covered with a thick sheath of ice. Teamsters had hauled in supplies and all was now ready for the winter's work.

On clear mornings I could smell the smoke from the camp on the island and hear the ringing axes and the crash of trees. Later when I came to board near my schoolhouse in the stormy days of winter, I could hear the men at work while I, a laggard in bed, awaited dawn. At my evening meal they were still at work—twelve hours a day, with an hour out for the noonday meal.

It was not cold and snow alone that stopped my walks: there was danger. As the teams came swinging down the road with their loads, I often had to get out into the deep snow a rod or two to escape instant death from the swerving timbers. True, I could hear them coming a mile away, bells clanging and jingling, the bobsleds squealing on the icy road like stuck pigs; but no sooner was I out of the way of one load than there was another. I was often late in getting to school.

The greatest delays were on the hills where snub lines had

to be used. When the jingling bells, the crunching, squealing sleds, and the loud-mouthed drivers told me a load was approaching a hill that was to be 'snubbed down,' I had to find a safe place and wait until the operation was over. I waited so often that I came to know every detail of 'snubbing down' a hill.

At the top of the hill, the load was brought to a standstill. One end of a heavy rope was attached to the rear beam of the sled, pulled tight, and coiled around a tree. Two men slackened the rope to let the load with its own momentum slide down the hill. The horses under the skilled hands of the driver guided its direction. If the rope parted, teams and driver might go to their deaths. A driver knew by the 'feel' of his load, as strands snapped, when the rope was breaking. A quick leap and the driver could save his own life, but only a coward would leap from his load. Quickly swinging his horses to right or left, he might swing the heavy load broadside to the road and check the downward plunge. Many times drivers thus saved their teams.

In my comings and goings to this camp I came to know a standard Michigan lumber camp of sixty years ago, and all that went on in it from the time the first man came until the last one left.

A long, low log structure furnished quarters for the men. It was roofed with unplaned hemlock, between the cracks of which snow and, happily, fresh air found entrance. A little light came in from small-paned windows. The long building was divided into three compartments, the largest for sleeping, a smeller one for eating, and a still smaller one for cooking. The eighty men slept in three tiers of narrow bunks spiked to the sidewalls. In one corner of the room was a barrel of water, tin basins, soap, towels, and a small mirror. In the center of the room was a huge box stove. Scattered about were benches for seats, card tables, bootjacks, and a sloping chair for barbering.

Shadows moved on the benches and capered over the floor from two smoky hanging lamps in each room.

On the tables, when they were not in use for card playing, lay two or three fiddles, an accordion, and an array of harmonicas—a lumberjack must have music. For reading matter there were ancient weekly papers, copies of the *Police Gazette*, and dime novels in plenty.

A long table flanked with benches ran through the center of the dining room, broken in the middle by an open space for a stove. The tables were ornamented with gaily colored oilcloths. On the rough walls were pictorial calendars, almanacs, and advertisements.

The food in a lumber camp was good. Fried salt pork heaped on plates, with pancakes and golden cane syrup, and dried apples, was the daily morning meal. For dinner and supper slices of salt pork covered pans of white baked beans. Pork, hams, and shoulders, sliced by the cook, varied with corned beef, were the only meats. Bread and butter, boiled potatoes, and cabbage or turnips were served also for dinner and supper. The desserts were cookies, doughnuts, and dried-apple pies. Three times a day there was coffee. Only on Sundays were the meals flavored with conversation.

Close to the men's camp a log stable sheltered forty teams of horses. In a snug little hut, John Billings, the scaler, had his office and living room. The scaler, a tall, thin-lipped Vermonter, represented the lumber king; standing at the skidways with his scaler's rule, he determined the number of board feet in each squared timber, discarding all that did not come up to requirements. The scaler in a lumber camp is less popular than an umpire in a ball game, and Billings deserved his good pay for the abuse heaped upon him.

Lumber camps have many odors. Besides the smells of food and tobacco, there are the pungent odors of wet horse blankets, dirty clothes, lines of drying socks and mittens, human bodies, liniments, oil lamps, tallow for hands and boots, oils for harnesses; the pitchy smell of pine; and the odors of patent medicines, of which woodsmen are as fond as old women.

The men were awakened before dawn by the cook's noisy call: 'All up! All up!' Work began with daylight. Men working within a mile of camp came in for the midday meal; those farther away took a cold luncheon or had a hot meal brought to them by a 'cookee.' Work ended at dusk, when men hurried to camp for a hot supper.

Supper over, the men whiled away an hour or two mending garments or playing cards or checkers. A few read; others listened to the fiddles and watched a jig, a hornpipe, a fling, a double shuffle, or a breakdown, dances popular in all lumber camps. Jokes, raillery, and repartee passed around freely. Some nodded over tedious twice-told tales, each to be capped by that of another romancer. Only a laureate was ever *asked* to tell a story; others began when they could break in. Visitors were hospitably welcomed. No minister ever went away empty-handed.

Work stopped on Sundays; on this day the week's working was done. Letters were written; some did a little reading. Occasionally a preacher came in and all listened with respect and interest. There was a good deal of noisy singing at these Sunday services from Gospel Hymns, which the preacher brought in book or sheet music, accompanied always with an accordion rather than a fiddle.

The camp had its aristocrats, to whom all made obeisance. They were the men who used best the ax, the saw, and the peavey; who had the surest eye on a load of logs; or persuaded their horses to pull the largest loads. Aristocrats came into being in the first month in camp among men who in all else lived in a pure democracy. Men quickly find their places in competitions involving muscle.

On our farm we began cutting firewood for sale in early December and kept at it, on and off, until sugar-making time about the first of April. Father would not bother to sell the wood in town, and for years we sold it to Steve Manchester for fifty cents a cord; Steve sold it here and there in town for a dollar a cord; he made two trips a day, hauling three cords each trip. In the middle of the forenoon, and again in the afternoon, we might expect to hear the jingle of Steve's sleigh bells and then his cheery hail.

Steve hauled wood on a two-horse bobsled on which rested the frame of a heavy wood rack. In this frame were tall sturdy white ash stakes against which the wood could be piled high. Steve would work only when the sledding was good; in a heavy snowfall or in a thaw we never saw him. He liked cold weather and came without fail when the thermometer was below zero, his moustache and whiskers bristling with icicles.

Cutting wood in winter was pleasant work. One enjoys going into the snow-covered forest in winter. The saplings, swayed by the wind, murmur to themselves, accompanied by the louder soughing, almost a moan, higher up in the thick foliage of the tall hemlocks, the giants in our forest. As we came in and out of the forest, we were sometimes startled by the whir of a partridge rising from a warm lair in the deep snow.

The commonest winter bird about our working places was the fluffy, black-capped chickadee, whose cheery call-note, *chick-a-dee, dee, dee, dee,* could be heard all the daylight hours. The most conspicuous and noisiest of the winter birds was the blue jay, and though he seemed to like human company, he scolded all day long with a harsh, discordant *jay, jay, jay.* Usually we could hear in early morning the two kinds of woodpeckers drumming and tattooing on a dead tree or a hollow stump. On a dark day or as night came on, we occasionally heard the bloodcurdling scream of the barred owl whose rather pleasant call note is *whoo-whoo, hoo-hoo-too-too.*

Always in the dead of winter, there were riflelike crackings of frozen trees. The man-made noises of our tools were pleasant to hear. The clack of the ax, the heavy thump of the maul striking the iron wedge, the whir of the biting saw, the jingle of sleigh bells and the noisy greetings of teamsters coming for a load of wood. The most welcome sound of all to hungry men was the whistle of the 11:45 train at the head of the bay.

It is remarkable how many smells trees give forth. In our forest of mingled hardwoods and hemlocks, with a rare fir, the wood of each species had a distinct smell as you cut through its bark. Very often a falling maple or beech, brought down branches of a hemlock and the pleasant, pungent aroma of the wood filled the air; a crushed fir had an even more tingling odor. The bronze-reddish twigs and wood of black and yellow birches gave off the delicious odor of wintergreen. The freshly cut chips and sawdust of maples have a sweetish fragrance foretelling sugar-making time. The reddish wood of the beech is redolent with a sour, musky odor.

The most remarkable scent in winter woods is that of large ants which we found occasionally in cutting into decayed trees, as we must sometimes do in preparing the couch for firewood timber. Often so great a space was honeycombed by a nest of ants that we might easily have collected a quart of them. When we cut through the nest many ants were crushed, giving off a strong smell of formic acid. Madame Pettier told Mother that trappers in the Hudson's Bay Company ate these ants as a cure for scurvy. The large, shiny-black 'hind-body' of this ant was filled with a clear liquid that tasted like a sour grape. At the first opportunity we saved a handful for Joutel. Sure enough, he ate them by the dozen, taking the whole ant in his mouth. Mother would have nothing to do with them, but my brother and I cut off the swollen hind-bodies and found them very refreshing for a mid-winter titbit.

XXIII

Parker's Store

SOON after we came to northern Michigan, W. E. Parker established a department store and became a merchant prince. The store was called by everyone 'Parker's,' but the owner was called by all, even children, 'W. E. Parker,' a name more familiar to most of us than George Washington. The goods in the store were said to have cost $10,000. Besides the store, W. E. Parker owned a sawmill on Devil's Pond, at the base of Harbor Point. One sold logs to the mill owner and took his pay in goods at the store, or in lumber.

W. E. Parker undertook to supply all in our land with food and raiment and the tools farmers needed in tilling the soil; wagons and sleighs plied between the store and lumber camps laden with flour, pork, sugar, salt, coffee, hardware and horse feeds; sailors and fishermen got their wares at Parker's. There was everything in the store that human beings needed from the cradle to the coffin. Parker's took in exchange all the products of the virgin forest, and everything that could be grown on new, fertile land. The several kinds of fish in Lake Michigan were salted and sold to this establishment; in pigeon years, the store bought the birds and sold them in distant cities, cleaned and packed in barrels. When Parker's failed, it seemed to us that universal bankruptcy was at hand.

The wooden edifice that housed the merchandise of this tycoon was of vast size. It was long and wide, two stories high, with a cellar beneath that put bowels in the inert earth. Nor was this enormous building all of Parker's busy mart. A great lean-to at the rear of the main building sheltered the heavy armament needed by farmers, lumbermen, and fishermen—the side arms were kept in the main building. In the lean-to were wagons, sleighs, plows, mowers, harrows, chains, anchors, coils of heavy rope, and coarse sea gear. All shone with the vivid colors of newness—the rainbow shades and deeper hues of freshly painted farm machinery as it tarried on the way from manufacturer to user. From morning to night the lean-to rang with the assembler's work and the testing blows of buyers.

At the rear of the lean-to was a long, low shed. Here were stored the inflammables: kerosene, turpentine, linseed oil, tar, brimstone (sulphur), paint, and charcoal, all in such quantities that there would have been a veritable inferno had a fire started.

Separated from this shed by a narrow road and a strip of beach was a long wharf on which were piles of corded wood for furnaces to make charcoal; hemlock bark for distant tanneries; lumber for Chicago and Milwaukee; and cedar shingles for many parts. Always there was a ship or two, under sail or steam, coming or going, loading or unloading. These forest products gave off woodsy smells: pungent hemlock bark, the soothing odor of pine lumber, redolent cedar shingles, and the rough smells of the hardwoods. On a summer day it was delightful to sit, bamboo pole in hand, in the shade of the piles, listening to the tall tales of sailors or woodsmen and occasionally catching one of the perch or bass that nibbled at the bait.

The front of Parker's store would not impress those accustomed to modern 'emporiums.' Parker's was elegant in its simplicity. It was an up-and-down wall rising from a rough board platform to a high false front that made the building look as though it had three full stories. On the towering super-wall was painted in huge letters 'Parker's Store.' After a year or two, the white paint began to peel off and the building became the silvery gray of a yellow-jacket nest.

Besides white customers, there were some Indians, old and young, drunk and sober, all hungry or wistful, standing or sitting on the front platform, now and then peering through the windows. The glass was so wavy that they couldn't see what was inside. Only when the wide doors opened could they get a good look at the wares. Then they would sniff odors so delectable the Indians were compensated in part for their long wait in the summer's heat or winter's cold. No one was welcome in Parker's unless he had money or credit—few Indians had either.

You entered the main room of the big store through doors as wide as those in Father Zorn's church, into a long customer's hall, flanked to right and left with counters on which were showcases of crystal-clear glass. Near the windows on the right side was an upright showcase to which a boy went first to feast his eyes on an assortment of guns and ammunition; next on this counter was a case of knives, razors, and scissors; then a case of musical instruments, among which mouth organs and Jew's-harps predominated; another counter held watches, rings, and other jewelry; still another, combs, brushes, and perfumes.

The wall shelves on this right-hand side contained drygoods, paper collars, hats, and suits of clothes for men; ribbons, hats, and bolts of dressgoods for women. In the rear was a counter, filled with cases and bins of footgear, and as I look back at it, there seemed to be greater variety than in modern stores. There was a large assortment in rubber, felts, and stockings, for outside wear. The fancies of farmers, lumbermen, fishermen, and townspeople were widely different for footwear. For dress occasions in the 1880's both men and women wore high patent-leather, kid, and calfskin shoes, which buttoned a little to the left of the middle with black, shiny, beadlike buttons, which required a buttonhook to fasten or unfasten them, an article that was always getting lost. Fashion for men's shoes also called

for congress gaiters, made in fine leathers with inserts of elastic
on both sides, thereby doing away with buttons.

Supplying women with their wares was a complicated business. There was much cloth of many kinds for dresses, but few
ready-made garments. Dresses and underwear for women were
made at home. Parker's specialized in gloves, bustles, blouses,
and black cotton stockings. Tight-fitting jerseys were the fashion
for young ladies stepping out socially. The style in jerseys had
been set by Lily Langtry, the Jersey Lily; sweaters were not
known.

On the left, as one entered, was a counter loaded with plug,
fine-cut, and smoking tobacco, with a long case filled with pipes
and boxes of cigars. There were many kinds of plug tobacco. It
came in bars of several plugs each, to be cut off at marked spaces
by a small heavy machine fastened to the counter. Fine-cut
chewing and smoking tobacco came in pails and was sold by the
pound; it was then just beginning to be put up in small bags.

Cigarettes were not sold in Parker's store. Preachers, teachers,
doctors, and parents all condemned their use. Smoking cigarettes was a vice of boys too young to smoke cigars. Saloons sold
them at ten cents for a packet of ten. I do not remember that
there were any brands, certainly none of the standard brands
were known then. Cubebs, a cigarette wrapper filled with a spice
from some tropical country, were frowned upon but not forbidden.

In common with every other boy, I bought and smoked
cigarettes. The tobacco was strong and vile, and I could well
believe, as I had often been told, that a cigarette was a 'coffin
nail,' and that if a boy smoked steadily, he would end up in an
insane asylum.

Every boy in our land made collections of odds and ends.
On every plug of tobacco was a bright metal tag, which gave
name to a brand: Indian Chief, Tomahawk, Spearhead, Andrew
Jackson, and so on, into scores of kinds. Cigars, then as now,

came in boxes, and each cigar had a fancy name. These metal tags, the boxes, and the bands were choice collector's items. Of equal value was the small picture of some celebrated woman that came with every packet of cigarettes. While in high school I became the possessor of a number of these, of which my favorites were Carmencita, a Spanish dancer, who danced a rollicking cancan to the tune of the popular Ta-rah-rah-boom-de-aye; Lily Langtry; Modjeska, the greatest living actress of those days; the beautiful bride of Grover Cleveland; Sarah Bernhardt; and Ellen Terry and Lillian Russell, both of whom were coming to the peak of their fame.

Next came caddies and canisters of tea, coffee, cloves, cinnamon, pepper, and allspice, with emblems showing the brands and the countries from which they came, names of perennial fascination to a boy. There were Hyson and Souchong teas from China; coffee from Mocha and Java; spices from Ceylon, Bengal, the Celebes, Borneo, and the piratical islands of the Pacific. What adventures had the producers of these wares had with ferocious animals? With slithering serpents? What fights with cannibals and pirates? What calms and hurricanes had they encountered?

Near by were the candies: peppermints, brown paper-wrapped lozenges, chocolates, cream candies, and gumdrops. Ranged on the shelves back of the counter in glass jars were a variety of stick candies and large round suckers of several flavors, gorgeously colored with stripes. In open wooden red pails were horehound, lemon, and mint drops, of which kind-hearted clerks gave youngsters a small handful when a considerable purchase of groceries had been made. There were no boxes of candies; a wooer gave his ladylove candy in a prosaic paper bag.

Among the jars of candies, there were several of licorice root and stick licorice. Licorice root came in straight brownish sticks, yellow inside, several inches long, while stick-licorice, an extract of the root, was as black as night, the same length as the pieces of root but much thicker. The two licorices and horehound candy were standard remedies in our household for sore throats. We children used the three confections as preventives as well as remedies.

Parker's did sell gum, but not much. There were several brands, of which I remember Spruce, Lady Washington, and Rubber gum. Spruce gum was a clarified product that might have come from our forests; Lady Washington was snow-white and crumbled within an hour after we began chewing; Rubber gum was the kind we now know, then just coming on the market. I do not remember that grown-ups in the 1870's and 1880's ever chewed gum and it was a pleasure (if it be a pleasure) forbidden well-bred youngsters.

On the coffee counter was a big red coffee grinder for those who wanted to buy ground coffee. My mother greatly preferred unroasted coffee, which she roasted and ground for herself. When we had threshers or other workers in numbers, she bought 'Arbuckle's,' roasted, ground, and put up in pound packages. The coffee grinder at Parker's was usually operated by Benny Ettawagesicks, an Indian interpreter and chore boy for the store. Benny was a friend of mine and passed me out many a bite of this or that edible, in return for which I lent a hand in grinding coffee.

Then came barrels of brown and granulated sugar from Cuba and Louisiana; boxes of prunes, raisins, figs, and dates from the Mediterranean countries; sometimes there were crates of oranges and lemons from Florida; here were boxes of smoked herring and codfish from the St. Lawrence, Nova Scotia, and Newfoundland. We could learn something about all the continents, islands, and countries of the seven seas, as well as the states of our own country, from the merchandise in Parker's store.

On one counter was a circular Cheddar cheese, two feet in diameter and a foot thick, a greater or lesser segment always missing. The cheese was covered with a heavy fine-wire screen to keep flies out. When the clerks cut a segment of cheese as a purchase, a small slice stuck to the knife and was handed over to a hungry boy. Near the cheese were slabs of dried beef, with a machine to cut thin slices, one slice of which went to the customer to eat at once.

In close proximity to cheese, dried beef, and smoked herring was a barrel of crackers. For 15 cents we could buy a sufficient quantity of these to make a good meal—strong fare for husky men and boys, cheaper than a meal at the Star Hotel, which cost a quarter.

This right-hand counter was divided in the middle by a raised dais, railed in and lighted from the back with a double window with larger panes than those in the front of the store. From here W. E. Parker governed his dominion, though because of his many outside interests, the great merchant was seldom on his throne. In his absence, Mr. Crandall, the book-keeper, reigned. Though a kindly man, well liked by all, his keen eyes could look you through and through when by chance he raised them from his doomsday book for unfortunate credi-tors. In our mixed population, no doubt it was necessary to eye every man who asked for credit as if it were certain that he was contemplating default of payment. (Is there in all time a moment so grim as that in which a man without a penny in his pocket must ask for credit?)

None except visiting salesmen from distant cities, the captains of ships, lumbermen, or other men of large business ever dared cross the threshold of this sanctum in Parker's.

Visiting salesmen were called 'drummers,' and most boys looked forward to being one someday. We all admired the cut of their clothes, their free and easy ways with old and young, their popularity with the young ladies of the town, and the smell of their cigars. They knew all about the outside world, and talked politics knowingly. In winter they sat around the great rectangular stove swapping yarns with townspeople.

To the rear of the dais were items in stock of little interest to a boy: furniture, carpets, wallpapers, hardware, and tinware. As these commodities were not in great demand by settlers, who brought such wares from former homes, there was seldom much business in this quarter of the store.

Many customers came for the goods found on one long shelf. Patent medicines in bottles and boxes were thickly set on this shelf. Pills and nauseous draughts are daily bread for backwoods people. Hostetter's Celebrated Stomach Bitters was a popular cure-all for all ailments of the alimentary canal. St. Jacob's Oil for rheumatism was next in point of popularity. Then came Warner's Safe Cure, and Pierce's Golden Medical Discovery, with several kinds of pills as runners-up. Lydia Pinkham's Vegetable Compound (Pink Pills) was another favorite. Castoria and paregoric were stand-bys with mothers who had babies.

In front of the shelf of medicines were almanacs. They came as a herald of the Christmas season and lay in piles on the counter where everyone might help himself. Before New Year's day every home had an almanac, and in our house of readers there were many, all of us finding that the jokes and witty sayings made good spice for our scant literature, pleasant to pick up on winter nights when boards creaked and snapped with cold, and wind and snow beat against window panes. Almanacs were more than simple reading matter. Without the almanac's calendar, some families would have lost track of days, dates, and months; through them pioneers kept track of sacred and secular festivals; from them people got a smattering of what then passed as science, of which simple astronomical facts were fairly accurate; some laid great store on the prophesies of weather to come. The most popular almanac in our house set forth the virtues of Hostetter's Celebrated Stomach Bitters. It hung year in and year out behind the stove on a loop of string in the upper backstrip corner. The wrappers were green and on the front cover was a picture of St. George, on a prancing charger baiting the dragon, into whose open mouth the saint was about to thrust his spear.

Through the winter a long box stove glowed red in Parker's. In transactions of the unofficial business of the community, in this part of the store such quantities of tobacco venom were ejected that the stove had to be guarded on its four sides by boxes of sawdust. Here I often sat, munching whatever my pocket could afford, listening to the wisdom of village sages. The talk was good: most often accounts of personal experiences of veterans of the Civil War; sometimes politics or religion; or village gossip and Rabelaisian stories; or prices and values of forest and water products. The conversations were forthright, homely, and honest. In the years that have followed I have spent many duller hours, listening to the sophistication of brilliant talkers and the hollow echoes of social discourse.

I knew all of the hangers-on in Parker's store and though they seemed commonplace enough then, many of the richly flavored figures round the big stove—discussing the affairs of our little world, while the winds stormed outside and the snow sifted silently down—come back to me now with all the relish and vividness of characters in a great novel.

In the cool, moist cellar of Parker's establishment were goods for lumber camps and the shipping trade. Here were barrels of pork and corned beef; of brown sugar; golden Orleans and blackstrap molasses; chests of tea and coffee; round boxes of cheese; boxes of dried apples, prunes, and raisins. The rafters were hung with smoked hams and slabs of bacon; there were crates of dried cod from the banks of Newfoundland, and mackerel from other depths of the Atlantic. Coming down the steps to the Stygian gloom of this crypt with its strange forms and odors, we never knew what might lurk in the darkness. The scurry of rats gave further zest to the adventure.

Above the store was a barnlike hall used for church services, Sunday school, lodge meetings, political gatherings, oyster suppers, and dances. The room was lighted by kerosene lamps fastened to the walls around the sides, above each of which smoke-blackened areas showed on the timbered ceiling. At one end was a raised platform, which served as a pulpit for preachers, a rostrum for speakers, and upon which the musicians sat as they fiddled for dances. It was a place of torture for children who were called upon to speak pieces at socials and school exercises.

Out of all these activities, the dances come to mind most clearly now, though they were events at which as a child I could be but an onlooker. The orchestra was composed of a first and second violin and a bass viol. The shining floor was thronged with dancers, swinging and whirling, jigging and bowing, to the old-time quadrilles, polkas, and schottisches; the waltz in our community was not quite respectable. Invariably dances ended with the Virginia reel. Never since have I seen dancers more liberal with hands and feet; never since have I heard music more exhilarating.

Just before W. E. Parker went out of business in the harbor village, he created a sensation by hiring Frank Franks, a Jew, to take charge of the store. Few of us had ever seen a Jew, and we all hurried to town to see what manner of man a Jew was. It turned out that everybody liked him. He selected and fitted suits to men and boys; chose hats and dresses for women of all ages; sold or gave perfumes to debutantes, cigars to men, furbelows to women, candy to children. Soon he called everyone in the whole region by his first name and knew everyone's affairs; soon he had the whole store shipshape. It was a pleasure to do business with Frank Franks; he talked and laughed with all his customers, meanwhile weighing coffee or tea, or measuring calico with lightning speed. He totaled your bill, counted your coins, and gave you back your change so quickly it took your breath away. Many boys came with written lists from mothers and sisters, which they could not read; Frank Franks read scrawls that could hardly be called writing. Everybody was sorry when, after a time, Frank Franks went back to Chicago and set up business for himself. For years when any of our people visited Chicago, Frank Franks was most hospitable and asked about his old friends.

XXIV

The Blacksmith Shop

SOMEONE from our farm had to go to the blacksmith shop nearly every week in the year. I, being of least worth on the land, usually went with the horses to one or the other of the two shops, and always they were thrilling and wonderful places. Sparks flying, the clang of heavy hammer on the anvil, a kicking or biting horse being shod, the labyrinth of old wheels, parts of plows, pieces of cultivators, odds and ends of metal, tires being set, bobsleds shod or mended, a hame repaired, or the thousand other jobs for farmers, lumbermen, sailors, or fishermen made a blacksmith shop a pleasant place to visit.

Besides, our two shops were so rushed with work that it was necessary for me to wait an hour, two hours, or a half a day, thus getting away from hard work on the farm. If the wait was to be short, I loitered about the shop, taking another look at the tools that lay about, or examining the diversified oddments that hung from pegs driven in the solid logs of the framework. When the wait was moderately long there was time to look about town or do a little fishing off Parker's dock. Often I had to have something to eat at the noon hour, and went to one of the grocery stores and spent 15 cents for cheese, smoked herring, dried beef, or bologna sausage and crackers. A leisurely day in the blacksmith shop in the midst of haying was a godsend.

The two blacksmiths were picturesque characters. George Lewis was the proprietor of the first shop established in the village and he had imported Barney Bester as a helper. After a few months, Barney went into business for himself. Both were Canadians. George was a Protestant and an ardent Orangeman; Barney was a Roman Catholic, a follower of the green—of course they couldn't work together. They were alike only in their grimy hands and faces and in their leather aprons. George was short and stout; Barney tall and slim. Of the two, I liked George the better, since Barney, of German descent, spoke with an accent I could hardly understand. George, also, was the better smith—a true artist.

The two shops had been one-room Indian houses substantially built of logs. Both had front and back doors, and small-paned windows, so covered with soot-filled cobwebs that not much light came through. Both had the same satisfying smell, an aroma made up of fungous rot in the logs of the building, the damp soil of the floor, pungent horse droppings, old leather, ammonia of scorched horse hoofs, the sweaty blacksmith, burning charcoal, wagon grease, horse liniments, and harness grease.

The anvils had a smooth upper surface upon which iron farm tools and shoes for horses were shaped. One end of the upper part of the anvil had a conical, horizontal projection, which George Lewis called 'the beak' and Barney Bester 'the horn'; on this the curved pieces of iron were hammered out. On the other end of the anvil were holes of several sizes in which different kinds of cutters, dies, and shaping-tools were inserted. The smiths called these accessories 'swages'; holes for swages on occasions served as cannons. On the Fourth of July the anvils were taken to an open place and at dawn the holes were loaded with powder, stoppered with cloth or sod, and a cannonading lasting an hour ushered in a long day of celebration.

The only time I ever saw these anvils loaded and fired was in 1884 when Grover Cleveland was elected President. Father, my brother, and I were in the depot all night, and when in early morning it was certain that Cleveland was elected, the Democrats of the town joyously brought forth the anvils to celebrate. For an hour we kept the cannons roaring. The boys in the happy throng had to gather material to stopper down the powder. We used handkerchiefs, the tails of our shirts, wet newspapers, and pieces of sod to make ramming material. It was a wonder that none of us was killed, as sometimes happened in firing anvils.

Charcoal was burned in the forges, which were substantially supported by stone foundations. Over each forge there was a big leather bellows with heavy wooden handles. The bellows, when pumped, forced a noisy rush of air on the flaming charcoal, quickly changing iron from black to cherry red and on to white heat. The blacksmiths found it easy to persuade boys to pump. In my own case, before my teens I groaned in misery at the thought of turning the grindstone, but in the magical shrine of a blacksmith shop, even on the hottest day of summer, I would pump and pump until every stitch of clothing was wringing wet.

In a row around the forge were hammers, tongs, and huge shears. On one side of the forge was a tub half filled with water. Opposite this working end of the shop were heaps of discarded iron articles. Here were worn-out wheels, parts of plows, cultivators, and harrows—odds and ends of every conceivable thing made of iron. In one corner was a pile of old horseshoes saved for a leisure moment when the blacksmith could make them over, after which they were hung in shining array on the walls of the shop. These shoes were of sizes and weights for dray horses, draft horses, and dainty light wear for a buggy horse.

The piles of old iron implements and broken bits to me represented utter confusion, but George and Barney could put their hands on any piece wanted, seemingly knowing exactly where a bit of iron discarded months before had been thrown.

They never sold or threw away scrap iron; in their shops conservation was practiced.

On one side of the back door was a strong, well-fastened ring to which animals to be shod were tied. The most fascinating thing a boy could see in a blacksmith shop was a horse being shod. A colt having his first shoes or a vicious horse was exciting, no matter how often it was seen. To the impassive blacksmith any horse to be shod was just another horse.

He dropped the shoe on the bed of charcoal in the forge, started the bellows with one hand, and poked the coals around the shoe with the other. When the shoe was red-hot approaching white, he snatched it out with his tongs, laid it on the anvil, and quickly hammered it into shape, myriads of sparks flying 'like chaff from the threshing floor.' The shoe was then dropped in the tub of water, from which a cloud of steam rolled to the roof. While it was cooling, he lifted the leg of the horse, deftly pared the hoof, and then fitted the shoe, still so hot that the shop was filled with the acrid smell of ammonia from the scorched hoof. With sure strokes the nails were driven home and clinched. It only remained to smooth the edges with a coarse rasp.

Not all horses permitted the smith to lift their feet without objection. Blacksmith shops were provided with a hoist from above, whereby a horse was encircled with a broad band around his middle and lifted from the floor. A horse so 'swung' was helpless. Sometimes one leg was hobbled; a horse could not stand on three feet and kick. A biter had his mouth drawn tightly to the ring at his head and held with a heavy halter. Jack, one of our mules, was the meanest domestic animal that ever lived. Always, Jack had to be swung. Jenny, Jack's mate, was quieter, but was so unreliable that she too was always hung up. Whenever we drove this team past a blacksmith's shop, as the noise and smell of the shop came to their ears and nostrils they began to prance and act up generally.

The blacksmiths were busy in winter as well as in summer.

Sleighs of all descriptions had to be 'shod'; chains were in constant need of repair; cant hooks and peaveys were made and re-sharpened; horses unshod in summer must wear shoes in winter. The commonest work was changing calks on horseshoes. A calk on a horseshoe is a sharp-pointed piece of the shoe projecting downward. When roads are icy, the calks must be sharp; dull for work in deep snow. Many good horses were ruined by working in deep snow with sharp calks; if the hind hoof wearing a sharp-calked shoe overlapped and struck the front leg, or if a floundering horse struck the leg of a teammate, a disabling wound might be made.

The most satisfying time to visit the blacksmith's shop was mid-winter, when sparks were flying in all directions and the fire in the hearth heated the shop while snow was falling outside and an Arctic gale blowing.

It is sad to have to record that neither George Lewis nor Barney Bester made money. In the rush and confusion of their sooty shops, neither kept accounts, and their customers' memories were short, so that much of the work these smiths did was never paid for. In old age, each eked out a poor living on a small farm.

XXV

A Little Learning

I DO not remember who taught me to read. My three half-sisters were much older than I, all schoolteachers. I have vague recollections of my being carried to my eldest sister's school when I was little more than a babe in arms by my two next oldest sisters, both of whom were preparing to teach. No doubt these two tyros tried their 'prentice hands on me and early taught me to read; at any rate, my earliest recollections are embellished by schools and books. Mother recorded my progress in reading by telling all and sundry that her youngest son had read the Bible from cover to cover before he was eight years old.

In my first years, I was much in the care of my half-sisters, who, of course, spoiled me and made me an insufferable little prig. My brother, two years older, very robust, and no farther along in his reading than I (he had not 'read the Bible through') was a self-appointed monitor to see that I did not become too conscious of my mental and spiritual attainments. On one occasion, when Mother was bragging of my having read the Bible through at such an early age, one of the women to whom she was talking remarked: 'That boy is too smart; he'll never grow up.'

This was too much for my brother, and I had to take a good trouncing at his hands.

My first school in northern Michigan has been described in

a previous chapter. After we had spent a few years in this town school, our seat of learning was of necessity changed to a country school near our farm. The school and the building were at that time new. No one could mistake the building for anything but a schoolhouse. It was a small, boxlike structure with one door and four pairs of windows. Its only ornament, outside or inside, was a belfry in which no bell ever hung in my day. Yet the building with its simple lines was attractive. (There was not money enough in our school district to build an ugly school-house.)

In summer, you saw through the open door and windows a pulpitlike desk at the front; in the rear, a long bench loaded with dinner pails; at the sides, pupils' desks and seats, girls and boys on separate sides; in the center, a large acorn stove. In school hours, you might see on a front bench a row of pupils reciting, or a platoon of standing spellers, whose high-pitched voices, a wearisome sing-song, poured from doors and windows to compete with the notes of summer songsters, or furnish amusement to ribald blue jays and chipmunks, which, in the freedom of their surrounding woods, chattered their derision at the unhappy prisoners in the schoolhouse.

In winter, the interior would be changed only to show a red-hot stove and a half-cord pile of wood. Instead of the noiseless tread of bare feet, you would hear the tap, tap, of heavy boots and shoes on feet so woefully uncomfortable with chilblains that children were allowed to take off shoes and stockings to relieve the unendurable pain and itching. The thin framework of the schoolhouse in winter let in piercing draughts of sub-zero cold, which the stove could never vanquish. Happily the frosted windows shut out the sight of falling snow, which sifted down continuously, making the clearing outside spotless as ermine, a calm and tranquil world, but dreary, oh, so dreary, when one had months of it.

In winter we schoolchildren came wading through the half-broken roads out of the deep woods into the brighter light of the clearing. Our steps quickened and our faces brightened as we came in sight of the schoolhouse with its blue smoke curling peacefully up from the chimney. The head of each youngster was bundled and mufflered, and before each face was a thin mist of breath congealed in tiny icy particles by the bitter cold. In the schoolroom all were stamping, sneezing, coughing, blowing chilled fingers, wiping running noses. Older sisters and brothers comforted the smaller ones, who were crying over frost-nipped extremities. The cares and furrows of maturity showed on the faces of older children as they looked after the young in their charge.

In mid-morning and again in mid-afternoon we had a recess of fifteen minutes and an hour at noon, when, with whoop and hurrah, we tumbled out to play in mimic warfare with snow-balls, 'Fox-and-Geese,' 'Prisoner's Base,' 'Wait till the Black Man Comes,' or 'I Spy,' much like what the youngsters these days call 'Hide and Seek.' When there was no snow on the ground boys liked best 'Two-Old-Cat,' 'Duck-on-the-Rock,' and 'Anti-Anti-I-Over.' The teacher called pupils in from recesses by ringing a heavy hand bell, and was importuned by the six-year-olds: 'Teacher! Let me ring it!'

The noon hour made a pleasant break in the school day. Our dinner pail, filled with food for three, was especially made with a tight-fitting top. Its contents were supposed to be a surprise, but at recess we all made explorations. Usually there were sandwiches, hard-boiled eggs, cold meat, dried-apple pie, and cookies.

My sister took great pride in 'setting the table.' A cloth was spread on a desk and the food divided in three neat piles. My sister made her brothers 'mind their table manners.' We were very proud of our good school dinners and often divided them with the children of families who had little.

In mid-winter, when storms raged outside, we played games indoors. The small children stuck pretty closely to 'Pussy Wants a Corner,' but the oldsters found most entertainment in kissing games. There was no billing and cooing; the pleasure was rather in the singing and movement. 'London Bridge is Falling Down,' 'King William was King James' Son,' 'Post Office,' and 'Drop the Handkerchief' were fun without the touch of lips. 'Button-Button, Who's got the Button' entailed forfeits, the redemption of which were as ludicrous as childish minds could make them.

At four o'clock, when the sun, far to the south, had completed its brief sojourn, we took our way homeward, our playground soon to be wrapped in that frozen splendor that night unrolls in forest lands of snow.

The pleasantest day of the week in our backwoods school was Friday, when in the afternoon we 'spelled down,' had 'debates,' or 'spoke pieces.' Along with a good deal of nonsense, we recited the literary gems from dime books called 'speakers' and various school readers: 'Thanatopsis,' 'Casabianca,' 'John Gilpin,' and parts of 'Snow-Bound,' 'Enoch Arden,' and 'The Rime of the Ancient Mariner.' My taste ran to the lachrymose; and I spoke with much pathos parts of 'Enoch Arden,' 'Curfew Must Not Ring Tonight,' and 'The Dead Child's Ford.' My brother took to oratory, and thundered out every year in our school and at exercises in other schools 'The Drunkard's Daughter,' and John B. Gough's 'Power of Habit.' He 'rendered' these two favorites with so much fire and movement that his voice filled the schoolroom and echoed in the woods outside. He used many gestures, and was very fond of the last verse in 'The Drunkard's Daughter,' which ran:

> Tell me I *hate* the bowl;
>   Hate is a feeble word;
> I *loathe, abhor,* my very soul
>   *With strong disgust is stirred*
> Whene'er I see, or hear, or tell,
>   *Of* the DARK BEVERAGE OF HELL.

The last lines in the 'Power of Habit' were even more dramatic: (Gough's oration, as all old-timers know, is a comparison of habit with Niagara Falls):

'Young Men, Ahoy!
What is it?'
Beware! Beware! The rapids are below you!
Now you see the water foaming all around. See how fast you pass that point! Up with the helm! Now turn! Pull hard! Quick, quick. Quick! Pull for your lives! Pull till the blood starts from your nostrils, and the veins stand like whip-cord upon your brow! Set the mast in the socket! Hoist the sail! Ah! ah! it is too late! Shrieking, howling, blaspheming; over they go.
Thousands go over the rapids of intemperance every year, through the *power of habit*, crying all the while, *'When I find out that it is injuring me, I will give it up!'*

Some schools held an exhibition on the last day of school, but in all the district schools I attended or taught we spoke pieces in the afternoon of the day school was over and hurried through, pleased to begin the long summer vacation. To not a few boys and girls who had had or were approaching their eighteenth birthday it was the end of an epoch in their lives. The younger children waited with eagerness the awarding of prizes as the last part of the day's exercises and then whooped out with the cry: 'School is over!'

To the teacher, too, it was often the last day of school or a change to another district the next autumn, for which child and master might rejoice or feel sorry.

Who among moderns knows what a 'headmark' is? Let me explain: just before noon and again before school was out at four, there was a spelling class for advanced pupils who spelled orally, standing in a platoon of twenty or more. He who missed a word was required to give up his place to the one lower down in the rank who spelled it correctly. When the head of the class

missed, he had to go to the foot and seek again to come to the
head. Each pupil who attained the head was given a headmark
for each class. He who had the most headmarks at the end of
a term was given a prize, always a book. I still have three prizes
so won: *The Works of Robert Burns*, Moore's *Irish Melodies*,
and Whittier's *Songs of Three Centuries*.

Sometimes we debated. I was not much of a debater, as I was
always so frightened that my voice trembled and my knees
shook. One debate still stands out in my memory. The subject
was: 'Resolved that Good is Overcoming Evil.'

Father undertook to coach his sons, with me on the affirmative, my brother on the negative side. My chief argument was
that no two opposing forces are equal, and in this case good was
stronger than evil; therefore, given time, evil would disappear
and good would fill the hearts of all. My team presented its
arguments with much oratory and I was sure that we should
win, but to my great disappointment the judge awarded victory
to the negative, adding the gratuitous opinion that there always
had been and always would be the same proportion of good and
evil in the world. The judge was a minister visiting the school
that day. Father roared when my brother said the affirmative
might have won had I not, when I had uttered my trump
argument, added, with a great show of satisfaction, that when
good did drive evil out of the world, there would be no need
of churches, ministers, and Sunday schools.

The day on which this debate took place is one of the lesser
landmarks of my boyhood. It was the Friday before the Tuesday
of the election in which Garfield defeated Hancock. Four years
before, in 1876, Hayes had defeated Tilden, at least it was
finally so decided, although every Democrat in the land believed
that Tilden had been elected. Father, who did not go to the
Civil War, was ready to shoulder a rifle and go to Washington
to seat Tilden. We children were quite as excited as our parent;
and on 4 March 1877, when Hayes was inaugurated, my brother
wrote a poem:

Old Hayes, by Tilden he was beat,
But Hayes, the thief, stole Tilden's seat.

On the fourth day of March,
All stiffened up with starch,
Old Hayes took his seat according.

In 1880, Father was sure the people of the United States would repudiate the Republican party for this theft; surely Hancock, the Democrat, would be elected. As everybody knows, Garfield went to Washington.

Only once did I ever win a debate when pitted against my argumentative brother. The question was: 'Resolved that the Pen is Mightier than the Sword.' As usual, I was on the affirmative side, and my brother, who could never chop off a chicken's head, had no heart for the negative.

In our district there were two terms in the school year, a summer term of three months and a winter term of four. Women teachers were the rule for the summer session, men for the winter. After moving from town to the farm I had but two summers in school; at ten years I was called upon to work in the field with the men. So far as my education is concerned, this did not matter, for schooling under women then did not amount to much. The women taught until they married, teaching being the only means at that time whereby they could earn money. Not so with the men; they were professional teachers and did their work well. In our country school I had two men teachers: Mr. Cox for three winters, Mr. Richardson for two.

When Mr. Cox came to take charge of our school, he was looked upon as a great find. He had several qualifications to commend him. Chief of these was that he had attended a normal school, and he had had experience in schools in the outside world. A third qualification was that he taught music as well as the three R's; for, strange as it may seem, our woodsmen-farmers had high regard for singing. Still further, he was married and had a house, so that there was no trouble about a boarding place. Also, Mr. Cox was very strong in arithmetic, especially mental arithmetic, being 'a lightning calculator.' In our parts a learned man was not learned unless he was good at 'ciphering' on paper and at calculating orally.

Mr. Cox was as handsome a man as one could wish to see. He was big, broad-shouldered, with arm and leg muscles so well developed that every boy wished he might some day have the like. He had a fine head, shingled with black, curly hair; a ruddy face, a good mouth, and perfect teeth. This admirable body he favored with very good clothes when he had money, which was not always the case, for there were not many schools at which he could or would teach.

My parents liked Mr. Cox because he was a good Presbyterian and looked after our spiritual as well as our mental needs. He was a hidebound Calvinist, would accord no liberty of thought for those not of his faith, and was very hard on Mr. Parmalee, turned Seventh Day Adventist, and Father Zorn, the Roman Catholic priest, both of whom will be described in other chapters.

I was not a favorite with the excellent Mr. Cox. I was born wholly tone deaf in music and was also a half-wit in mathematics. How could one hope to find favor in the eyes of a music teacher and a lightning calculator? Neither was I a good penman, and Mr. Cox wrote a copybook hand. That I was a prize-taker in spelling and had some talent in reading, grammar, geography, and history counted as nought with Mr. Cox. What misery I suffered in his mental arithmetic class! He called upon me to make quick calculations about sales of farm and forest products; to take journeys hither and yon and compute the miles, and to make a thousand similar calculations that he called 'practical problems.' I was slow, seldom accurate, sometimes heedless, sometimes sullen. Mr. Cox's canny eyes, never humorous, sometimes terrible in sternness, were always upon me. He despised trying to teach me as much as I hated being taught by him.

Mr. Cox was successful in keeping up a spirit of competition among his pupils, and kept us alert and industrious. He saw to it that taking the prize for the most headmarks in spelling, solving all the problems in Ray's *Higher Arithmetic*, standing up longest in spelling school, or winning a debate gave a boy fame in our countryside. Mr. Cox had also an admirable sense of independence and assurance, which he imparted to his pupils, so that, while we were but children intellectually, yet in these qualities and in the desire to get on in the world, we became under his tutelage remarkably mature.

The teachers before Mr. Cox had much trouble with textbooks. Readers, spellers, arithmetics were of several kinds. Mr. Cox insisted on one standard text for each class. He wanted to make another change, but only succeeded temporarily. Work that modern school children do with paper and pencil, in pioneer schools was done with slates and slate pencils. The work on a slate was erased with the fingers wet with spittle, a very unsightly and insanitary procedure. Mr. Cox made us buy penny sponges, which, wet with water, made acceptable erasers.

Mr. Richardson followed Mr. Cox. The two were very unlike as men and as teachers. Mr. Richardson was small and so dark in complexion, hair, and moustache that we called him 'the Spaniard.' His manners, features, and clothes were all good, so that one might be sure that he was a gentleman. He never whipped, was mild, easy-going, and very absent-minded. Mr. Richardson was studying to become a Seventh Day Adventist preacher, and spent so much time over his religious books that we had long recesses and few working hours.

He opened school each morning with a chapter from the Bible and a long prayer; all knew he was practicing for his vocation. The school board gave Mr. Richardson orders not to mention his religion, but somehow we came to know that he thought Christ's second coming was due, and Doomsday was at hand, and that he kept Saturday for Sunday. There was something more to think about than when our Presbyterian preacher was holding forth with his 'Thou shalt nots.'

All considered, Mr. Cox was the better teacher, but I fared better under Mr. Richardson. He liked arithmetic, music, and writing as little as did I. He let us study much as we pleased, but I, having by this time reached that estate in a district school called 'a big boy,' kept at my books. In my last winter under Mr. Richardson, I became very proud of my ability to parse words and to resolve sentences into their grammatical parts by means of diagrams on the blackboard and liked to think of myself as a 'lightning parser.'

There is much to be said in praise of these old schoolmasters. They were masters of their schools, not stifled servants of school boards. Their methods of teaching were simple and direct without experimental fluctuations; they did not glorify teaching methods; they impressed their personalities on their pupils to a remarkable degree. There were so few aids in our barren schoolhouse that it might truthfully be said that all teaching equipment was carried in the heads of the masters. Nonetheless, they got what they knew into the heads of their pupils.

Every winter there were three big days in the district schools in our land. Wide-awake schools in winter held a spelling school (similar to the spelling bee), gave an 'exhibition,' and all celebrated St. Valentine's Day. Spelling schools and exhibitions were always held at night. St. Valentine's Day was an affair for individual schools, carried on in school hours, though sometimes it required the aid of the postmaster to exchange messages between the beaux and belles of neighboring schools.

Spelling schools followed the accepted pattern of those in all the little red schoolhouses in our broad land for generations down to the advent of graded schools and modern methods of education. The best spellers in two opposing schools stood up, each on his own side of the schoolroom. A teacher from a neighboring school pronounced the words. When a word was misspelled the speller must take his seat. The contest was over when all the spellers on one of the sides were seated. Sometimes there might be two or even three 'spell-downs.' Often parents 'stood up' with the school spellers. Father was a good speller and when he could be persuaded to go and 'stand up' with our school he was considered a real asset.

It was a valuable experience. Some spellers could spell every word in any of the several spelling books then in print, and the pronouncer had to take to the dictionary.

The exhibitions, also, followed the pattern of most of the country schools in America in the last century. The exercises began with vocal music, followed with declamations by timid little boys and girls whose fond mothers wanted to show them off. Older pupils then 'spoke pieces,' with vocal music interspersed. Nearly always there was a 'play' on a raised platform with curtains that could be drawn. Everyone in the neighborhood loaned a kerosene lamp to light the schoolroom. After the play, the real elocutionists of the neighborhood had their turn, most of whom we had all heard many times. A Mr. Leatherman, an ex-schoolteacher, with a wife whose tongue was as curt and shrewd as Xanthippe's, often spoke 'Xanthippe Was a Scold,' making the schoolroom ring in the best style of country elocutionists. A Mrs. Johnson, another one-time schoolteacher, was always called on for 'The Raven' and for an encore, 'The Bells.'

My brother was under great nervous tension at these exhibitions. He knew that toward the end the teacher would announce: 'Wilbur Olin Hedrick will now render John B. Gough's "Power of Habit." '

His effort was followed by thunderous applause and he was called upon for one and sometimes two encores, which he varied at every exhibition to surprise and please his audience.

We liked these spelling schools and exhibitions best when the land was deep in snow. The means of transportation were bobsleds for the old and very young and a horse and cutter for older boys and girls. Great fun it was to cuddle down under buffalo robes in straw-lined bobsled boxes; and wrap up, never more than two, under a buffalo robe in a cutter. Sleigh bells jingled all the way.

The fourteenth of February was a red-letter day in every school in our parts. On this day we fondly commemorated St. Valentine, but whether his birth, his death, or deeds of goodness, none of us knew, nor for that matter none knew who St. Valentine was. Nevertheless, we kept his memory as green as if he had been of our time and country and not a vague figure of centuries ago in ancient Rome.

In our school we celebrated the day by sending valentines. The younger children sent gaily colored penny thrillers, humorous, ironical, or tender, but the big boys and girls chose very elaborate works of art in paper lace, perfumed and bearing tender poetical messages. As a sixteen-year-old, I spent a whole Saturday afternoon looking through the 'large and elegant assortment' of valentines in the local drug store, for a valentine to send to the young lady who had taught during the summer term in our school and gone in the autumn to a normal school. The search ended in my selection of a heart-shaped box at least a foot in diameter, two inches thick, in which was a large lace valentine, very neat and dainty, studded with hearts, and with forget-me-nots around an affectionate, robust message, such as I conceived the young lady of my dreams would find fitting.

When St. Valentine's Day came in Leap Year, the sending of valentines continued intermittently until the extra day in February. All the girls in school exercised with a vim their right to do the wooing. Anonymous proposals were received by every well-favored boy in school. In our parts, of a certainty, 'man was the pursued' in these fifteen days in Leap Year.

At about this time of the year all of us who could read and write got out our autograph albums to make sure that everyone for miles around had inscribed a sentiment on a special page. Since the book was open to inspection of all, these inscriptions were never tender sentiments but usually a few lines of original poetry or a quotation. Emerson was by far the most popular author quoted.

There was great elation in the educational centers of our land when, in my fifteenth year, it was announced that there was to be a high school in our harbor town. My brother and I immediately set our hearts on going to this new seat of learning. At first there were difficulties. The poor, sandy land of our farm hardly sufficed to support our little family, and to take two grown boys from the winter's work in the woods would be a heavy drain on our resources. Besides, there would have to be books and better clothes. How could we stand the cost of four years of high school?

The matter of time we solved by studying through the summer and then boldly telling the superintendent (self-assurance outweighing education) that we were qualified to enter the junior class, thus cutting four to two years. Getting to school was a problem. It was three miles to town, and a horse could not be spared at any time of the year for transportation. Of course we must walk, not so difficult in spring and autumn, but a hard pull in winter when the snow was deep and the temperature often 20° below zero. Besides, there were our chores to be done morning and evening.

Then came the problem of extra money for books and clothes, which we knew we ourselves must somehow earn. Here Father came to the rescue. He gave us as many trees in our woods as we could cut into stovewood. A cord could be sold on the ground for fifty cents. Thus we were assured of money. On Saturdays we could cut four cords of wood.

As so often happens, much money made us more and more avaricious; we had to have money in plenty. Autumn, winter, and spring, when avarice gripped us, we set out two or three nights a week, after the evening meal, to cut wood. A cord was our stint, nothing less would satisfy. From seven until ten we made the saw hum, the ax ring. Boys of our age that could not cut, split, and pile in three hours a cord of eighteen-inch wood were of small account. The work was difficult only in the gales and zero weather of winter, when, after having battled with the weather to and from school, we again faced it to cut a cord of wood.

In winter, besides shouldering a crosscut saw and an ax, we had also to carry a shovel to dig our way about in the deep snow. On dark nights we had to take a lantern. We liked the work best on nights when the moon shone, making the snow-covered forest as light as day. Rarely the Aurora brightened the sky, filling the northern heavens from east to west with rose, red, crimson, and blue, under which the snow sparkled as if covered with diamond dust. Often the mercury went below zero and we had to be careful not to freeze nose and ears; sometimes a gale blew; most often, snow, white and silent, dropped endlessly down.

I must not make the work seem harder than it was. To cut a cord of wood did not require a whit more effort than it does to play an evening game of basketball. The fight against a gale of wind was so fine a combat that we worked in a furious ecstasy. Cold and rough weather was an exhilaration quite comparable in a bad night to a stiff climb on a high mountain. Pulling a saw and swinging an ax hardened muscles so that we had a fine feeling of fitness. After a tree was felled, the limbs lopped, and the wood piled in a neat tier eight feet long, four feet high, we went home glowing with the feeling that in a day or two another half dollar would be jingling in our pockets. We liked the life. A night in the woods was like a deep drink of a potent liquor, a drink that made the blood dance in our veins, our bodies tingle from head to toes; a keen edge of pleasure came from defying the weather. I do not remember other hours when it was such a joy to be alive; other days, when, if things had gone well at school as well as in the woods, one could say at night with greater gusto: 'This has been a day of magnificent accomplishment!'

We found the principal of the high school a man of warm personality, with a genius for making the most out of the raw material that came to his hands. He was not sufficiently trained to be a really good educator, but he gave us many fine thoughts and strengthened the ambitions of all who had a grain or two at the start. I am afraid he let us off in our work pretty easily. Had he been relentless in examinations, my brother and I should never have got into high school, and would have been dropped long before the end of the first year.

Ours was the first class in the new high school. There were eight of us, four girls and four boys, an odd lot of fish, such as is usually to be found in an American high school. At the time we rated ourselves high, and we did turn out well; all became schoolteachers; all but one went to college; all came to something worth-while in after life.

No one would believe that a person now living, born and bred in civilization, could come to his fifteenth year without having seen or heard a piano. Yet, not until I went to high school and began to know the families of my schoolmates had I ever seen any other musical instruments than organs, accordions, and fiddles, nor had I heard music other than sacred music, the lively tunes of country dances, and the scraping of fiddles by our hired men. When I began high school, there were two pianos in the harbor village.

Soon, to our unspeakable joy, my brother and I were invited to a musicale, and I knew that I should hear a piano and real singing. I can still remember some of the pieces on the piano and some of the songs of that evening more than sixty years ago. Who would not remember 'The Blue Danube' and Chopin's 'Funeral March'? How could I forget 'The Night Hath a Thousand Eyes' and ' 'Tis the Last Rose'?

As my brother and I walked home in the cold, blustering

night after the musicale (what a lovely word 'musicale' seemed!) our hearts danced with joy. Could there be anywhere on earth better music, more admirable people, refreshments more delectable? Truly, the world was treating us well.

When the Northwest Territory was divided into named territories, far-sighted statesmen decreed that certain lands in every township be set aside to be sold for educational purposes. A wise administration provided that a part of the money be spent to equip each township in the territories with a library. In due course, several yards of book-laden shelves came to each of the townships in the Land of the Crooked Tree. These libraries were second only to schools and churches in furbishing the minds of pioneer families.

The law at the time put these libraries in the hands of town clerks. This was not a good arrangement, because the libraries moved about as election followed election, and some clerks discouraged readers. In our own township, the town library was for several years in Thompson's drugstore, the proprietor of which stood over me, looking me through and through until I took a book—often, in my hurry, one that I did not want. The place was to me a cemetery for books where one read titles as he would epitaphs on tombstones. A library where patrons cannot browse is no library.

An adjoining township had a real library, where the town clerk, elected year after year, let a boy browse at will in what seemed a world of books. Here you could take as many books as you wanted to and keep them as long as you wanted them. The books, when I first saw them, perhaps four hundred, were new, and the odors of leather, cloth, and ink were intermingled with the odor of the white pine out of which the bookcases were made. Not a book had a dog-eared leaf, not a broken hinge, or a scuffed back, a chipped spine, or a loose signature, not even the mark of a soiled thumb. A dealer in rare books would have rated every one of them as 'immaculate.'

The librarian was prouder of his cases than of the books they contained. He had selected clear white pine and had planed and grooved shelves and cases to a perfect fit. He preferred to be known rather by his carpenter's chips than by his books. The cases must have made an impression on me, for the clean smell of white pine often takes me back to the long-ago and far-away backwoods library that helped so much to let me into the world of books.

The town-clerk librarian kept a boardinghouse for the workers in a near-by sawmill. Any one of the mill hands might have passed pleasant hours with the books, but I never saw one of them with a book in his hand. The bookcases stood near the door between the living room and the dining room, and, as the men passed in and out, they instinctively shied at the books as if to touch them would have been a desecration—they would as soon have handled mummies of authors. In my eighteenth year, as a schoolmaster, I boarded in this house with the library, and came to know the mill men well. I think they had little respect for me as a teacher, and twitted me at every meal on my ignorance in woodcrafts, but my familiarity with books filled them with awe and respect.

Considering those who were expected to read them, a more curious collection of books could hardly have been sent into our wilderness. Whether they had been brought together by chance, were publishers' remainders, or had been selected by some state authority who had taste in reading, I do not know. As I recall the titles, it is certain that the books were selected for the exclusive use of booklovers. My guess is that some be-spectacled, bookloving scholar in the State Library (possibly a bluestocking) had made the selection.

Here are some of the books that were on the shelves of this backwoods township library: volumes of Scott, Dickens, and Thackeray; *Jane Eyre*, in green cloth covers and small type; Burns and Thomas Moore, each in a single volume, very hard to read because of the fine print; several volumes of Hawthorne,

including *The Scarlet Letter,* which I read in my fourteenth
year; a splendid set of Parkman in dark red (first editions all);
there were both *Peru* and *Mexico* by Prescott, in dark red;
Lavengro, Romany Rye, and *The Bible in Spain,* which gave
me undying love for George Borrow; Shakespeare in three
volumes; *Don Quixote; The Confessions of an English Opium
Eater;* a volume of Lamartine; Irving's *History of New York
by Diedrich Knickerbocker;* and odds and ends of the New
England school, mostly poetry, but several Emersons and at
least one Thoreau, *Walden;* but no Melvilles. (What a joy it
would have been to have read while still a boy *Moby Dick,
Omoo,* and *Typee!*) Out of this library I got most of Cooper,
whose every book I read with rapture.

The partial enumeration of these books at my command may
suggest that I had a high-brow literary taste in my childhood.
Far from it. A printed page was to me a printed page. I read
avidly dime novels, the love stories of Mary J. Holmes,
E. P. Roe, and Augusta M. Evans; seed catalogues and Patent
Office Reports; magazines and newspapers of any kind that
came to hand; almanacs; Sunday-school books; and I never
went to town on a Saturday afternoon without visiting Lem
White's barber shop to have a peek at the *Police Gazette* (very
disreputable in that day and age). Much of the reading of my
boyhood was cheap stuff, to be remembered with rising gorge
as one does the nauseous drinks and cheap candies of the circus.
I am not one who can point a moral from his boyhood reading.
I did not read by system or to improve my mind. I read without
plan or purpose other than to gratify an appetite for reading.
Worst of all, I was a skimmer. In one of my readers was the
precept:

> Learn to read slow, all other graces
> Will follow in their proper places.

This precept I wrote in my copybook hundreds of times, but
to no avail. I could not wait for the copulation of ideas, but

snatched the joy of reading in gulps, as if I expected that I should shortly go blind and ever after would have to think how much there was in the world that I had not read.

There was never time in my forest home to read as much as I wanted to. I had to skim. Much of my reading had to be done when I was expected to do something else; when I had been told twice or thrice to come to a meal, or go to bed; or to do this or that chore; or on a Sunday morning when I had been told several times to get ready for church. My greatest joy in reading came when driven indoors by rain to my mean little room, which was transformed for a few hours into a paradise where I might lie on the floor, my eyes riveted on a book, oblivious to the carking cares of the world. Reading was the greatest pleasure of my boyhood, one always within reach, a pleasure curtailed only by lack of time.

For a family always short of cash, we spent an inordinate amount of money on newspapers and magazines. Father subscribed for the two local papers, in every issue of which the editors showered abuse on each other. Both papers had eight large folio pages, the four outside ones filled by home talent and home advertisement; and four 'patent insides' printed in Chicago, which told us how the world at large was wagging. Father had read the *Baltimore Sun* from boyhood, and continued to read it to the end of his life. For state news he took the *Detroit Free Press,* then strongly Democratic. I saved enough pennies to subscribe to *The Youth's Companion;* my brother took *Harper's Young People;* my sister, *St. Nicholas.*

The days and nights in my boyhood were much longer than modern days and nights, which have been cut short by a hundred modern inventions. The smell of kerosene lamps seventy years ago whetted the appetite for reading. In our home, the kitchen was the chosen place in which my brother and I read on cold nights. The unshaded small wick lamps had to be directly in front of our eyes; so we knelt on hard kitchen chairs, elbows on the table, and read and read, until the fire ceased to crackle, and all sounds stopped—except the ticking of the clock and the gurgling of the lamps—until the icy cold, our aching backs, stiffened knees, and smarting eyes sent us to bed. My brother could stick out the cold longer than I, and came later to our bed to crowd me over that he might steal my warm place and cuddle his icy feet in the calves of my legs.

XXVI

Preachers and Churches

MR. PARMALEE, the Baptist preacher, was born in the northern country, and knew every part of it. He came to our part of the country as the pastor of the Baptist church, but soon fell into disrepute with the clergy of the town because of 'unorthodoxy.' True enough, he was unorthodox. One Sunday he announced himself a Seventh Day Adventist and resigned from his Baptist pastorate. What a commotion it made! You would have thought he had gone over to the Prince of Darkness. Since there were at the time few Seventh Day Adventists in the neighborhood, he had no salary and no church and thus had to preach his new faith in hired halls and schoolhouses. His was a voice crying in the wilderness.

Of all our clergy, I liked Mr. Parmalee best. He had much to do in shaping my terrestrial life, and should I by happy chance come to a celestial one, he as much as any other of the men who have tried to teach me right from wrong set me on my way. His sermons were so short and simple, and his diction so pure and dignified, that it was a pleasure to hear him. It was commonly said that he suffered from the effects of too much learning; some thought he was a little mad, and this, with his being an 'apostate,' gave interest to his sermons for me.

In the days when Mr. Parmalee was a Baptist clergyman, with a good salary, he had had many friends; but when evil days fell, the poor man lost most of his friends and went from neighborhood to neighborhood preaching and lecturing for the few pennies he could pick up. But he was well liked by non-Baptists and so had no difficulty in getting meals. It was harder, however, for him to come by a bed, as houses were small and crowded and Mr. Parmalee was fastidious.

He worshiped cleanliness. As a guest, he asked to have shirts, socks, and underclothes laundered. He was the only man I knew who always had a clean handkerchief. He would not sleep with any other person, and was particular about bed clothes. Worst of all, at our house, where water was often scarce, he wanted a tub in the kitchen and a little hot water every night. In a house where three children must scrub hands, feet, and faces at bedtime, taking a full bath once a week, it was hard to entertain a guest who wanted an 'all-over' every night. On the other hand, Mr. Parmalee was a most helpful guest; he would help with every kind of work and so more than paid for his keep.

The preacher and Father were great friends, so that in spite of the trouble his visits gave Mother, he came often and stayed long. We children liked him because he helped us in our studies, had an inexhaustible fund of information, and would tell story after story. In truth, he was a vessel filled with learning, into which he loved to have thirsty children dip. Mr. Parmalee was a lover of Dickens and impersonated characters in the great novelist's books with voice and gesture; so we often had a play presented in our living room with an actor of no little ability. Who would not like such a man?

The Reverend Mr. Parmalee had two distinct compartments in his brain, one for religion and one for science. In his sermons he accepted every statement in the Bible as word-for-word truth; in conversation he was an up-to-date scientist. He was the first man I ever heard mention Darwin, and he often affirmed to my father his belief in evolution, which at that time nearly all clergymen were denouncing.

Father once said to him: 'But, Mr. Parmalee, it seems to me Darwin and Moses do not agree.'

The preacher replied dryly: 'Moses was not a scientific reporter.'

All through my mature years, I have been associated with scientists, but, of the hundreds I have known, none has had so fine and delicate a feeling for nature as Mr. Parmalee. He and I were tramping early one spring through a beech and maple forest in which trilliums were as plentiful as the stars in the heavens. Mr. Parmalee could not restrain himself:

'O, lovely, lovely! . . . See how bravely they break through the snow! . . . What a perfect white! . . . How spotless the leaves! . . . It's Nature's perfect flower! . . . *Trilium grandiflorum,* a perfect name for a perfect flower!'

The name, he told me, came from the Latin *tres,* three. First, he called my attention to the three large leaves. Pulling a flower apart he showed me three sepals, three petals, six stamens, six styles, six lobes to the ovary. Every part of the floral design, he pointed out, was perfectly balanced.

Digging down into the ground he pulled out an onionlike corm and said: 'The Creator has stored food in the corm and has willed that it be so delicately adjusted that with the first burst of sunshine in the spring this perfect plant springs from the dormant corm. Who could doubt the greatness of God?'

Preachers were fairly common in the land of my boyhood. Most of them were elderly men with austere countenances. Mr. Parmalee did not run true to type. From his figure, face, and dress one would have said he was a teacher rather than a preacher. He was a tall, thin man, straight as an arrow, with coal black hair, worn rather long and covered out of doors with a broad-brimmed black hat. He had a pale, ascetic face, which the sun did not burn; a sensitive mouth, humorous eyes, and a brow that often showed lines of care and worry. In the pulpit he wore an ill-fitting frock coat, a survival of better days, in which I always suspected he was most uncomfortable. Blue serge was his choice for every-day wear, plain and cheap but well-fitted, so that his clothes as well as his face bespoke him a gentleman to our farmer folk.

When Mr. Parmalee greeted you his face lighted up with a pleasant smile; behind the smile was a lovely spirit. Outside the church he was one of the people; inside, he was every inch a preacher. Our Presbyterian preacher, the Reverend John J. Cook, could not on Sunday surpass Mr. Parmalee in dignity, though in length of sermons and prayers he could and did outdo his Baptist rival every Sunday in the year.

Mr. Parmalee was greatly interested in astronomy. I remember one night when he held me spellbound with talk about the stars. We had gone across Little Traverse Bay in the afternoon in a two-masted Mackinaw boat. Coming home in the evening, we were becalmed. As we lay on our backs beneath the starry skies, he told me that there were millions and millions of stars that we could not see, although we were now looking straight at them. He explained how Venus was at the moment the brilliant evening star and would in a few months be a brilliant morning star. He named the stars, the planets, the constellations he knew; he told me about light-years; the Star of Bethlehem, and such other astronomical lore as he thought a boy's mind might grasp. Always he qualified: these were the impressions of astronomers whose information might not be trustworthy. Poor man, the two compartments in his brain were always at odds.

It was midnight before his talk came to an end, with a moral lesson that I afterward heard him set forth in sermons and that at the time impressed me as very wise. He said that if trouble makers, busybodies, and those who had petty disappointments and worries would only get out under the open sky and study the stars, their troubles would disappear.

On this night, becalmed on a motionless sea, with stars twinkling and meteors shooting, as I listened to the wonders revealed by Mr. Parmalee, my delight was so great that something clutched my throat. When he had finished, he quoted some verses that, he said, were among the best in our language. They seemed to me then to have been written especially for that night. The first one was:

> The twilight hours, like birds flew by,
> As lightly and as free;
> Ten thousand stars were in the sky,
> Ten thousand on the sea.

Sometimes Mr. Parmalee's scientific knowledge was of use to the homesteaders among whom he worked, and once, at least, it brought great comfort to some of them. It was at the time of the great fall of 'brimstone.' One June morning everyone found a film of 'brimstone' on the quiet waters of barrels and ponds. Some of Mr. Parmalee's Adventists believed it was the first act in the destruction of the Sodom and Gomorrah in which we lived. Wicked and good alike were pleased when Mr. Parmalee came with his microscope and a branch of a pine tree and showed us that the 'brimstone' was pollen carried by the wind from the great pine forests southeast of us.

Mr. Parmalee was full of fine projects. He intended to write several books that he felt certain would enlighten the world. The one he wanted most to write (his *magnum opus*, he loved to say) was on the Mound Builders, about whom he thought he had knowledge possessed by no one else.

It was he who first put it in my head to go to college. He said to me time and again: 'Hitch your wagon to a star, boy! Go to college! There is more to the world than you can see in these woods! . . . Hitch your wagon to a star! . . . Go to college.'

Mr. Parmalee was only one of four Protestant ministers who brought the Word to the whites in our sparse community. Every Sunday morning the bells of five churches sounded forth in harsh, jangling discord to emphasize the disagreements of

Christians. The four Protestant sects lived in smug self-righteous contemplation of the Roman Catholics, who were mostly Indians. I never saw an Indian in a Protestant church. Red men in our community were to the Protestants as are the untouchables to the chosen of India. All of our Protestant churches sent money to foreign missions, but the red-skinned pagans all about us were not thought worth saving.

The preachers in our land were all bedrock Calvinists. They made a sharp division between Sunday and weekdays and kept a heavy Puritanical sabbath. Twice each Sunday I had to listen to a long sermon that was but sound in my ears and an opportunity to build castles in Spain. The boredom of church services was especially bitter in daytime, when I could see happy little Indians scampering on the green or paddling on the lake. At night I did not mind so much; the sermon was shorter, and I liked the bright lights and the goings-on of the young people in the back seats, in which as I grew older I took part.

Terrible sermons they were to sit through, with one religious precept after another crammed in our ears; but from them we could not fail to learn right and wrong. Presbyterianism is a very inconvenient faith. I have never been able to sin with any pleasure; to swear as vehemently as I wanted to; to lie, often needful in the complex affairs of our civilization; or, as a boy, to steal from an apple orchard or watermelon patch without twinges of conscience; or to covet my neighbor's rare books and fine pictures, a grievous sin of my later years. Whenever I have been tempted to do these things, there was always the admonishing finger of a Presbyterian preacher pointing at me and commanding in a loud voice: 'Thou shalt not!'

The Presbyterian preacher of that time was traditionally an exhorter who sought to save immortal souls by vividly picturing the torments visited upon the sinners who sat before him. Human fancy ranges far and wide, but nowhere else, in my experience, has it taken such flights as in the sulphurous realms pictured by these old-time Calvinists as they discoursed on the punishments that after death are meted out to all except the chosen few. Reverend Mr. Cook I recall as a normal and most likable man except when he stood behind his pulpit preaching hell-fire. In a sonorous voice he described the torments of the doomed. He painted his picture amazingly well, and filled his hearers with terror, alternating his sorrow for our fate with a note of hope that we should get what we deserved.

After hearing sermons by these worthy men, the children in our family speculated on the fate of people we knew. Who would be saved? Who damned? (We were afraid that heaven would be overrun with Republicans, but were sure that the best people there would be Democrats.)

In winter, Methodists and Baptists buried their creeds and united in 'protracted meetings,' which lasted three or four weeks and stirred the emotional life of the villagers to a religious frenzy. My parents stood a little aloof from the winter meetings; but my brother and I, craving excitement, went often, and came away ill at ease, embarrassed, and bewildered by the flood of promises and condemnations of the preachers, and by the confidences of wintertime converts who confessed their sins. These upheavals of mind and soul seemed to us a very painful way to attain salvation, especially since some thus saved needed to have the process repeated winter after winter.

The impressions children get from sermons take very remarkable turns. At revivals we were asked again and again: 'Are you washed in the blood of the Lamb?'

There were no sheep in our part of the world, and I could not see how I was to be washed in the blood of a lamb.

'The Lord God is a jealous God!'

Why?

'Are you ready for the Judgment Day?'

To me, getting 'ready' was a matter of clothes.

I loved the phrase 'the trump of doom.' It was a favorite expression with one of our Methodist preachers, and I was disappointed if he did not use it several times in a sermon, making the words resound from every part of his little church. Should I hear the trump at the resurrection?

Of course, I could not comprehend the plan of salvation. Nor could I understand the Trinity. I had definite mental pictures of God and of Christ, but I could never bring an image of the Holy Ghost to mind. Even now in old age, after having listened to three thousand or more sermons (a very modest calculation), many of the things that preachers talk about are not plain to me.

Mother's faith was superb. She was a dyed-in-the-wool fundamentalist and took every statement in the Bible literally (as she did every word in the village newspaper). For her the sun did stand still and Jonah was swallowed by the whale. She walked by faith for three score and ten years in a family half pagan. To Mother, a preacher who spoke without notes delivered a message straight from God, whereas one who read a sermon spoke merely as a man. She wanted her bread from a primal source, not second-hand. Mother would never argue religion with any of her family, though she hammered it into some of her neighbors.

Each of the churches had its place in our community. The Episcopalians 'came out of the top drawer' (at least they lived in the best houses and wore the best clothes). All acknowledged the Presbyterians to be the intellectuals of the town; to those of us who belonged to that faith, it was *the* Church. Baptists and Methodists, at that time at least, were less well endowed in mental and cultural attributes, and members of these sects were seldom found in the 'higher society' of Episcopalians and Presbyterians; some of them came over to the Presbyterians 'for the sake of the children.' Only Indians went to the Roman Catholic Church, though Father Zorn was the best-loved preacher in the town.

It was always a pleasure to me to see my parents dressed for church. Father wore a blue broadcloth suit and a handsome pair of high boots, the tops underneath his trouser legs. How old the boots were, I cannot say. He wore them during all the years I can remember up to my eighteenth, when they were showing wear, but were still neat and unpatched. The boots were hand-made and cost eighteen dollars. Mother's dress of black silk and her black hat were as old as Father's boots, but every summer when my half-sisters came on a visit Mother's clothes were remade, after endless discussions, to conform to the prevailing style. Generally Mother's black silk had a very full skirt, which fell from a tight basque buttoned in front.

Mother's best hat matched her best dress in material and in length of service. It was of black velvet, with a silver bar, and a fine egret feather. She had also an ostrich plume. Both of these feathers had been given her by her step-daughters, who made the hat over, changing feathers, and adding flowers to make it appear that she could afford a new hat every year. There was always, also, a new ribbon to be tied demurely under the chin.

Once I overheard a neighbor woman say: 'Mrs. H. is stuck up in her black silk dress and ostrich-plume hat.'

I told Mother, and how the fur flew when the woman appeared at our house a few days later!

Family prayers in our house went and came with the seasons. In spring and summer, when all were hard pressed by toil, morning and evening worship were forgotten; but after the autumn equinox, for most of the winter, morning prayers were fairly regular. Sometimes the stress of work cut them short or brought them to an end for a while. My father's faith was sometimes shaken by the persuasive writings of some agnostic; and then, since he was never a hypocrite, there was no morning worship.

My brother and I knew that Father could never withstand the glowing rhetoric of Robert G. Ingersoll, and we often borrowed books and lectures by Ingersoll from Dave Hartzeler, a neighbor who was an out-and-out free-thinker, to see what the effect might be on our family's religious life.

Dave Hartzeler was the only free-thinker in our community.

He was a good neighbor, one we all liked, and his wife was long intimate with Mother, as were her two daughters with my sister. Dave's children were well behaved, a surprising fact in view of what the preachers said of life in a family where there was no religion.

Mr. Parmalee and Dave Hartzeler were warm friends, and every now and then it was rumored that Dave, the atheist, was about to be baptized a Seventh Day Adventist. What a triumph that would have been for Mr. Parmalee!

In the 1880's, social activities in our land were carried on mostly through the churches. In our village there was hardly a week from October to May in which one of the four churches did not have a dime social. These socials were announced with much unction on Sunday in the schedule of events read by the pastors. One always looked in the two weekly newspapers for the heading 'Dime Social.' Then followed either an announcement of a social to be held, or a report of one that had been held.

These socials were held under the auspices of the Women's Auxiliary of the church sponsoring the event. They were held at the homes of prominent members of the church, from six to ten in the evening, furnishing a supper to all who attended. Anyone might go and would be welcomed.

Dime Socials followed one pattern in food and exercise. Food came first as the important part of the program. You might always count on baked beans. To flavor the beans there was an assortment of catsups and chili sauces; other accompaniments were coleslaws and pickles in variety. There were platters of sliced ham and cold chicken. The bread was customarily hot soda biscuit and for dyspeptics, whole-wheat bread. Lastly, for dessert there were five-layer jelly cakes, sponge cakes, angel-food cakes, cookies, and doughnuts. Coffee for grown-ups and milk for youngsters was the rule.

How could so many foods be furnished for a dime? To begin with, in the 1880's a dime went as far as five dimes go today.

Also, the food was largely homegrown, homecooked, and donated by women members of the church, who thus showed their skill in cooking. The left-overs were given to the preacher's family, and the dimes helped pay his salary.

A variation of the Dime Social was the Donation Party, held once a year in late autumn at the preacher's house. There were about the same foods for supper, but everyone was expected to bring a liberal donation of some substantial food as well. The usual donations were pork products, flour, vegetables, canned fruits, cakes, cookies, preserves, and pickles. Without a Donation Party the preachers in our land would have starved. Their salaries were never more than $600, part of which was paid by home-mission funds and the rest raised in church subscriptions and Sunday collections. The churches' only annual expenditures were the minister's salary, donations to foreign missions, hymnals, and prayer books.

After the suppers at socials and donation parties, there were 'exercises.' The head of the organization giving the social presided and began her program by announcing: 'Our pastor will make a few remarks.' These remarks, as the newspaper usually said a few days later: 'Were in lighter vein, but carried a message.'

Next it would be announced that some 'miss' would play the organ 'or sing a solo.' At every social, several children would 'speak pieces.' The church quartet choir would sing a tune or two, and all would join in singing 'Blest Be the Tie that Binds,' 'Lead, Kindly Light,' and at the end, 'Till We Meet Again.'

Each of the four Protestant Sunday schools annually celebrated two great events. Christmas and Easter were observed in all the churches much as they are in Protestant churches today.

Christmas observance in early homes was very different from that in modern days. There was little Christmas shopping; we never sent or received Christmas greetings, not even from brothers and sisters away from home. Christmas presents were articles of clothing that we at home gave each other, though my sister always expected a china doll. My brother and I expected caps, mittens, socks, and were disappointed if we did not get a book.

At Christmas my small-boy mind was burdened with the names of four messengers from the Christ child: Belsnicker, Santa Claus, Saint Nicholas, and Kris Kringle. The four to my mind were brothers very like the modern Santa Claus and all came with jingling bells on sleds drawn by reindeer. Belsnicker was the herald of Santa Claus to see how the children in the family had behaved during the year, and at our house his coming visit provided the first mention of Christmas by the older members of my family just a few days before. His duties I understood perfectly, but the business of the other three I could not quite comprehend—perhaps they divided the work of distributing presents to the children of the world?

Dinner was the most important part of our celebration of Christmas. The meat was roast turkey with bread and oyster stuffing, the well-browned bird being surrounded with sausages. With the turkey, sauerkraut and mashed potatoes were served. On side dishes were celery and pickles. Hot soda biscuits and cream gravy took the place of bread and butter. Coffee was served with the dinner, which always ended with mince pie. Every viand in the dinner, except oysters, sugar, salt, and pepper, came from our own farm.

Easter was kept in our Protestant churches exactly as it is kept in them today. We made a great ado about eggs on Easter at our house. When we were children, Mother or the older girls colored hard-boiled eggs red with cochineal, blue with bluing, and brown with walnut husks, and hid them about the house. The youngsters, having been told that rabbits had laid them, spent an hour before breakfast looking for rabbits' nests. At breakfast we ate boiled, fried, and poached eggs, from two to eight or ten apiece. At dinner we had as a side dish hard-boiled eggs pickled bright red in beet juice and vinegar.

XXVII

Father Zorn

FATHER ZORN, the Roman Catholic priest, long antedated any other clergyman in our village. Though I seldom went inside Father Zorn's church, and lived in an atmosphere wholly prejudiced against any but Protestant churches, still I knew Father Zorn well, and as years have passed I have come to admire him more and more.

Probably I should never have known Father Zorn except by sight had it not been for the cold winter and my sickness, about which I have already written. During that time I was expected to get a little air when the weather permitted, and, as I was not to be trusted alone, I was often put in the hands of Juliette, the half-breed girl of my pigeon excursion. Juliette very often had other fish to fry and would leave me with her aunt, who was Father Zorn's housekeeper. The aunt, in turn, would pass me on to the friendly priest, who seemed not in the least averse to having me in his living room. After a few of these enforced visits a friendship was struck up between us.

The rectory was a long, low wooden building with a living room, dining room, and kitchen downstairs. I never knew what was upstairs. The whole place, inside and out, had been sadly neglected—no paint, plaster falling down, and none of it kept very clean by the old half-breed housekeeper. I suspect that Father Zorn would have said that he cared not for a perishable home, and that this house was but the temporary lodging of a wayfaring man.

Upon entering, one came first into the living room, where there was a faint mouldy smell like that of fungi, whether of decay or of books, I do not know. Walls, tables, and chairs were loaded with books. Over the door was a framed motto in Latin: *Et ne nos inducas in tentationem, sed libera nos a malo.*

In one corner of his very large room was a cupboard, its panels cracked, the hinges and hasps of the door loose; in it my inquisitive eye caught glimpses of faded and tarnished lace and scarlet and purple vestments. By the side of the cupboard was a *prie-dieu*, over which hung a crucifix.

In the living-room there were three large pictures in color and the largest mirror that I had yet seen. One of the pictures was of St. Francis feeding birds. The colors had faded and St. Francis had so sour a face that I found it hard in later years to associate him with anything so happy as birds. Across the room from St. Francis hung a picture in a heavy gilded frame, chipped and tarnished, of Abraham and Isaac. Isaac lay bound on a pile of faggots; Abraham, dressed in disreputable garments, stood over his son, knife poised in air. At one end of the room was a painting of Christ looking down from the cross on Pilate's soldiers, above him the inscription in Latin: *Hic est Rex Iudaeorum.*

The large mirror, which hung opposite the picture of Christ, seemed to me a wonderful glass, especially as, in one position, its waves distorted my face, making it look like a full moon.

'It makes a sad face merry,' Father Zorn once said to me.

Father Zorn's rectory stood on the south side of the main street at the western boundary of the town. A few rods distant, blocking the street, stood his church. It was an antique in new land, looking down disapprovingly on the upstart houses growing up on either side of the street over which it had so long presided. Its builders had raised a structure of heavy, squared timbers of pine, symbolic of the Church. Some later builder boarded the timbered frame with wide silver-gray unpainted boards. The building was rectangular and devoid of churchly ornaments on the exterior, except a high spire, gilded with glistening copper and surmounted by a huge cross that shone in sunlight like gold; but the fancies of many blossomed in the interior. Through a deeply recessed portico with inner and outer doors, you saw straight ahead, behind the altar, a barbaric ornamental screen of carved and painted woods, on either side of which were heavy hangings, changed in color with the church seasons. Parts of the reredos were life-sized pictures of Christ and of the Virgin, both decorated with brightly colored paper flowers. Christ was pictured without a beard, since Indians, having no beard, disliked them. The pictures were in full face, because to an Indian a face in profile is but half a man. On the altar was the cross, made of brass, but polished to shining gold that shimmered in the light of tall candles.

On the long sides of the church were two series of pictures, conceptions of some painter with the imagination of a Dante. One side was given up to angels, some in Heaven, some helping souls from Purgatory to Heaven; on the other were sinners in Hell, tortured by horrid grinning devils. These devils goaded condemned souls with tridents and pitchforks from a cliff into deep abysses of Hell, which were surging seas of flames. There were, as well, two or three pictures showing serpents and dragons feasting on the entrails of sinners.

In our first years in this country of the Indians, Father Zorn's was the only church. Protestants had as yet no meeting place and only occasional sermons by visiting missionaries. For a half century before the coming of the whites, this old church had been the only authority for morals, the only guide to God, the only seat of culture, the only sanctuary of art, the only civil authority.

Here alone might one learn of the mystery that surrounds death. The bell in this lonely church rang with no answering bell; rang with seeming inconsequence at all hours of the day; rang the hurried call for Mass; rang the Angelus; rang the tranquil curfew; rang joyously on festal days; tolled for the burial service. Even the old rogue Joutel disliked to be long away from its sound. Usually his excuse to go home was 'I lik' to 'ear ze bell.'

On three sides of the church was a graveyard enclosed by a rickety picket fence, a yard where the graves of Father Zorn's flock lay thickly clustered. The rank of those in the graves was indicated by the size of the wooden crosses, ranging from massive timbers for those who had died while high in the esteem of the Church to tiny markers made of laths to mark the resting places of illegitimate babies or children. None was marked with a name. Many crosses had fallen, and the mounds of old graves were sunken. The graves of late-comers in the yard were ornamented with wreaths of cloth flowers, bits of pottery and glass, so that the Indian in his last illness might look forward to being borne to the splendors of the grave.

Here, standing outside the tumble-down fence, one cold winter day I saw the burial of one of my Indian playmates. He was put in a shallow grave dug in frozen ground as hard as iron. His coffin was a drygoods box much too large for his small body. I had seen him carry the cross on Saints' days, and now wondered what marker his grave would have; I was pleased when I found that someone had carved for him a cross very like the one he had been accustomed to carry. I had disliked the little barbarian and had fought with him time and again, but seeing his body put into this cold, hard ground saddened me.

While a student in college, I found that this graveyard had a most varied flora, so many species that one summer I was kept busy for several days, botanizing over the graves of Indians whom I had known in life. Coarse, rank-smelling burdocks, sticktights, and beggar-lice crowded and elbowed one another, bristling with burrs and ticks. There were jungle spots of nettles; tansy grew wild; nightshade, supposedly deadly poison, clambered over the rickety fence; several species of sedges and grasses not found elsewhere in our region grew here along with the foxtail, redtop, and wild oats. On the graves, out of the paths where they would have been crushed, there grew a remarkable assortment of delicately patterned mosses.

I never have seen a place where there were so many wasps and spiders, no doubt attracted to a good hunting ground for other insects. The yard was rich in crickets and grasshoppers that chirped and shrilled in the luxury of summer. Nowhere else have I ever seen so many ants in so small an area, or elsewhere ants so industrious, or with such strength in dragging burdens heavier than themselves. Here in God's acre, plants made an extra effort to reproduce, a fact of which the bees must have been aware, for they came to the graveyard to roll in the pollen and saturate themselves with the nectar of the weeds and grasses.

Father Zorn was not a priest to let slip the observance of any church day. In particular, Corpus Christi was for him a marked day of the Christian year, and one in which most of his flock were ever ready to take part. This holy day follows Easter by some sixty days, and so came at about the time the Indians for immemorial years had celebrated the pagan rites of the Strawberry Dance.

The strawberry, to the Indians of the Upper Lakes, is the fruit of life, held in reverence by all the tribes; and the custom with all had been to celebrate the ripening of wild strawberries with music, feasting, and dancing. Roman Catholic missionaries, quick to seize such opportunities, had turned the pagan orgy of the Strawberry Dance into the Christian festival of Corpus Christi.

In the mission of L'Arbre Croche, Father Zorn began the day with Mass at eleven o'clock, at which he wore his most sumptuous vestments and performed the solemn rite with pomp and dignity worthy a cathedral service. Mass was followed by a procession through the aisles of the church out into the sacred field of the dead, where, under a gigantic cross, the litanies and benedictions prescribed by the Church were said.

The procession from Mass to the cross in the cemetery was headed by a choir of small boys, who chanted in clear, fresh voices the sonorous service, which for centuries had animated hearts in the Old World and now gave faith to a race new to the Church in an obscure corner of the New World. The somber church was dazzling in its bizarre dress of artificial flowers, its lithographs of saints, its gilding of candles, and the brilliant noonday sun.

After the choir came the little girls of the mission, carrying crosses decorated with white paper flowers. Then came ranks of older girls, rosaries in hand, holding aloft the banner of the Virgin. This group of adolescent girls formed the largest division of the procession. Juliette led them. All were Indians or half-breeds; all had black hair, which reflected the sunshine in tones of black, violet, and dark purple. There was about all a luxuriance of figure common to children of Nature. They walked erect, lithe, alert, statuesque, with a firm step and a fine carriage of the head. Their lighted faces revealed a fervor of spirit hardly to be expected.

After the girls came the women, in black dresses, heads covered with shawls, faces silent and reserved. Even the touch of summer, as they came out of the church, caused no brightening of countenance. I doubt that they were much stirred by religious zeal—only appetites of the body could greatly interest them. A straggling division of old men came last, for they alone among the males of the parish showed concern in matters of religion. Young men and those of middle age in active life preferred to be indolent onlookers.

The churchyard was sumptuously carpeted with the rich green growth of June, and on this verdant carpet the procession knelt before an altar under the great cross. Father Zorn read his lessons, the choir chanted its litanies with murmured responses from the kneeling people, benediction was said, and dismissal came in the noisy clanging of the bell high above in the steeple.

Another of the Indian festivals that the Roman Catholic missionaries combined with one of the red-letter days of the Church came in October. Autumn was a time of plenty, when, for ages past, the Indians had held their Feast for the Dead. Always the feast was followed at night by the ritual of shooting the devil to protect their dead against his onslaught in the feeble time of winter. This festival of our Upper Lakes Indians coincided in time, and somewhat in purpose, with All Saints' Day, which the Church celebrated. Thus, *la Toussaint* of the French became the *Tu-san-wong* of L'Arbre Croche Indians.

Fire is an Indian symbol, as I suppose it is in some degree a Christian symbol. Our Indians were past masters in making bonfires, having had long experience in a region hardly to be surpassed in the whole world for abundance of material. In the dim light of early night a great pyramid of dry resinous logs from the forest and driftwood from the shore was kindled, and, as darkness came on, a whirlwind of leaping flames sprang from the pile—the devil must have felt quite at home.

The place the Indians chose for shooting the devil was at the base of the long point that made our harbor. Here there was a calm, serene little body of water called 'Devil's Pond,' said to be bottomless. In after years, it was filled with sawdust and other debris from a mill built on its banks, and now not a trace of the beautiful little pond is to be seen. To the east of the pond lay the harbor; to the west, Lake Michigan. There could not have been found a more beautiful place for the evening rites of All Saints' Day.

First, there was a feast. After the edge of appetite had been dulled, the Indians were ready for the great ceremony. The bonfire was burning in great fury. The wild throng, both sexes, now circled about the pool. The air vibrated with shattering gunfire, staccato calls, whoops that a multitude of devils could not match, the beating of drums, the clanging of bells, the clatter of metals, and wild cries above all other noises. At last, with ammunition spent, all hoarse with shouting, it was adjudged that the devil had been driven away and the pagan rite came to an end.

Once this celebration of All Saints' Day coincided with a remarkable natural phenomenon. Northern lights, which came every winter, were early this year. No one had ever seen the sky so brilliant, nor in all the years that have followed have I seen Aurora's lights in so grand a display. Night after night for several weeks darkness was ushered in by a light crimson vapor. Gradually this brightly lighted vapor filled the northern heavens from east to west, from horizon to zenith. The world seemed to be on fire, and the terrestrial fire at Devil's Pond was but the flicker of a firefly. Great clouds of crimson, red, orange, yellow, and blue enlivened with darting rays of rainbow hues, rolled up from the northern horizon to the center of our sky. Later, wise men said the beautiful northern lights of this autumn were due to fine dust that filled the heavens of the whole world. An island in the East Indies, Krakatao, had blown up and it took months for the dust to settle, during which time sunrise, sunset, and northern lights were bathed in brilliant colors.

I remember well my last sight of Father Zorn. I was soon to leave for college, and went to take a look in the old church, thinking it might be my last. I saw again the trembling candles, smelled the mingled odors of summer flowers and incense, and heard the droning voices of unregenerate youngsters. Father Zorn stood before the altar facing a row of copper-skinned children, in rapt attention as the priest taught them to kneel, to pray, to make the sign of the cross. A few careworn women were passing in and out; a girl with a baby in her arms, her face hidden in a shawl, stood in a shadow-draped corner waiting to have her child baptized; or, possibly, to confess her sin.

XXVIII

An Ancient Capital

WHEN my brother and I came to what is now boy-scout age, the spirit of adventure moved us to go camping from time to time. We made trips hither and yon to explore the country, to fish, to hunt, or just to camp out where fancy might suggest. In June of the year when I was twelve and my brother fourteen, we got permission to visit the ancient capital of L'Arbre Croche. There had been something in the newspapers about the place, reason enough to satisfy our parents, although between ourselves the trip was planned to rob Indian graves, which were thickly sprinkled about the old capital, and from which might be taken arrowheads, beads, tomahawks, and silver trinkets used as money by the old fur traders.

Leander, our half-breed schoolmate, was to join us in this ghoulish enterprise. The site of the old Indian capital was some twelve or fifteen miles from our home. Early in the morning of a summer day, my brother and I joyfully set out to survey the wonders of a part of our country we had never seen, full of hope that we should find a fortune in Indian graves. We left home in a light, one-seated spring-wagon drawn by a horse so old and lame that our parents were sure we should not have a runaway or get too far from home. In the village, three miles on our way, we picked up Leander, glad to have him in the wagon, as we had been afraid he would back out.

Our adventure started with all in high spirits. The sky was

pure blue from horizon to horizon; soon we were in the glory
of a rising sun. Caroling birds and chattering chipmunks enlivened our way; a doe and her fawn crossed our road, mere
streaks of color.

The country through which the road ran was typical of the
northern woods, and never had anyone a better opportunity to
see flora and fauna than we had in our dawdling, snail-pace
journey. The way ran in and out of the highlands of hardwoods,
through dark ravines of hemlocks and an occasional cedar
swamp. Most pleasant on this dewy morning were the sunlit
clearings skirted by briars, sumacs, aspens, chokecherries, and
balm of Gileads, every species distilling into the air its own
special odor so that the earth was covered with a sweet and
wholesome fragrance. Now and again we stopped to eat a snack,
to drink from some spring, or to strip and plunge into a creek.

In early afternoon we pitched camp on the shore in the
middle of the site of the ancient capital of the Ottawa, the
Indian metropolis of the northern lakes, the center of Indian
agriculture and industry for hundreds of miles in every direction.

When the French came to northern Michigan, they found
the shore studded with Indian wigwams for a distance of twelve
or fourteen miles. Most of the land near the shore was under
tillage, for L'Arbre Croche Indians were farmers as well as
hunters. Probably, when the settlement was most prosperous,
there were as many as a thousand camp fires. When the fur
companies of the Northwest established themselves at Mackinac
Island they depended upon the cornfields and sugar bushes of
L'Arbre Croche for maize and maple sugar, the chief foods of
trappers in their expeditions to far-away parts.

In its golden years this ancient capital was the seat of the
foremost of Indian industries, the making of canoes. Within
sight of our camp were all the materials for making a bark
canoe, indispensable to these lakeside Indians. Here were canoe
birch for the shell; cedar wood for slender ribs; fibrous roots
of juniper for stitching; fir and balsam to furnish gums for

caulking the seams; roots and berries for dyes; and the proper hardwoods for paddles.

Many evidences of old Indian inhabitants were still there. We saw the remains of Indian gardens: raised rows where corn had been mounded spring after spring; beds with paths between; cone-shaped pits, which had been caches for corn and potatoes. Along grass-grown trails were well-marked spots where wigwams had stood. We were looking for graves, and soon found the mounds on a ridge of ground overlooking the lake. In the whole world the dead could have no resting place more beautiful than this part of the shore of Lake Michigan.

Impatient for the treasures we were to find, we put our spade and pickax to work in a group of graves. The dry, friable soil was easily removed. Each spadeful of sparkling sand seemed to our wrought-up imaginations to be grained with gold. Without proper gravedigger's tools, the Indians did not dig deeply to cover their dead, and we quickly came to birchbark cases filled with bones. It was a horrid sight, and through the first two or three diggings my stomach was squeamish; I should gladly have turned away to the green woods, but the clink of arrowheads, beads, and silver bangles spurred me on.

Happily for us, novices in robbing graves, freezing and thawing and the lime in the soil had made the bones clean and white. In some graves the dead had been seated with the knees tucked under the chin, faces toward the setting sun that so often at this place and in this season of the year, as on the day of our visit, was of supernatural glory and splendor. One of these sitting figures had the frame and skull of a giant, majestic in death, no doubt once a chief, now still sitting as on a throne. About him were many spangles, an iron tomahawk, and a rusted sword with a French inscription. His mound was larger and higher than any other, so that from it he might see his capital.

Next to the skeleton of the giant was the delicate frame of a woman, possibly the chief's daughter or wife. It was a beautiful skeleton, perfectly formed, the bones as white as ivory. As the exquisite ruin lay uncovered before our profane eyes, my brother, becoming sentimental, dwelt at length on the fact that once the Indian maiden had walked hereabouts, beautiful in the flesh. This skeleton, which seemed nearer to our time than any other, brought a shadow over all of us, and without a word we stopped digging, filled the graves, the last one most carefully; and, believing our fortunes had been made, began to take stock of our treasures.

We took our relics down to the clean sands of the beach, and spent an hour washing and cleaning our graveyard booty, and then took a long swim, with the hope, I suspect, that the pure waters of Lake Michigan would cleanse us of the day's sacrilege.

When the fur traders' money brought the old metropolis into the full tide of prosperity, the well-to-do Indian brave was as much a dandy as any man that ever walked the streets of London or Paris. He bedecked himself with the richest clothes his furs could buy, and bespangled them with coins, ovals, disks, and crescents of silver; bands of silver encircled his arms; silver pendants hung from his ears and his neck. Ornaments of bright metals glittered and jingled from every part of his body as he walked or took part in the ceremonial dances. He carried a bow and a quiver of stone-tipped arrows, a stone or iron tomahawk and scalping-knife, and always a pipe of stone or metal. Similarly, his spouse and daughters were bedizened with gaudy calicoes, gay shawls, strings of beads, and lesser ornaments of silver, especially crosses and crude figures of Christ and the Virgin. Death did not separate Indians from their belongings, and it was the silver ornaments that constituted most of our treasure.

What riches did the silver from the graves bring us? The jeweler to whom we took our plunder told us that our wares were German silver, a cheap alloy without value. What cheats the old Indian traders were! For all our precious metal we did not get a single penny.

Out of this grave-robbing, there came a gnawing conscience, which has taken no vacation in the years that have elapsed. I try to forget this shady episode in my early life, but always conscience is in ambush ready to spring. Only a few years ago, the still small voice came again to wound me grievously. Near my home is a burial mound of the Seneca Indian, which a remnant of the tribe visits occasionally to lament for their dead. These Senecas, friends of mine, asked me to become the Keeper of the Graves. Arrant hypocrite that I am, I consented. I, a robber of Ottawa graves, became a keeper of Seneca graves! Suppose the Senecas, even yet, should call me to account? The Ottawa, in the Happy Hunting Ground of their tribe, many of whom the Senecas had sent to their graves, must have taken my appointment as another insult from their ancient enemies.

The most pleasing memory of this wicked expedition is of our camp. The site was a place of drowsy peace in open glades of small trees and clumps of junipers—a place where one might pitch a tent or break ground for a summer cottage with only an hour or two of labor. When the Ottawa came to these shores three centuries before, a fugitive horde from the all-conquering Iroquois, they found, according to the French who visited them at the time, one vast continuous forest of maple, pines, hemlocks, and hardwoods. Inland from the shore of the ancient capital this forest still existed, but was being destroyed to the last acre by the settlers.

To the early Indians, the lake must have been more impressive even than the forest. On it they had come in their canoes; from it they might expect their enemies. From the bluff it was always in sight, and in stormy weather its roar was always in their ears. From it came fish, their chief means of sustenance. All the things they know were reflected in its waters—sky, clouds, moon and stars, trees, their own faces. The lake must have been to the Indians the most wonderful thing in the world. So it was to the three small boys camped on its shore. We saw in it all that the Indians saw, and more; for at all times there were the sails of passing ships greater in size than any Indian could conceive. Even less could he have imagined a great steamboat, the hulls and smoke of which we saw by day and the clustered starlike lights at night, or lighthouses, the lights of which we saw as darkness came on at Big Beaver, Ile aux Galets, and Waugashance.

Near our camping-place was a creek teeming with brook trout. We had neglected to bring fishing tackle, but Leander found nails in the driftwood out of which he fashioned a spear, and soon we had a fine dish of the speckled beauties. We had brought sausage and a frying pan, a coffeepot, cold baked beans, pie-plant pie, and doughnuts to dunk in the coffee. As green foods we had young onions, and now, all about in the old Indian gardens, we found quarts of wild strawberries, dead ripe and full of juice. Food cooked in the open over a wood fire cannot be beaten; and the smell of herbs and strawberries, the open air, the soft wind from Lake Michigan, and the setting sun made a delightful spot for our banquet. We watched the west turn from gray-blue to rose-pink, and then the great golden ball dropped down, in burnished crimson, into Lake Michigan.

Before we had finished our evening meal, the dews of the summer night were falling; the earth was fragrant, as were the sheltering trees, and the ferns, mosses, and wild flowers. There were the songs of thrushes, the caterwauling of whippoorwills, the zooming flights of nighthawks, and the screeching of owls. Nearer to us were sounds that only those who have spent a summer night in a forest have heard: whisperings of leaves, twigs and boughs rubbing; the soft footsteps of foxes or porcupines investigating the odors of our food; the lapping of wavelets on our sandy beach; and noisy smacks of leaping fish on the water. Taken together, birds, odors, and noises lent our camping-place enchantment.

So wonderful is the fascination of a fire for boys camping

out that building it is a chief event in an outing. It is a return to ages past, when all men lighted fires to keep beasts away. We could hardly wait until our evening meal had been eaten to make ready for night a campfire of driftwood. We achieved a blaze that furnished enormous light and intolerable heat. In the quiet air the smoke rose in a straight blue column, which broke into wisps of clouds above the treetops. As the flames whirled up, they gave to the heavens a more alarming gloom. Close to the heat of the fire, I was uncomfortable, and yet feared the pitchy blackness away from its light. The light pine and cedar logs and planks we had used to build it sent up sparks like clouds of fireflies, pretty enough to look at, but dangerous as they came down half extinguished and sprayed us with ashes.

When our fire had burned low so that a seat near it was endurable, we sat down to discuss the events of the day, but soon drifted into talk of the ancient capital in whose ruins we sat. My brother, who had a bent for history, had been reading Parkman and was full of knowledge on the history of L'Arbre Croche and its capital. He told us that L'Arbre Croche was an important place in the time of Pontiac's War. The great chief himself was, my brother informed us, an Ottawa, and while it was not certain that he had been born or bred here, certainly he had been here, and he had commanded the Ottawa at the memorable defeat of Braddock.

From history the talk drifted to the 'Little People,' suggested perhaps by the unexplainable night noises all about us. Asked point blank whether he believed in the fairies or Little People that Indians talked about, Leander could only say: 'Not in reason, but there are things in the world for which no one can give a reason.'

He said he had never seen any Little People, but that was not strange, for they had the form of spirits and could not be seen by all.

His grandmother had seen them, and he had heard them and had been scared stiff by them. It was these spirit-beings that made night noises; that set dogs barking in the night; that threw stones at one in lonely places; he himself had often been seized at night with unearthly fright that had made his hair stand up like a porcupine's quills. We should, he said, have done as the Indians do when they finish supper—left something for the roaming fairies. My brother scoffed in derision. I was a little creepy. As we sat talking, Leander suddenly exclaimed in a loud whisper: 'There come the Little People!'

The night had been as silent as starlight. There had not been a breath moving in the treetops; not a ripple on the lake; the smoke of our fire rose in a spire to the sky. Now there was a murmur far away in the woods; then a whisper; then a sibilant swish. The leaves on the aspens, firs, and birches were all a-quiver, those far away bordering a hemlock forest moving first. Something was coming out of the gloom of the hemlocks.

'Little People walking in the sky!' Leander said.

They were scuffling their moccasined feet in the treetops. In a minute or two they had passed over us out over the lake. In the light mist I could see their white moccasined feet (or was it wisps of smoke?). I was terror-stricken. I put my hands over my ears and shut my eyes. Of course there were fairies. I had seen them, I had heard them.

Our fire had burned low, and we were shivering in the chill of the night, with nothing to fear, yet fearing everything, so that we could not close our drowsy eyes. It must have been midnight before we crawled under our blankets. The two older boys were soon sleeping peacefully, but I lay sleepless on my hard couch, alone with the Little People, the twinkling stars, the dark forest, the uneasy lake, and the bones of dead Indians.

The shadow-stricken past took possession of me. I saw the ancient forest of L'Arbre Croche, peopled with Indians. I saw painted savages flitting silently from tree to tree. Whenever I closed my eyes, grinning skulls and white skeletons appeared to torment me. Sometimes the skeletons were lying as we found them in the graves; sometimes they swaggered about, their loose-jointed bones miraculously holding together without sinews or flesh. In my dreams, Leander was dressed in paint and feathers, carried a bow and arrows, a tomahawk and scalping-knife. Leander had said that many of the Indians in the graves hereabouts had died of smallpox. Of a certainty I was now infected with this dreadful disease. The night terrors of my more youthful days were back again. There was no comfort in starry heavens, the lake, the forest, in the sounds of the waves, or the wind in the trees.

When dawn came, though our beds were not places of luxury, since it was Sunday of a summer day and no one to rout us out, we took pleasure in lying long at ease. Yawning, we came to life, ate a warm breakfast, and were ready for the last adventure of our outing.

Word had come that Joutel had been drowned when his Mackinaw had been wrecked during a gale, and that the boat had come ashore near the ancient capital. My brother and I felt that we ought to find the wreck and shed a tear for the old sinner. A mile from our camp we found the boat, stove in, half buried in sand. Vandals had stolen masts, cordage, and whatever had a penny's value. How Joutel would have cursed! We regretted that we could not hear the picturesque oaths of which he always had had so generous a mouthful.

Poor Joutel had always been afraid that he would die in his sleep and not be able to make a death-bed confession. His death by drowning, in full consciousness that no priest could reach him, was worse than death in sleep. He would have chosen, too, to have people about. We could be sure that he was talking when death came, if not to his Maker, certainly to himself. Joutel would have liked a funeral with a priest, a procession, and a tolling bell, but his body was never found. He had always said that when he died his belongings were to be sold, the money to be spent for Masses. But all of his earthly goods had been in the boat.

'*Tout passe! Tout passe!*' he would have said.

XXIX

A Broken Leg

THERE was little sickness in our land; few died from disease. Providence was our doctor; toil, our medicine; fresh air, in God's plenty, our nurse. There were no undertakers, and physicians were so slighted that the wolf would have been ever at their doors had it not been for unexpected happenings to men in the forest. In every forest industry, Death stands ready to snatch a victim. A falling limb or a buckling tree may strike a chopper; the swish of a log may break a leg; a sharp ax is a dangerous tool. As I look back, however, it seems certain that God looked after our family well, so few were the mishaps.

In all our years in making a home in the forest there was in our family only one accident, and of this I was the victim. The accident came not in clearing land but in the simple task of hauling water.

It was the third day of July (I was planning for a glorious Fourth) in my sixteenth year. All the rest of the family were away from the farm on one errand or another. The weather was dry and our supply of water had to be supplemented by hauling from the creek a mile away. I put several barrels in a wagon, to which was hitched a pair of lively young horses. At the first turn of the wheels the horses were off on the jump. The devil was to pay!

The barrels spilled out; the wagon-box slid forward against the haunches of the running colts. Immediately they broke out of the barnyard, crossed a field, and came into some newly cleared land. I tried to steer them, but standing up in a rattling wagon box I could do little. The horses straddled a stump, which the wagon struck, and I went up in the air. Hanging to the reins in my effort to stop the runaways, I was dragged over humps and hollows among stumps and stones. At last the reins broke and I was free to get on my feet. But my left leg doubled between ankle and knee.

The pain was not great: in fact there was no pain, only a feeling of numbness. I tried again to stand and could not, nor could I crawl. Blood was flowing into my eyes, and for the moment I could not see. Lying on my back I began to take stock of my injuries, which were more than I at first had thought. The leg, I knew, was broken. The blood in my eyes came from a long gash high up on my forehead. I had no handkerchief and tore off a piece of my shirt to clear my eyes. The forehead wound, I concluded, was not very serious. Breathing was getting painful, and I found two broken ribs protruding below my lungs. I fainted in pain and horror. Coming to life, I took further stock and found that all my left side was raw and bruised. Here was a pretty fix! I was badly hurt; it was noon, with no chance for help until evening. The pain was becoming worse. I was bleeding badly and had no bandages. There was a broiling sun and no shade. I was thirsty and had no water.

As I sit in old age listening for his footsteps, Death seems a kindly old gentleman. May not his coming be a comfort rather than an affliction? A boy of sixteen has no such thoughts. To him, with all the world ahead, Death is a fearsome ghoul, truly the King of Terrors. No! A thousand times: I did not want to die. I clenched my fists to struggle with Death.

The pitiless sun, a red-hot ball, glowed in a cloudless sky, scorching by bruised body, on which there was scarcely a rag left. At first my skin was moist with blood and perspiration; then it became dry and began to burn with fever. My body was caked with dirt; my heart throbbed like an engine; my temples pounded; my throat was parched. If only I could have a drink of water! It was my first experience with pain, fever, and thirst.

Yet, through all these ills, my sense of hearing was curiously alert. In the neighboring forest, I could hear blue jays and red squirrels quarreling, the raucous voices of the birds and the strident chattering of the squirrels; from farther away in the depth of the forest came the twittering melodies of song sparrows. Near by a catbird was scolding. I could hear wagons on the road passing our house, but knew that they could not hear me, shout as loudly as I might.

A cloud of half-starved houseflies buzzed about in a mazy whirl, their drone as much a torture to my ears as their creeping feet to my body. Fortunately, the mosquito season had passed, and black flies would not come out of the woods into the open clearing.

I had little use of my eyes. They were nearly closed with sticky blood, and the sun blinded me. Late in the afternoon I forced them open to look at the forest—green, cool, beautiful, and sublimely peaceful.

Toward evening I felt a draught of hot air, and, opening my eyes, saw a swirling, cone-shaped wraith of dust, dried leaves, and dead grass gliding toward me. Seen in the mellow light of the dropping sun, the eddy was ghostlike and, recalling that Joutel said these 'roun's and roun's' had in them a soul, I wondered if my spirit was about to pass. The skirts of the whirligig covered me with dust, but a cool current of air followed the vortex and much refreshed my fever-burned body.

The rhythm and rhyme of words have ever been pleasing to me, especially in times of pain, sleeplessness, and trouble. Lying helpless on my back, I sought to repeat this or that poem, but without success until at last I found myself saying over and over, in a mild delirium, a jingle I had strung together when a child, of the names of places in our part of the world:

Charlevoix, Menominee;
Mackinac, Sault Ste. Marie;
Cheboygan, Petoskey;
Wequetonsing, Mononoqua;
Waugashance, Ile aux Galets.

Sometime late in the afternoon, for the sun was dropping into the western forest that shaded our clearing, I heard my name called and recognized first my sister's and then Mother's voice. On their way home from some neighborhood visit, they had found the horses loose at the barn. The broken fence, the scattered barrels, the wreck of the wagon had given them a clue to my whereabouts. They tried to help me to the house, but could not. Soon, however, with my sister holding the pail and Mother the cup, cold water was pouring refreshingly down my throat. My sister went for help; Mother stayed to dress my wounds and to relieve, as best she could, my pain.

Mother knew that she could do nothing for me with household remedies and that I must have a doctor. Meanwhile she straightened my leg, bathed my wounds, pillowed my head, covered my body with her skirt, and kept the cloud of flies away. Best of all, she cleansed my eyes to assure me that my sight was not failing. To see her face and hear her voice gave me new strength.

My sister had sent a passer-by for help and a doctor. In a half hour, I was being carried on a cot to the house and then, at last, the doctor came. The house had been quiet, and everybody had the sad look of relatives at a funeral. The bustling doctor changed all that. He opened a black bag and took out implements and bottles. He asked what had happened, when and where; he cut off my shoes; ordered the family to do this and that. I asked if I should ever get well.

'I think we can make you as good as new,' he said.

It was very hot, and the doctor said I should suffocate if people did not get out of the room. He ordered everybody out except Father and Mother, a druggist, and a lawyer, whom he had brought with him. They put me on a table and made a great fuss over the best way of giving me chloroform, a curious smelling yellowish liquid poured drop by drop on a cone held by the druggist over my nose. The last I knew the doctor was telling about how he had set two broken legs for a man a few days before, and the lawyer was protesting that the smell of drugs made him sick and that he would have to light a cigar. I went to sleep to the smell of chloroform and a cigar. In due course, I came to life to hear the doctor complaining that he had forgotten his needle and had to give me morphine in powder form, instead of injecting it subcutaneously. The druggist thought the powder was better than 'these new-fangled needles.'

What did the doctor want with a needle! I had never before heard of a hypodermic needle.

After the morphine, there was a night of deep sleep, and the next morning the accident seemed like a dream. My leg was in a plaster cast; my body was girt with bandages from head to feet. Uncertainty of the future troubled me greatly. I knew nothing of broken legs. Should I be lame, and limp for the rest of my days? The possibility of death or perpetual lameness haunted my first waking hours.

Worries subsided with the coming of people. Word of sickness was carried by mouth from house to house for extraordinary distances in our thinly settled region, and was listened to more eagerly than rumors of great happenings in the outside world. It would be hard to say how many callers I had the day after the accident, each one with tales of relatives or friends who had had their legs broken. By the end of the first day, I had information on broken legs that would have filled a book. All came bearing gifts. I did not know there were so many good things in the world to eat, and people from the village sent so many books and magazines that I began to glory in the prospect of being a cripple for life with nothing to do but eat and read.

Now I must go back three years to my thirteenth summer. I was then a dealer in flowers and berries from the woods, and frogs and minnows from the waters. The fish-bait branch of my business made necessary a trip on a ferryboat, where, sitting on a new minnow pail, squeezed tightly between two men in the bow of the boat, I became perforce an eavesdropper. One of the men I knew, a Dr. Young, a regular summer visitor; the other was a much younger man, whom I had never before seen. I could tell from their speech that both were from the deep South.

At first their conversation was commonplace enough—the charm of the day; the surpassing beauty of Little Traverse Bay and its shores; the happy relief from hay fever, from which they both suffered. Then they turned to books. The stranger said he had brought nothing to read and asked Dr. Young what he had. Dr. Young ran over a list of books he had brought and ended by recommending Rabelais to relieve boredom. He said he always kept a copy at hand and often prescribed it in certain mental cases. Then followed an animated discussion of Rabelais, whose name I was hearing for the first time. Was Rabelais a man or a book? I could not make out. I must know something more about this wonderful man or book, and Dr. Young gave me a clue. As we drew near our wharf, he said to his young friend:

'By the way, John, do you know Miss Jane Carter? [Cahteh, the Southerner pronounced the name.] She is a librarian, knows books, and may have brought some with her. She is stopping in the yellow cottage next to mine.'

Now it happened that Miss Jane Carter was one of my summer joys. She was a liberal buyer of my flowers and berries, generous with pastries and sweetmeats, and had a heart full of kind words uttered in the soft voice of the South.

Walking home with my minnow pail, I reflected that I might get on a better footing with Miss Carter if I talked with her about books and said less about the sordid details of my business. The next afternoon when I delivered fish lures for some male members of the Carter household, I asked for Miss Carter. The maid said Miss Carter was giving a tea, but that she would speak to her. Word came back that I was to come to the front of the house.

Miss Carter met me with her purse in hand, thinking it was money I wanted.

The tea drinkers stopped their chatter and called to Miss Carter: 'Bring the young man up.'

At first I was covered with confusion. The beautifully dressed women so overwhelmed me that I was tongue-tied, but they were delightfully polite and friendly—as agreeable as if I had been the Prince of Wales. Why not? I had on shoes and stockings and was wearing my best clothes; my hands and face were well polished; I had remembered to take off my hat, and my hair was immaculate.

The environment was perfect. Little Traverse Bay, its peaceful waters spreading to a line of blue hills in the distance, was never more beautiful. Between the summer cottage and the water were clumps of white birches and aspens, through the foliage of which the sun streamed, transmuting the leaves into gold; the dark shadows of spruces and balsams tempered the glow of the sun. The day was as beautiful as days can be only in the northern lakes region.

The handiwork of man was wholly good, too. The floor was covered with gay rugs, and there were cushions and bright stuffs on the chairs. The tea table was laid with snow-white napery, cups and dishes of china, and spoons of silver, which sparkled in the sunlight. I was poured a cup of tea and given a dish of cinnamon toast, a delicacy I had never tasted before. Miss Carter's guests gave greater beauty to the world than sun, water, trees, or the lovely furnishings. They were good to look at in themselves and were dressed in becoming bright summer stuffs, with lace, ribbons, and broad-brimmed hats. On their wrists were bracelets of gold; diamonds sparkled as they raised and lowered their cups.

Surrounded by so much beauty, tea, and toast, I became expansive. Glibly I answered all their questions. Women, I thought, mostly read Mary J. Holmes and E. P. Roe, and to their books I turned for conversational openings. These authors did not meet with much favor with Miss Carter's guests, and Miss Carter herself disposed of them by saying: 'A boy should not read love stories.'

Finally the tea came to a close. As I was about to go, Miss Carter said she wanted to talk to me about the books I was reading. In the next three years, bringing us to the time my leg was broken, Miss Jane Carter took my reading in hand and patiently tried to enrich my untutored mind through good books. She weaned me from the trash I had been reading. From her own library, she put in my hands *Huckleberry Finn, Tom Sawyer, Two Years before the Mast, The Oregon Trail,* the two books about Tom Brown, and bade me read Cooper, Scott, and Dickens from our town library. She did her best to polish my English, which she found quaintly larded with backwoods idioms and mispronounced words.

To return to the broken leg. A few days after the accident, Miss Carter came from the South for the summer. She was told that nearly every bone in my body had been broken and that it was doubtful whether I could live. Almost immediately she came to our house. Bandaged as I was from head to foot, my brother had begun to display me as the 'family mummy,' a joke not too bad for the neighbors, but I did not want Miss Carter to see me in the mummy bandages, nor did I want her to come into my mean little room, and only after an argument with Mother would I let her come upstairs.

Miss Carter tiptoed to my bed. Her voice pitched in the low sick-room key was golden sunshine. She had, she said, telegraphed to Dr. Young to put forward his vacation and come at once.

What with all Miss Carter's unexpected kindnesses and my

shame at not wanting her to come into my room, tears began to flow and I had to do something. I was reading Captain Burnaby's *A Ride to Khiva*. She did not know the book (which I still think is one of the best books of travel I have ever read) and I launched into its praises so enthusiastically that the broken leg was forgotten by both of us.

I remember that I told Miss Carter that the names of the places Captain Burnaby visited seemed most pleasant in sound: Afghanistan, Samarkand, Mesopotamia, Bokhara, Tashkent, and so on. It then occurred to me that in my half-delirium on the dreadful afternoon of the accident I had wondered how my jingle would sound if a Southerner said it and asked Miss Carter if she would repeat my rhyme:

> Charlevoix, Menominee;
> Mackinac, Sault Ste. Marie;
> Cheboygan, Petoskey;
> Wequetonsing, Mononaqua;
> Waugashance, Ile aux Galets.

Her rippling voice made the jingling words seem to me a kind of bird language.

A few days later Miss Carter brought Dr. Young. The great surgeon timed his visit to me with that of our town doctor, and with him took a look at my injuries. When the examination was over, my parents and Miss Carter came into the room to hear the verdict. To Miss Carter's questioning glance, he said: 'Of course he is going to live. I wish you had as good prospects of a long life.'

Then to my parents: 'No, he will not be a cripple; in three months he will be quite himself; there is just a broken leg, a few broken ribs, and some nasty scratches and bruises.'

Convalescence was a pleasant experience, one that I still treasure. For a few months I lived, as it were, in the lap of luxury and no one begrudged me comfort and ease. Neighbors continued to bring me food that was the fat of our land. My

little room was filled with books and magazines. All day for
two months before I could hobble about, I lay in bed reading,
dozing, daydreaming. I felt as though I were in a new world.

My bed was beside an open window through which at dawn a
flood of music came from the birds in the forest across the road
from our house. From morning to night, a pair of catbirds sang,
or scolded in strident calls, darting about with a great flurry of
wings. Robins were busily feeding on our bit of dew-soaked
lawn. All day I could hear the whistle of trains and boats that
carried me away to the world outside, which I so much wanted
to see. The treetops touched the sky. Sunset brought the songs
of thrushes, and in the afterglow of the summer days there was
the call of whippoorwills; later the zoom of nighthawks, the
hoot of owls, and the cries of tree toads.

I took a great fancy to catbirds that summer. The dreamy,
softly rising and falling cadences of the catbird are not less
melodious than those of its near relative, the loved mockingbird
of our Southern States. He has as great a variety of songs and
sings as sweetly as his famous relative, but, perhaps, and to his
credit, not so noisily. The male catbird across the road would
sometimes sing steadily from the same perch in a bushy chokecherry for a half-hour with no intermission. Again, on another
day, he could not keep his perch for two minutes and would
break his serenade with the most incongruous notes. It was on
such mornings that he would mew like a cat and emit a harsh,
sharp, crackling note like the snapping of dry sticks. My catbird,
as I think all of them do, would sing at any hour of the day;
there seemed to be added zest to his singing on gloomy, rainy
days; and I am sure that I heard him a few times at night.

After Dr. Young had been to see me a few times, Father,
who would owe no man a dollar, began to worry about the bill
he expected to have to pay. We had heard that this noted
surgeon sometimes charged as much as $500 in his own city,
and here he had come a thousand miles from home. If our

farm and all our belongings were sold, they would not bring much more than $500. But when Father asked for his bill, Dr. Young said: 'If I were on the road to the poorhouse, I would not charge you a penny.'

Then he added: 'I am Miss Carter's slave, and came because she told me to. Besides,' he said in his whimsical way, 'I am indebted to any Southerner in the North who dares to keep the *Life of Jefferson Davis* next to his Bible!'

Dr. Young came to our shores only a few more summers. I never knew what became of him. Cheery old Rabelaisian, he healed many a body with his surgeon's skill, many a soul with the mirth and jest of Rabelais.

In the autumn of the year I broke my leg, Miss Carter married, and her husband, in the country's diplomatic service, took her to Naples to live, whence she sent me a card at Christmas. The next summer, we heard of her death.

XXX

Mormons and a Cow

MORMONS settled on the Beaver Islands, just off the shores of the Land of the Crooked Tree, in 1854. The leader of this group of some seven or eight hundred was James Jesse Strang, who maintained he had been named by Joseph Smith, martyred founder of the Church of Jesus Christ of Latter-Day Saints. Strang set himself up as a king as well as a prophet, and in time had all the trappings of a monarchy in his capital of St. James on Big Beaver Island. Soon King Strang had most of the troubles that beset thrones. His subjects were rebellious; he quarreled with his neighbors; and, after a reign of but a few years, the monarch was killed by one who had been his right-hand man. A band of fighting fishermen loaded the poor Mormons of Beaver Islands in boats and took them away, much as Evangeline's people were taken from Acadia.

A few Mormons escaped deportation, and several families of them came to our country. From a son of one of these exiles, who lived some twelve or fifteen miles from our farm, Father bought a cow. I was sent to bring the animal home.

The long, hard journey was to be made the day before Thanksgiving. At daylight I left home, carrying a leading-rope, my luncheon, and sixty silver dollars in four bags in four pockets. At the start the weather was not bad, but when dawn broke a malignant sun scarcely cast a shadow. Soon the air was filled with large snowflakes lazily drifting down, but it was not cold and there seemed to be no wind except an occasional long-drawn sigh that seemed to come from some Arctic giant. By noon I was wading through snow halfway to my knees. I ate my luncheon in a thicket of evergreens where every branch was weighted down with snow.

By mid-afternoon I was plowing through a level of snow that covered stumps in the clearings. I could see but a few rods in any direction and became fearful that I might lose my way. The world was as silent as a tomb. No other creature was astir. The rope halter and the silver dollars had become burdensome, but I bore another load that could neither be shifted nor laid down.

That summer I had been sowing wild oats, and now as I trudged and wallowed along, my sins seemed so heavy that a millstone hanging to my neck would not have counterbalanced them. I had been smoking; swearing with or without provocation; I had investigated saloons, not to drink but to slake my thirst for sinful sensations; my ungovernable appetite had led me several times to a neighbor's melon patch; and I professed to be an agnostic and a socialist. (These two words have ever charmed me as a snake's eyes charm a bird.) Here I was, I reflected, in my seventeenth year a hardened sinner.

All that summer, our old Presbyterian minister had thrust his sermons at me. My brother, the reformed thresher, had pronounced me 'bad.' There was, too, a young lady who had persuaded me to read the *Idylls of the King* and had said if she were a man she would try to be a King Arthur and search for the Holy Grail. She even said: 'If I were a man, I would try to live exactly as Jesus Christ lived.' (I did not tell her that I was then reading Rabelais.)

Had she been old and ugly, I should not have listened to her, but she was young and comely; moreover, she owned one of the two pianos in town, and she played the 'Blue Danube' and 'Narcissus' admirably, and sang 'O Promise Me,' and 'The Night Hath a Thousand Eyes' divinely.

This was not the first day of self-searching in my youth—days of wondering what I wanted, of asking what I was to have in the years to come. But now conscience took me to task at an untoward time. Nature could have provided no better setting for conscience to consort with me than this snowstorm.

Late in the afternoon I came to the end of my long, hard journey. The house of the Mormon was a little cabin at the foot of a hill, down which I forced my way through the snow, foot by foot. It was an eerie place, a bowl on the rim of which hemlocks were so large and thick and black that a pall seemed to hang from the clouds to the earth. The snow-covered stumps in the little clearing of four or five acres looked like an army of ghosts.

The cabin contained only two rooms, a downstairs living room and one for beds upstairs. In these two smallish rooms the Mormon and his wife and six children were crowded. Where was a ninth person to find a place for the night? The children ranged in age from a suckling to a rabbit-eyed girl of about my age. If there was a place to lay my head, could I endure such quarters for a night? The snow had nearly sealed the lower room, and a red-hot cookstove filled it with heat and steam to suffocation. The evening meal was being prepared, and its odors, intermingling with the smell of children, were not appetizing even to a half-starved youth.

More and more my simple errand took on the quality of an adventure. I knew that my host was a Mormon. I knew, too, that he was English, and I found now that I could hardly understand his brand of our language. Moreover, this man had told my father that his father had worked for Charles Darwin, against whom all our preachers were then hurling epithets. A Mormon, an Englishman, a Darwinite! I had been taught that all of them were bad; this was to be an adventure indeed. But I liked the man.

The Mormon's wife was a ghost of a woman, shriveled and

sapless, worn thin with hard work and the bearing of many children. Poor creature! One could see that her food had not nourished her, and could surmise that there had been in her life little of ease, pleasure, romance, or sight of beautiful things. The lonely life in the little clearing was telling on her; yet she laughed at the children's capers and had a kindly, motherly way with them.

We supped on bread and molasses, fried salt pork, potatoes, and tea. This was the first time I had seen English people at tea, and to see old and young toss down cup after cup made me fear that the smaller children would be dissolved. When supper was finished, all of the youngsters, excepting Rabbit Eyes, were put to bed.

Meanwhile the old man was taking off his shoes and stockings preparatory to baking his feet to 'cure rheumatism.' He put a stick of wood in the oven; on it he placed his heels. Half his legs below the knees were thus put to roast. From time to time he took them out to cool; had they been wooden, they would have caught fire.

Sitting thus baking his shins, this English wanderer, who had no hope of ever seeing home again, told me the tale of his life.

Now past middle life, he had been born and reared in Kent, England. As I have said, his father as a youth had worked in Darwin's garden; but not liking gardening, the father had learned the printer's trade in Canterbury, which was his wife's home. Life had been uneventful until a Mormon missionary came along, and in the very shadow of the great cathedral's towers converted the two to the faith of the Latter-Day Saints.

After a time, they undertook the long journey to Utah, but in Buffalo met King Strang. This wily monarch persuaded the converts to desert Brigham Young and come with him to St. James on the Big Beaver. Here the Englishman had helped King Strang set up a printing office, which we called his 'Royal Press.' When the Mormons were expelled from their island home, my host's family had been visiting English friends at

Charlevoix on the mainland, and had neither means nor desire to follow the fortunes of the deported Mormons.

Although these people had nothing in common with our family and were in no sense neighbors, they knew that my father was a Southerner, a Democrat, and a Presbyterian. They knew that I had had my leg broken—Rabbit Eyes had read about it in the weekly paper. She had seen me win a dollar in a foot-race for boys on Fourth of July a year before. They knew quite as much about all our neighbors, and yet the woman, at least, was no gadabout, for she had not been to town in the four years she had lived in the woods. She did not go, she said, because she had no clothes.

Meanwhile, I was nearly dead with weariness. I was worried, too, about where nine people were to sleep in two rooms. Also, there was the important question of how I was to dispose of the sixty silver dollars for the night.

It turned out that the two old people slept in the bed downstairs; the two youngest children in a trundle bed pulled out from under the parental couch; the big daughter with a smaller sister, and the two boys in two beds, in the upstairs room. The old man told me that I was to crawl in with the boys, one feather bed on top of us, another beneath. The house had been poorly shingled, and the floor and bed were well dusted with snow.

I folded up my outer clothes, the silver dollars in the pockets, and put them under the bed. Keeping on my underclothes and socks, I snuggled up to a little Mormon and in no time was asleep. The next morning I dressed and went to a window, and saw at once that I was snowed in. Snow covered the stumps and fences in the little clearing. It had taken so long for the green of the forest to grow, and now in a single night there was no bit of green to relieve the eye, nor could one have told that the fantastic shapes in the forest were trees. It was a strange, motionless world, with no living thing, plant or animal; never had life seemed to me nearer death. There was no road to take me from my prison, and this was Thanksgiving Day.

I went below to another meal of bread, pork, and potatoes, a meal that differed from that of the evening before only in the substitution of pork-fryings for molasses. We ate our meal without a word. We were crowded in a little room filled with steam and the odors of food, children, clothes, a dog, and a cat. A cur chained in a crowded hen coop would not have been in worse case than I.

Casting about for a printed page, I could see nothing but the newspapers pasted on the walls. These had a strange look. I soon found a front page: *Daily Northern Islander*. It was a Mormon paper published on Beaver Island. Some of the papers were upside down, and all were wrinkled and askew, so that to read I must turn and twist. My host, seeing how I was laboring to decipher the print, told me he had a box of the papers and some Mormon books upstairs that I might read. Up we went. A box of food on a desert island could not have been more welcome to a shipwrecked sailor. There were several volumes of the *Northern Islander*, a Mormon Bible, and three or four books from King Strang's Royal Press.

Soon I was in the mysteries of Mormonism. I read of the golden plates and the 'peepstones' of Urim and Thummim; of the travels and adventures of Morona, Nephi, and other saints, of the Land of Zion, the Pearl of Great Price, of resurrection, revelation, temples, tabernacles, and tithings. As I sat in my little upstairs room on this wintry day, thoughts came of Utah, the Great Salt Lake, the City of the Saints, the deserts, the Danites, and other things true and fanciful that I had heard about Mormons; so that now with all my new knowledge, in my youthful exhilaration, I could have said, had my host been a missionary: 'Almost thou persuadest me.'

My host had set type for all of the books published by King Strang at the Royal Press in St. James. In his box-library, he had, so he said, copies of all the king's books. What a treasure-trove this box of books would be to a collector of Americana! I remember very well that there were several copies of *The Book of the Law*, written by Strang; copies of another on the resources and natural history of Beaver Island—a book I should now much like to have. Besides, there were volumes of the *Northern Islander*, including the last issue, which contained an account of the martyrdom of King Strang.

At noon, when Rabbit Eyes called me down to another meal, I was loath to go, so interested had I become in Mormonism.

As I went down to Thanksgiving dinner, I stopped at the little window in the north, rubbed clear a space of glass, and looked out on the world of snow. The sky was flawless, the bluest blue that I have ever seen above a snowy earth. I went to the south window that I might see the sun, but the dazzling glare and the sparkling diamonds in the field of snow were so bright that I dared not stay long at the window for fear of snow blindness.

Again, the food was bread, pork, potatoes, and tea, which we quickly gulped. After dinner I returned to my reading, the family to their various tasks. The Mormon would not let me help with the snow shoveling.

'There is but one shovel. . . You are still tired. . . You want to read.'

The man spoke kindly and his face showed such good will that he was excellent in my sight, as no doubt he was in the eyes of God.

It seemed to me that the afternoon had hardly begun when dusk began to fall. My garret was too dark for reading, and I went below and out of doors to join some men with oxen and horses, who were breaking the road—treading down the snow, not plowing it out as is done in these days of automobiles. Another party of road breakers we met said that the way to town was now open, and I trudged back to the cabin, happy in the thought that the next morning would see me homeward bound.

For our evening meal, the food was the same as the preceding ones I had eaten in this poverty-stricken home. I had almost forgotten it was Thanksgiving Day, and now, remembering, I was suddenly stricken with the most dreadful homesickness. It seemed to me that I was a thousand miles from home, that I had been away a thousand years, and that I might never again see my home. I swallowed tears to keep them from my eyes. It was homesickness in its most heartbreaking, crushing form. All that was going on at home flashed through my mind. Melanchthon Miller, a boyhood playmate of my father in Virginia, was visiting us for the day, and my mother would be expected to prepare a dinner in Virginia style. The main dishes would be turkey, ham, and pickled oysters; the table would be loaded with breads, vegetables, and side dishes of pickles and conserves. The feast would end with mince pie. My mind rang with the refrain:

> Turkey, ham, and pickled oysters;
> Turkey, ham, and pickled oysters.

I knew there would be loaves and fishes of the noonday dinner left—turkey, ham, and pickled oysters; my mouth watered. Turkey, ham, and pickled oysters—I must go home at once.

Besides missing a good Thanksgiving dinner, I now feared that I should not get to see Melanchthon Miller, a man I liked very much. Besides my father and Perry Nelson, Melanchthon was the only other Virginian in our region. We always had him with us at Thanksgiving or Christmas, though Mother objected in a mild way, because he had an enormous appetite and a body so long that special preparations had to be made for his bed and its coverings. Melanchthon was a widower. He lived at Mancelona, forty miles away, and Father always explained to Mother when he wrote asking him to come: 'A lonely man since his wife died.'

He was a Southern Democrat and an ex-Confederate—the only man to whom Father could speak freely; and I knew there would be much good political talk as well as tales of faraway Virginia. Miller had been a captain in Lee's army, and at Gettysburg had ridden at the head of his company with Pickett in his famous charge. Father and my brother would get him all worked up over Gettysburg, and I had missed having a part in it.

Besides, I was sick of the hutch in which I was cooped, of its cramped quarters, its dirt, its smells, and its family. The woman of the house gave me the shivers, she resembled so much a corpse risen from the grave. I did not want to sleep again with the smelly urchins. Rabbit Eyes got on my nerves. I did not want to sleep another night in the same room with her. During supper I turned the thing over in my mind, eating as one compelled to eat to live. At last my mind was made up to go at once; yet I could not go without the cow.

So when supper was finished, I took the four bags of silver and counted out sixty dollars in four piles and announced that I was going home and wanted the cow. My host protested: 'It is dangerous for you and the cow. You can never make it. The cow will founder in the snow. . . You are welcome to stay another day. . . I will help you on the way tomorrow . . .' and so forth.

His arguments were of no avail. I must go. I made several lame excuses: I had been indoors all day and needed the walk. . . I didn't want to miss school the next day . . . there was a guest at our house that I wanted to see . . . this was the first Thanksgiving I had ever been away from home. . .

It was a case of bad excuses better than none, but I made it plain I was going home. Had it been necessary for me to tunnel my way through the snow on my hands and knees, I should have started. Never before had home seemed so sacred a place. I could see from his face and from his words that the kindly old man was grieved at my going, but at last he consented to turn the cow over to me.

When we went to the barn it turned out that the fine lady I had been at so much pains to acquire did not like my company. She refused to go with me. The author of evil had filled her heart with a determination not to leave home, just as he had set my heart firmly on going home.

But I had had much experience with balky cows and knew exactly what to do. The cow had planted her hoofs in the door of the barn and stubbornly refused to budge. I made a half-hitch in my leading rope and slipped it over her nose. She had to come or be strangled. But when she came it was with her head down, nostrils distended, tail up, and eyes evil. This, too, could be remedied. There was a fork handle in the barn; and I attached it to the half-hitch so that it was as effective in keeping her back as a bull pole is in keeping back a bull with a ring in his nose. There would be no more dangerous charging. Again we started, the farmer whipping from behind. He went with me a good two miles, alternately whipping and soothing the poor beast, his voice trembling because of the cruelty he felt compelled to practice.

When the old man left me, I was tired in body and low in spirits. In the icy silence my breath curled up and covered my eyebrows and the fringes of my scarf with frost. The long road ahead through the forest, up and down hills, was a nightmare. But madame had learned that she was the weaker vessel and was now thoroughly tamed. My second wind came and we plodded along mile after mile.

The road curved from clearing to clearing through heavy forest growths. At first there were lights in the houses. Through the windows I could see rooms bright and twinkling with the glow of stoves and lamps; shelves of shining dishes, pans and kettles; beds covered with patchwork quilts; clothes hanging on the walls; people, old and young, resting or moving about.

It was amazing to see all these snug corners in a world of snow and wilderness. No sounds came from the houses. Except for the occasional bark of a dog, the only noise in the quiet night was the squash, squash, of the cloven hoofs of the she-devil I was dragging behind me and the crumpling of my moccasined feet in the frozen snow. In the forests, branches were bending and underbrush was crushed earthward, laden with the heavy weight of snow. There was one stretch of hemlock forest in which the snow covered the canopy of verdure high above the earth, making arches of marble supported by lofty black trunks, pillars in a structure more vast than any ever built by man. Falling snow from over-weighted branches sounded faintly, magnifying the calm of the windless night, as a whisper intensifies silence in a church.

The black, glacial sky was bright with countless stars; never had they seemed so cold and lonely. Nothing in the world is less companionable to a boy alone in a forest than stars. The full moon would have been a good companion, but the twinkling, pin-point stars gave me no joy as I led my cow through the woods and clearings. I had then some fear-pervading superstitions, acquired from the Indians. That night, there was a creepy, uneasy subconscious feeling that the Indians might be right in their belief that the stars in the Milky Way were passing souls, ghosts on their way to the Happy Hunting Grounds.

It was well after midnight when, coming out of the winter darkness of the woods, on the last lap of my journey home, a light glimmering in the window of our living room heartened me. (Mother had psychic powers about her children, and said she knew I was coming home that night and had put the light in the window for me.) As I led the cow past the house to the barn I gave a halloo to let them know I was home. Before I could stable the cow, Father was in the barn to make sure that all was well; inside the house, Mother and Melanchthon Miller were downstairs to greet me.

Great was their curiosity to know what had happened. I told them that in the Mormon house there was little to eat and no place to sleep. There was nothing to do but to come home. I remembered that in the house of the Mormon, it had seemed that I had been away from home a thousand years. As I took off my coat, it seemed that I had left home but a few hours before, and I was ashamed of my silly homesickness. Melanchthon Miller helped me save face.

He felt my cold hands and, turning to Father, said: 'Ben, the poor boy is frozen, he must have a hot toddy.'

Then to my mother: 'Let's have some hot water. I'll be back in a minute.'

Up to his room he lumbered for a bottle of whiskey, which he handed to Father. The amount of whiskey poured in the glass seemed to Mr. Miller out of proportion to the water already there; he seized the bottle, saying: 'Give it more color! Give it more color!' and he poured until the mixture turned to a golden amber.

A warmed-up dinner is never much more than an unappetizing memory, but a picked-up cold dinner on Thanksgiving night is a banquet scarcely less delectable than one that comes steaming-hot from the stove. When the cold titbits were on the table, Father and Melanchthon Miller sat down to a second Thanksgiving feast and ate as if they, too, had just come from a winter-night's outing with a cow.

I knew it was coming. At the close of every Thanksgiving dinner, Father, pointing to one or the other of his sons, would say, 'You see there the consummation of a miracle—the contained is greater than the container.'

Though Mel Miller had heard the joke a dozen times before, his appreciation was as fresh and keen as ever.

The old Virginian was tall, thin, bony, with long arms and legs, and very large hands and feet. He had a zig-zag body made up of knock-knees, bent arms, and rounded shoulders, separated from his head by a long scraggy neck buttressed by an Adam's apple as large as a Bartlett pear. His head, too large for his body, had a great expanse of bald pate covered with bumps and hollows that would have delighted a phrenologist. His face was thin, smooth-shaven, and so bilious a yellow that we children, out of Father's hearing, called him 'Old Marigold.' His beak was like an eagle's, but his eyes were mild and kindly.

The picture is not complete without a few words about his midnight attire. He wore a heavy white woolen nightshirt (he was always half frozen) that did not cover his shanks. His feet were incased in two pairs of warm socks and huge, clacking slippers. To keep his head warm, he wore a woolen nightcap of the same piece as his body covering. Around his neck was a knitted scarf out of which his Adam's apple went and came as his neck lengthened and shortened.

Late as it was, I could not forego the pleasure of baiting the old rebel.

'Mr. Miller,' I said, 'a man in the *Century Magazine* says that Lee made a great mistake when he ordered Pickett to charge the Union army at Gettysburg.'

Aroused by my statement, he now refought the battle of Gettysburg, using every piece of furniture in the room to show the positions of Confederate and Union generals. Stamping up and down (by this time everyone in the house was up to see the battle), he showed us how Pickett and his men charged at Gettysburg.

'It was the most glorious charge in the war. . . Pickett left 3400 men out of 4500 men on the field. . . My regiment lost 90 per cent of its men. . . Every officer in my regiment was killed or wounded. . . I was wounded here, here, and here. . .'

He pointed to his wounds and pulled up his nightgown to show a shriveled leg.

'Where were you when you were wounded?' I asked mildly.

'Right up to the Union lines, by God,' he shouted, 'a dead horse under me and with a shattered leg. . . Two of my wounds were made by Yankee bayonets.' He pointed to his side and shoulder.

The battle would have gone on indefinitely, even though we had all seen it fought in our kitchen a dozen times before, had not Mother begun blowing out the lights, commanding all to go to bed. What with weariness, the toddy, the meal, and the battle, it was afternoon when I came down the next day. Melanchthon Miller had gone.

XXXI

Farewell to the Land of the Crooked Tree

THE year I was seventeen and my brother nineteen, we were graduated from the village high school. We wanted very much to go to college, but Father thought a college education for two sons would cost a fortune, and did not see how he could spare us from the farm. Then suddenly, he urged us to go, stipulating only that we do the best we could to pay our way.

The most agreeable road to money-making in our land was to teach school, and, despite our lack of years, we knew there would be little difficulty in getting schools, since teachers were scarce. Neither my brother nor I was much wanted in our own township, because it was a notorious fact that we both read novels, and neither of us was much good at 'ciphering.'

We found that we could have schools at the same wages in two townships, Friendship and Pleasantview. Friendship sounded best to my brother. I chose Pleasantview. The schoolhouse at Pleasantview Center was six miles north of our farm; school began in September. I could walk the six miles night and morning.

The morning of the opening day is an ordeal in any teacher's first school. Gravely alert, anxious to do my best, I came after my long walk (during which I had looked at my new silver watch at least once a minute) to face the shrewd eyes of forty youngsters, several of them as old as I was. Their eyes showed curiosity and appraisement, not hostility. I did not know a soul in the room and in my embarrassment could find no words of greeting to break the ice.

I had planned a dramatic opening. It was nine to the very second when I entered the schoolhouse. Eyes straight ahead, with brisk, determined step, I strode to the teacher's desk, seized the hand-bell, returned to the door and rang it until the clang could have been heard a mile away. 'Determination' was my watchword. Briskness inspired briskness; almost before I was at my desk the youngsters were in their seats, girls on one side, boys on the other; children in front seats, youths to the rear. Before the last tot was seated I announced that enrollment would begin with the oldest pupil and that all were to come quickly so that lessons might begin. A whirlwind beginning went off just as it had been planned.

This first day my pupils were nearly all girls, since the older boys were still working on the land. What an assorted lot they were—of half a dozen nationalities and as many religions!

The road to Pleasantview ran five miles north and one mile east of our farm. There were a hundred curves, a hundred ups and downs, and forty or more farms. Soon I knew every permanent feature of the fields and forest on the road, though all were eternally changing with season and weather. After a time I became weatherwise and could foretell by sky and cloud in my morning walk what mood would prevail at night or the next day.

In the autumn, as my school opened, the fires of the maples began to glow; some trees were like overgrown poinsettias. Leaves untouched by frost on all species of plants were ripening, their summer's green turning into yellow, orange, and red, and with every wandering breath of air in the forests, like gorgeous butterflies, they came floating down to earth. There could be no streets of gold, no pearly gates, no mansions in the skies to make heaven more beautiful than the forests through which my road took me.

Along the road were many succulent fruits of wild plants, pomes, drupes, berries, cradles of next year's seedlings. It was a good time to study fruits and seeds. There were windblown structures held aloft by down or parachute; pods and capsules bursting to shoot their contents afar; tumblers rolled by gusts of wind; burrs, which clung to man and beast; and berries distributed by birds and beasts.

By late November, winter was in full blast. A winter forest has its attractions. The fantastic forms of snow-laden evergreens and undergrowths are beautiful. The rounded anatomy of a hardwood tree is as lovely as the body of a woman; and the traceries of branches and twigs, the decorations of mosses and lichens, give to trees in a winter forest added beauty.

'Like a lovely tree
She grew to womanhood'

is more applicable to trees in winter than in summer. Every species has a well-remembered form. The beech, in northern woods, is the most beautiful.

I can see myself as clearly as if I were today on the road to Pleasantview, an awkward overgrown boy, cap pulled down over my ears, muffler about my neck, mittened hands carrying books, unencumbered by an overcoat—I did not own one. I can hear the crunch of the snow in the half-beaten road, the clop of hooves and the jingle of sleigh bells, the friendly greetings of passers-by, and their loud-voiced jocularities. I can see at the end of the homeward trip a light glimmering in the window of my father's house, sometimes faintly through myriads of falling snowflakes, sometimes so brightly as to be scarcely distinguishable from the evening star glittering on the horizon; and Mother as she gave me welcome, adding on Friday evenings: 'Another week is at an end.'

By January, my road was so swallowed up in snow that I could make the journey to and from the school only on Monday mornings and Friday evenings. Formerly someone had to 'board the teacher'; the custom of 'boarding round' had passed out before my day. By common consent the teacher's boarding-place in Pleasantview was with a German who had kept a hotel in the village until evil days fell upon him.

The quarters were rude, a huge rambling log house, shingled with unplaned shakes, through which the snow sifted and the winds ventured at will. Still, I was snug enough at night between two feather beds, with a warm living room to dress in. My landlady could bake, boil, broil, and roast the strong meats a vigorous youth likes. The flavor of a thriving farm with its abundance, its simple conveniences, its baking-day and washing-day smells, and intimate companionships made a happy fireside.

Early in the evening I frolicked with four children, helped them with their lessons, and sometimes took a few minutes to do the farmer's simple accounts, or to read to him from a farm paper. I gave him his only news of the stupendous doings of a world that was to him far away and full of mystery and wickedness. An hour after supper found the family in bed, and then the house was mine, to read and read until midnight. The old couple were up by four, the children by five, and I, a sluggard in the eyes of all, slept until seven.

My school director was also town clerk and town librarian, so that I saw him almost daily. Except for a kind heart and willingness to serve, never could there have been a shepherd of schools less like an educator in appearance and less well qualified for his tasks. I never saw him with a book in hand, nor did he ever enter the schoolhouse. He nevertheless had very original theories on every subject that ever came to his notice. Those on religion were many and novel. Some of his secular theories I give to exemplify the range of his thought.

He believed the earth was as flat as a pancake, had four

corners, and stood perfectly still: 'If it was a globe,' he said, 'the motion would fling us all into space, and pull the feathers off of birds and the hairs off of animals.'

The earth, to him, truly was a stage; its foundations cracked in every earthquake; one 'could walk and sail it from end to end'; animals, plants and men were made by a great manlike Creator. The stars were no larger than apples; the moon was the size of a milk-pan; the stars were hung above us and occasionally one broke loose from its moorings—one could see it drop; the sun was a large morning star.

The moderator of the school was a kindly old man who came often on Friday afternoons to hear the children 'speak pieces.' Sometimes in winter afternoons, when he saw the children leaving the schoolhouse, he would come in and ask me to read some of the 'pieces' in several readers that he had collected. The old man knew how to read, but his eyes were glazed with cataracts, so that he was shut off from printed pages. He liked poetry, and would ask again and again for 'The Old Oaken Bucket'; 'Woodman, Spare That Tree'; 'The Barefoot Boy'; 'Silver Threads among the Gold,' and 'When You and I Were Young, Maggie.' Narrative, romance, and poetry with prancing lines did not interest him. The picture of the old moderator abides pleasantly in my mind.

The treasurer of the school board was the owner of the mill that made the tiny hamlet of Pleasantview. Being a man of money, he thought the going wage of $30 a month too small, and insisted that I be paid $40. Here, then, was I, the youngest teacher in the county, yet the highest paid of any for miles about.

I had heard much about the millman. His was one of the largest mills in the county; he was worth $10,000, and hired ten men. I was in awe of a man with so much wealth and power, and dreaded having to meet him. The first meeting turned out better than I expected; soon I was quite at home with him, perhaps more so because I usually saw him in the presence of his wife, a most pleasant and agreeable woman.

The millman's wife was a different type of woman from any other in the community. She was town-bred and educated. Her clothes were so vastly superior that it was always a pleasure to see her. In the bloom of youth she must have been a belle; she had wonderful auburn hair and as fair a complexion as women ever have. Her eyes were what is called 'liquid.' She was the only woman in our region who year after year went 'outside' to visit, a more notable undertaking in our land than going to Europe would be to most of us now. She had time on her hands and was considered an authority on the novels of Mary J. Holmes, Augusta M. Evans, and E. P. Roe.

There were two children in the family, a daughter of my own age, the first pupil ever to enroll under my tutelage. The daughter was a rare treasure to any teacher. She chaperoned the older children and mothered the younger. In matters of dress, tidiness, and deportment she was an exemplar to pupils and teacher alike. She was the image of her mother, with her mother's auburn hair, charm of eyes, and fair skin, differing only in having the best galaxy of freckles I have ever seen, and the brightest coral-red lips. Like the mother, the daughter was voluble, and poured out a vast amount of harmless gossip and pleasant observations.

Often on Friday afternoons in winter the daughter drove me home in a cutter behind the family horse. Her image is almost as vivid now as when she appeared on these Friday afternoon rides—tam-o'-shanter, loose wisps of auburn hair, freckles on her face covered by the red of exhilaration, lips that needed no rouge; and a constant accompaniment of chatter to the rhythm of sleigh bells, a buffalo robe wrapped tightly about our bodies to keep out the bitter cold.

When the school inspector came, my pupils did not shine. They fell below in arithmetic, grammar, and writing, though they shone in reading and history. Most of the poor youngsters knew only toil, and I wanted to take them into some of the

fields of that mental enjoyment into which Mr. Parmalee had
taken me. The minds of my youngsters were as variable as their
faces, but they were alike in one respect, their lack of inter-
course with others outside their small family circles. They had
read no children's books, heard no stories, listened to no lulla-
bies, played without toys, prattled no nonsense, and had had no
daydreams. They existed to eat, sleep, and work. They were
children, yet grown-ups. Their outside knowledge ran to the
values of forest and farm products; their conversation to the
prices of groceries and dry goods, about which even the smallest
could haggle with merchants in town.

That year, fall and spring, flowers, trees, and shrubs—what
they were, how they multiplied, how they grew, their relations
—seemed to me the most important things in the world. I tried
to impart my meager botanical knowledge to my pupils. The
school board let me do as I pleased; so, as occasion offered, I
took the youngsters afield to botanize and had them bring in
specimens of wild things that we might talk about. So, while
my school fell short at the end of the year in formal branches of
learning, my pupils could name more plants and birds than any
teacher in the county; they knew more stories, poems, Indian
legends, and woodlore. I like to think that in years to come
they repeated these stray bits of knowledge as coming from
'an old teacher of mine.'

In the last days of school I was treading on air. My head was
in the clouds. I saw the world with enchanted eyes. The school
had been a success; college was just ahead.

The institution of learning of my choice was the Michigan
Agricultural College, where tuition was free and room and
board in dormitories were cheap. Besides, there were opportunities to earn money. The college required two hours a day
in 'farm practice' at eight cents an hour. To be sure, farm practice was unpopular. 'The wages of sin are eight cents an hour,'
characterized it in the words of students. However, my brother,

now a sophomore, was to turn over to me work he had done as an assistant in the library at twenty-five cents an hour. To me, the wages of heaven were twenty-five cents an hour.

I was well equipped, it seemed to me, to go to college; for, had I not a diploma from the Harbor Springs High School—a wonderful sheet of engraved sheepskin! It would enable me to enter college without an examination. I was proud of it and had had it framed. I left the frame behind.

I was proud, too, of my physical equipment. My wearing apparel was a brand new seersucker suit; patent-leather button shoes; a shining white-straw hat; and a splendid brown-leather suitcase, in which were all my other earthly possessions, except my money. After my railroad ticket was bought, I had $100 in my pocket to buy, in due course, a winter suit and a derby hat.

As our high-school graduation song, written by one of my classmates, said: 'The sad hour of parting is now drawing nigh.' For days before, Mother had been lecturing me on how to keep well; on the evils of smoking and drinking; and on keeping away from the bad companions I should find in college. As she kissed me good-bye, she told me to remember all she had told me. I am afraid I didn't remember quite all.

Betty, my little sister, now a young lady of sixteen, prefaced her good-bye kiss with 'You ought to be ashamed of your tanned face and hands.'

She told me what to do to improve their appearance. I didn't use her remedies.

I was also sorry to say good-bye to Father. His two sons, partners in creating 'our farm,' were deserting him in his old age. We had robbed the land of its magnificent trees, and had skimmed off the cream of the virgin soil, leaving Father only poor, sandy, good-for-nothing, sub-marginal fields, which none of us now loved.

Father had a redoubtable soul. After shaking hands, as I was about to step aboard the train, he said: 'Good luck! Work hard!'

I was off to see the great world.